DILEMMA OF DEVELOPMENT AMONG THE ONGE OF ANDAMAN

DILEMMA OF DEVELOPMENT AMONG THE ONGE OF ANDAMAN

DIPALI DANDA
SUMIT MUKHERJEE

MANOHAR
2021

First published 2021

This edition is for sale in India, Sri Lanka, Nepal, Bangladesh, Afghanistan, Pakistan and Bhutan

ISBN 978-93-90035-64-9

Published by
Ajay Kumar Jain *for*
Manohar Publishers & Distributors
4753/23 Ansari Road, Daryaganj
New Delhi 110 002
and
Indira Gandhi Rashtriya Manav Sangrahalaya,
Shamla Hills, Bhopal 462013 (M.P.)

Typeset by
Kohli Print
Delhi 110 051

Printed at
Replika Press Pvt. Ltd.

TO OUR BELOVED
CO-CITIZENS – THE ONGE

Contents

Foreword

The Onge of the Little Andaman Island, as claimed by the authorities concerned, is one of the four Negrito tribes who occupy the Andaman Archipelago of the Bay of Bengal. If the Great Andamanese, who presently have been rehabilitated on Strait Island, is taken as a combination of ten Negrito tribes, the Onge constitute one of the 13 Negrito tribes that ever lived on this island territory of India.

Since there is no Negrito population on the mainland of India, there are multiple speculations in circulation about the exact origin of the Onge. Whether they branched out of the African Negritos or are a distant kin of the Australian Aborigines is yet to be definitely known. Opinions of their possible independent origin cannot be ruled out altogether.

Nevertheless, the Onge constitute a small population. In fact, all Negrito populations, irrespective of wherever they live, are small in size. The present strength of population of the Onge is estimated to be around one hundred. Whether the Negritos of Andaman Archipelago ever lived in close proximity to one another is not known. Hence, how such a small population could survive in their apparent isolation but with their defined bio-cultural integrity, is a matter of serious speculation.

The Onge are hunter-gatherers who have been found to occupy a rather isolated island in the open sea, about 162 nautical miles away from Port Blair, the administrative headquarters of the Andaman and Nicobar Islands. When the first known contact with them was established, their population was estimated to be approximately 200. Whether because of the very nature of contact as such or due to some other reasons, their population appears to have assumed a declining trend. In fact, almost all over the world their downward trend in population strength seems conspicuous. In India, in particular, they have earned the distinction of being a threatened community.

The Onges' intense interaction with their immediate ecological niché set the rhythm of their cultural life. Like all other human populations everywhere, they have expressions of happiness, bereavement, love, enmity, friendship, sensitivity and other characters. In spite of that, the tendency of most of the contributors who studied them or worked among them appears to narrate the Onge as if they are an exotic people.

Dilemma of Development among the Onge of Andaman, the contribution of Dipali G. Danda and Sumit Mukherjee in this respect stands out quite distinctly. The monograph they produce speaks of their intimate interaction with the people, their ecology, cultural niché, psychology, economy and, in a nutshell, their way of life. The depth of their intimacy with the people presents a flavour hitherto unknown. Their apparent scepticism about the developmental initiatives undertaken by the Indian government is not only conspicuously evident in their account of the people, this also seems to be a major disturbing factor.

The degree of isolation the Onge experienced had a sudden change with the migration of non-Onge populations among their midst, particularly from the then East Pakistan (Bangladesh) and Sri Lanka. Besides, the representatives of the change agents have attacked the very vitals of their survival instinct. The two pre-published references appended to the volume, beside indirectly adding a sense of time dimension to the analysis, makes the issue of their survival instinct and agency rather explicit.

The administration is likely to benefit a good deal from the insights of the authors. On the whole, the treatise will be of much value to professionals, scholars, administrators as well as the change agents.

AJIT K. DANDA

Preface

It is primarily through exposures to anthropological literatures that we get to know the people like the Australian Aborigines, some tribes of Kalahari Desert, New Guinea, or Bolivia and the Negrito peoples of the Andaman Group of Islands, who are known for their hunting-gathering propensities. But most such people occupy terrains that are not very easily approachable.

The Anthropological Survey of India had been conducting field investigations among the Onge since the early 1950s. Expectedly, those surveys could generate a good deal of valuable basic information about the people. To begin with, such information was of great value for us. The early impressions about the area and the people have already been incorporated in this volume under the title, 'First Visit—First Impression'.

Our first brief visit nearly convinced us that the Onge have become virtually puppets in the hands of the members of so-called development agencies. Nevertheless, our knowledge about the history of cultures suggests that even in the most critical situation, the people under observation tend to maintain their distinct identity. They, too, try to preserve their respective cultures. That prompted us to appreciate that it needs a deeper probe to know the inner strength of a culture that enables its people to cope with fast changing situations.

Such an opportunity arose when a research team could be formed with a combination of two likeminded scholars – one, an anthropologist and the other, a human ecologist.

As a team, we conducted our work among the Onge of Little Andaman by living with the people for a good length of time during two different seasons. We intended to revisit the people during the third season too, so as to enable ourselves to observe their life-ways through all seasons. Incidentally, according to the Onge perception, there are three very distinct seasons in their habitat. Nevertheless due to reasons beyond our control, the proposed third visit could not take place.

We, however, were happy to have access to the early unpublished reports on the Onge as well as some old photographs taken by the research team of the Anthropological Survey of India (AnSI) that had visited the people for the first time (in 1955-6). We had the benefit of discussion with Dr Pranab Ganguly and Dr Anadi Pal who had studied the religious beliefs of the Onge for about eight months during the early phase of involvement of the AnSI in the survey of the people. That provided us with comparable basic information and thus facilitated our analysis of data. A summary of that report has been incorporated in Annexure I of the present volume. We have also incorporated a pre-published essay on the foraging economy of the Onge by S. Bose, who had worked among the Onge during the early 1960s. We were privileged to receive his guidance during his brief stay at Dugong Creek during our first field study.

We had started our intensive field investigation among the people with a great deal of enthusiasm. We lived with the Onge for several months and roamed about with them in the jungle during their hunting expeditions. Thus, through long association with them, we could feel the distinct flavour of the pristine Onge culture, which is likely to get blemished due to many encounters with and extraneous exposures to the so-called civilized people.

We are very thankful to the AnSI for providing us with the opportunity to live with such simple but very beautiful people for a reasonably long period. For various reasons beyond our control, we could not publish the present text on time. Some of the research findings of this study have, however, been published or presented in seminars.

We had no intention of writing a monograph on the basis of our study of the Onge; instead we thought of attempting a focused ethnography, particularly highlighting the power of adaptability of the Onge and the outcome of their exposures to the process of induced transformation. The present volume contains several of our published articles that have been written afresh.

There are many adorable features and valuable information on the Onge culture that qualify to be documented for the future generations of scholars. We apprehend the community may not survive with their distinctive identity for long due to the pressure of development and the consequent outcome thereof.

In spite of the continuous efforts of the administration to transform the Onge to fit into a tailor-made mode of life, the people appear highly attached to their age-old values. Till date they are able to make their living as they wish to and enjoy the pleasure of fairly unrestricted freedom. Modifications or alterations in this respect, therefore, have to be at par with their knowledge base and the experiences gained by them through the interplay with their life situations. The Onge culture may survive on the surface of the earth in their own desired form, provided they are allowed the free option of a choice by way of their style of living.

DIPALI DANDA
SUMIT MUKHERJEE

Acknowledgements

The authors express their sincere gratitude to the authorities of the Anthropological Survey of India, for providing them with the opportunity to undertake the study on the Onge of Little Andaman. The stay among the people as well as the job as such was undoubtedly arduous but extremely challenging. The local administration, including the Regional Unit of the Anthropological Survey of India (AnSI), was kind enough to extend logistic support. The authors are very much thankful to them. Some senior members of the AnSI, particularly those who had the previous experience of conducting a field investigation among the Onge, have made us indebted to them by providing valuable guidance and advice regarding field strategy in an isolated island.

Special thanks are due to Dr Pranab Ganguly, Dr Saradindu Bose, Dr Anadi Pal, Dr Manish Kumar Raha and Shri T.N. Pandit for their support and guidance toward successful completion of the project. The first three among them have made us particularly indebted to them by granting us permission to republish their works in the present volume. In fact, this help has added the valuable time-dimension to our analysis.

The physicians and their staff at Port Blair and Dougong Creek, particularly Dr Sahabuddin and Dr A. Mallick, deserve our special appreciation for their various support.

We are grateful to Prof. A.K. Danda, former Director of AnSI, for his continuous academic support and for writing the foreword to this volume.

We feel extremely happy to extend our sincere thanks and regards to the Onge, particularly to Sharvashri Totanange, Tambolai, Ramesh, Bairogegi, Kanjo and all ladies of Dugong Creek and South Bay Settlements who were actually the real friends and guides who looked after us in all situations, including the difficult ones.

We also thank Prof. Sarit Kumar Chaudhuri, Director of Indira Gandhi Rashtriya Manav Sangrahalaya, Bhopal and its Publication Officer, Shri Sudhir Kumar Srivastava, for their initiative and interest in the printing and dissemination of their work.

Dipali Danda
Sumit Mukherjee

Introduction

The highly contrasting existence of hunter-gatherer societies in the electronic era of this new millennium is a remarkable anthropo-geographic phenomenon representing very complex historical cross currents. Facts have already demonstrated that all such small communities have been thriving in close interaction with their neighbouring non-foraging and relatively more powerful people for centuries together. The foragers could not escape the greed of aggressive colonial rulers and traders totally and, therefore, have been forcibly brought under the control of the local or state administrations.

Nevertheless, with the beginning of systematic field studies, followed by the conference on 'Man the Hunter' in 1966, several ignorant and wrong notions about the foraging people the world over could be corrected to a large extent. The subsequent narrowing down of the perceptual gap between the researchers and those researched resulted in a number of meaningful studies of the so-called 'savages'. These developments resulted in the founding of several activist groups who raised their voices in favour of Marshal Sahlin's 'original affluent society'.

In tune with the global trend of research emphasis on the hunting-gathering people and their process of transformation, in particular, the Anthropological Survey of India took up a research project to cover the major foraging tribal groups of India during the early 1980s. Among the hunter-gatherers of the Indian archipelago, the Onge of Little Andaman Island, at that point of time, were modern-day foragers surrounded by the agrarian settlers from mainland India and were being regularly coaxed by the government 'welfare agencies' to swallow the imposed dosage of development. Being entrusted with the responsibility of evaluating the impact of such initiatives, both the authors, having a good deal of field experience, established a field camp right inside the rehabilitation settlements of the Onge. After an initial visit, two phases of intensive field studies were carried out during

1986-8 in two different settlements at Dugong Creek on the northeastern coast and at South Bay in the extreme south of Little Andaman Island, where a total of 96 Onge had been rehabilitated.

The Onge of Little Andaman, one of the surviving important Negrito communities in the world, have had a very static population for the last four decades. There have been several critical issues pertaining to adopting the induced changes in their habitat and economy.

The present volume is thus the outcome of a field investigation carried on for six months and research presented in the form of analytical and development ethnography with ecological, socio-cultural, economic, and political perspectives of a dwindling community listed under the Particularly Vulnerable Tribal Group (PVTG) of India.

The authors have tried to throw light on the degree of agreements between the induced change programmes and the age-old survival strategies of the people. Advantaged with sharing the same habitat for a reasonably prolonged period of time, an intimate relationship of mutual trust and the confidence developed between the researchers and the researched. On quite a few occasions, one of the authors was accepted to participate in hunting, fishing and canoe-making ventures as a team member of the Onge. There is hardly any such previous record in the history of the survey. Thus, in addition to participant-observation and collection of structured data, the research could extract and record valuable community perspectives and voices of the people themselves.

There are thirteen original chapters, some of which have been developed from articles published in national and international journals of repute. Two valuable pioneering research papers, written by earlier researchers of the AnSI on the Onge, have also been annexed to highlight the conditions that prevailed several decades back.

Chapter 1 presents the geo-historical perspective of the Andaman and Nicobar Archipelago with special emphasis on the natural, political, demographic and academic history of the study area, i.e. Little Andaman Island. The second chapter presents the first impression of the author, filled with the perplexity and awe of a mainstream Indian anthropologist on a first visit. The third and fourth chapters have spelt out the ecology and population of the Onge, discussing and incorporating their unique, rich knowledge system along with the most burning issues of the demography of the shrinking population. The Onge point of view on caring of their children, the most valuable asset of this small population, has been elaborated in the fifth chapter. Wide ranging facets of the hunting-gathering economy and the changes that have come about form the main focus in the following chapters that are divided into those dealing with subsistence activities, evolution of their techno-economy around hunting, and the role of the canoe as the most important material possession in Onge culture.

Perhaps the major transformational aspects have been reflected in the changing food culture of these people, having a wide range of fallout involving their economic pursuits, health and culture as a whole. The attempted comprehensive dole system from the government welfare agency that keeps them indirectly captured within the state's administrative domain is what Chapters 9 and 10 talk about. Finally, the tangible and intangible impacts, both localized and long-term, of the so-called 'development' programmes, have been summarized and critically considered in the eleventh chapter that focusses on development and their transformation.

With an objective of adding a new dimension, considering the Indian publications on ethnographic monographs, the twelfth chapter is composed of very selective excerpts from the field notes of both the authors. Those narratives originated instantly in situ, offer the readers the direct flavour of the field situation and the event.

A postscript is attached to the last chapter of this volume. This is an attempt by the authors to bridge the time that has passed, as the present-day Onge have almost given up their foraging economy along with their dignity of being 'the most affluent society'. Hence, it is not an exaggerated claim that this volume is perhaps the last record of the Onge population as a surviving community of hunter-gatherers in their own way of life as vividly recorded during fieldwork.

CHAPTER 1

Little Andaman: First Visit and First Impression

The very name Andaman creates a sense of wonder and admiration in the minds of every citizen of India. Several decades after joining the research faculty of the Anthropological Survey of India (AnSI), an opportunity to visit the fabled archipelago arose for the first author. It was a privilege to get posted at Port Blair, the headquarters of the Andaman and Nicobar Group of Islands. It provided a first-time opportunity to encounter its hunter-gatherer tribe.

Until then, the Jarawa, the Negrito inhabitants of the island, were yet to become sufficiently friendly. Another Negrito tribe, the Sentinelese of the North Sentinel Island (a tiny island of the Andaman Group), were altogether out of bounds. Nevertheless, occasional visits were organized by the Andaman Administration to the Jarawa territories in order to welcome the inhabitants into the fold. In view of the above, the author decided to direct her attention towards the Onge, yet another Negrito tribe inhabiting Little Andaman Island, and carry out intensive field investigations among them. The Onge were considered friendlier and relatively approachable compared to the Jarawa.

Little Andaman is the southernmost of the Andaman Group of Islands in the Bay of Bengal, about 44 km in length and 16-26 km in breadth. Once it was the exclusive habitat of the Onge. When the AnSI conducted a systematic study of the Little Andaman Island during the 1950s, there were no people other than the Onge living on it. By the end of 1960, Little Andaman had been opened to outsiders, particularly for the rehabilitation of the refugee populations from what are now called Bangladesh and Sri Lanka. It is a fact that the people like Onge, having a hunting-gathering economy, need a very large area for their sustenance. In spite of that, a large number of outsiders were made to settle there at the cost of the land and livelihood of the aboriginal people. During the 1950s, the Onge used to explore the entire island and at that time they were divided into as many as 24 local groups wandering throughout the length and breadth of the island.

In the perspective of a changed situation due to influx of other people in the Onge habitat, it was proposed to undertake an intensive study on them giving due emphasis on their neighbourhood and extraneous efforts due to various development and welfare programmes. Owing to population pressure and improved transport facilities, it was not possible for a simple community like the Onge to remain in relative isolation any longer. This was one of the factors which led us to undertake an exploratory survey of Little Andaman. We visited Little Andaman in 1984 to study the differential adaptive capabilities and strategies which might have ensured better adjustment of some of the groups vis-à-vis the Onge in the specific bio-cultural environment.

SETTLEMENT AT LITTLE ANDAMAN

Hut Bay settlement is the headquarters of Little Andaman. It is 100 km (by sea) away from Port Blair. To reach Hut Bay one has to take a night journey by boat. Some information on little Andaman is given below:

Geographical area	:	731.5 sq km
Area of reserved forest	:	699.79 sq km
De-reserved area	:	32.28 sq km
Number of villages	:	8
Number of families	:	680
Total population	:	7,209 (1981 Census, now above 10,000)

Source: Tahsil Office, Hut Bay, Little Andaman.

There is a Trunk Road from Hut Bay to the village at 22 km named Ramakrishnapuram.

The Forest and Plant Development Corporation is the most important government establishment at Hut Bay. Bengali refugees from the then East Pakistan were first settled at Little Andaman in 1969. All other settlements were established during the period between 1969 and 1979. Table 1.1 shows the community-wise break-up of families settled in Little Andaman.

Most of the families settled in Little Andaman are agriculturists. Only 26 families are engaged in small trade or other occupations. While going to Dugong Creek, we had the opportunity to have a talk with some of the settlers at Vivekanandapuram (Table 1.2).

TABLE 1.1: COMMUNITY-WISE DISTRIBUTION OF FAMILIES AT LITTLE ANDAMAN

Community	No. of Families	Year of Settlement
Bengalee	366	1969 to 1979
Nicobarese	165	1973
Tamil (Sri Lanka)	25	1977
Tamil (Burma)	8	1977
Mopla	83	1979
Onge	33	1976

Source: Tahsil Office, Hut Bay, Little Andaman.

Note: Though the Onge are an indigenous people they were settled in two different locations.

TABLE 1.2: VILLAGE-WISE DISTRIBUTION OF POPULATION

Name of the Census Village	Ethnic Group	Population		
		Male	Female	Total
Hut Bay	Mixed population	1,779	907	2,686
Ramkrishnapuram	Bengalee	840	961	1,801
Vivekanandapuram	Bengalee and South Indian	524	435	959
Harmeder Bay	Nicobarese	385	289	674
Netaji Nagar	Bengalee	521	161	682
Rabindra Nagar	Bengalee	142	136	278
Dugong Creek	Onge	–	–	102
South Bay	Onge	–	–	26

Source: Tehsil Office, Hut Bay, Little Andaman.

Besides these there are other people working in different forest camps, as shown in Table 1.3.

TABLE 1.3: POPULATION AT DIFFERENT CAMPS

Name of the camps	Population		
	Male	Female	Total
Forest Camp at 19 km	4	0	4
Forest Camp (3 nos.) at 14 km	159	10	169
Butler Bay Camp (4 nos.)	270	24	294
Red Oil Palm (Nursery)	48	9	57
Asia Match Company	23	10	33
South Bay Light House	2	–	2

Source: Tahsil Office, Hut Bay, Little Andaman.

It was reported that, due to uncertain rainfall, crop failure is a regular phenomenon in this area. There is no irrigation facility here. The soil of this area, with the exception of one village, is not suitable for paddy cultivation either.

We visited the Nicobarese village Harmender Bay. Owing to over-population at Car Nicobar, 165 families had been shifted to this village in 1973. The Nicobarese follow their traditional occupation of horticulture. The family cultivate coconut, banana, papaya, etc. The Nicobarese in this village are Christians by faith. The village was quite big and clean. The people looked healthy. Both the Nicobarese men and women are hardworking by nature. We observed that both the sexes carried loads of banana and other vegetables on their shoulder pole or on bicycles to the Hut Bay jetty to load them to the ship. These are transported to the Port Blair market from there.

The Nicobarese of Harmender Bay often visit Car Nicobar and take part in the annual boat race held there. As the Nicobarese settled in this village have a similar environment to what they had earlier, they did not have much difficulty in adapting themselves to the new settlement. The village is between two Onge settlements, one at South Bay and the other at Dugong Creek. The Nicobarese often come in contact with the Onge when the latter pass through the village. The Andaman Adim Janjati Vikas Samiti (AAJVS) also made a wooden hut as the resting place for the Onge at Harmender Bay. The Nicobarese of the village, in general, are friendly with the Onge, though sometimes they exploit resources reserved for the latter. It may be mentioned here that as both the Onge and Nicobarese are indigenous people of the region, they do not bear any ill-feeling towards each other. On the other hand, the refugee settlers have numerous misconceptions about the Onge, such as believing that they were criminals at one time, now settled at Dugong Creek, etc. However, they too bear the opinion that the Onge are very mild people. Due to lack of proper knowledge about the surroundings or history of the island, the settlers form their own ideas about the aboriginal people.

We visited the Onge settlement at Dugong Creek. In an attempt to make room for other people, the Onge of the island were rehabilitated in two different settlements. The population from around Butler Bay and Jackson Creek were rehabilitated at Dugong Creek and the people at South Bay were settled right there. Now the bulk of the Onge population is stationed at Dugong Creek. Twenty-six Onge households are here and there are seven at South Bay with a population of 76 and 26, respectively (Figure 1.1).

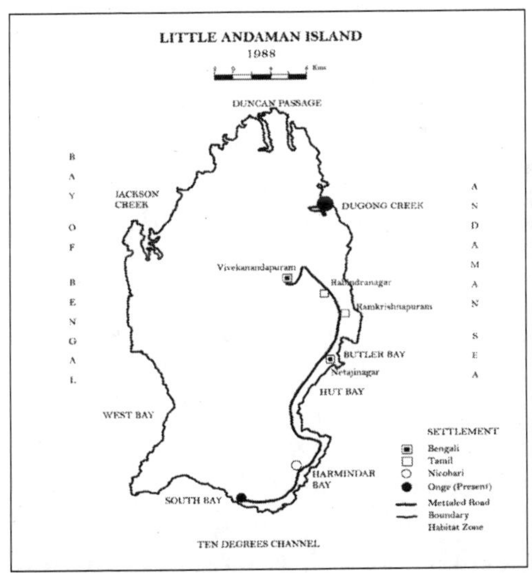

Source: Map prepared by the author.

Figure 1.1: Map of Little Andaman with settlements of various communities.

Dugong Creek is 46 km away from Hut Bay in the northern direction. To reach this settlement one has to go to Vivekanandapuram village by bus or by any other vehicle. Then the creek is to be crossed by boat. One can also reach the other end of the creek by walking through the forest. After reaching there, one has to trek about 14 km along the shore to reach the Dugong Creek Onge Settlement. We crossed the creek by a country boat. From the other end of the creek, which is locally known as Chota Nala, we walked the distance. We started from Hut Bay at 7.00 a.m. and reached Dugong Creek settlement around 1.00 p.m. At the resthouse for the Onge at Hut Bay we met two persons from the Onge community who accompanied us up to their settlement at Dugong Creek.

DUGONG CREEK SETTLEMENT

The Dugong Creek settlement was established by AAJVS in 1976. To settle the Onge, 26 wooden one-roomed pile dwelling type cottages were constructed. The cost of each hut was Rs. 20,000. They were later provided with electricity. These were allotted to each Onge head of the family. Till today their names are found inscribed in front of the house. These huts have no resemblance to the traditional lean-to shed shelter (*corale*) or the dome-shaped communal hut (*beyra*) of the Onge.

Every culture, by and large, is adapted to its ecology, Due to its close proximity to the sea and being in the tropical rain forest zone, it is very hot in summer where the Onge live. To avoid the heat, the Onge always constructed their huts in the middle of the forest having big shady trees. The huts were thatched with leaves of country palm. For making the new settlement for the Onge, however, these factors had not been taken into account.

Instead, at first, the forest was removed. The huts were provided with a G.I. sheet roof. As a result, the huts get extremely hot and very uncomfortable. As a consequence, most of the huts, with the exception, of two, are not in use by the Onge at all. Only House nos. 7 and 8 are still occupied and the remaining are all lying vacant in unusable condition. Neither the Onge nor the workers of AAJVS took proper care for maintenance of these houses. The huts are now in a dilapidated condition. The Onge made their own *corale* (lean-to shed) near these cottages. At present they live in three settlements. Eleven huts are located in the midst of the major plantation area and six on the opposite bank of the creek where the AAJVS establishment is located. Only four *corale* are found inside the AAJVS camps just by the side of the wooden cottages meant for the Onge. From the outward appearance of these hutments one gets the idea that these were rather casually built. The surroundings are also not properly cleaned. One traditional community hut made by the AAJVS also had electric fittings. But this is never used by the Onge for any ceremonial purposes. The *corale* inside the plantation, where the majority of the population live, is relatively better cared for by the people themselves. Now, due to the change in their traditional occupation as well as habits, the Onge need not move from one place to another that frequently. They dwell in one particular hut until it gets infested with ticks from the dogs or someone dies there.

It may be mentioned here that the Onge are very fond of dogs and treat them very affectionately. Sometimes, in a family, the dog population outnumbers its human population. In earlier days, however, dogs were very essential for the Onge, especially for accompanying them to the forest for hunting. So they developed an emotional attachment to them. These animals move freely in their settlements, share food with them and sometimes even the wooden beds. We observed that when a party of women went to the sea to collect crabs, dogs accompanied them in the boat. One or two who could not be accommodated in the boat, crossed the creek by swimming. Due to such intimate association with dogs who are not treated against ticks, Onge huts often get infested with ticks. Then the people leave the site and set up a new one. We saw some deserted huts both in the plantation area as well as in the rehabilitated settlement area. The belongings of an Onge hut are very simple – one or two plastic jerrycans for carrying water, aluminium pots, enamel plates, baskets, bows, arrows, *adze*, and so on. In one or two houses we found big *canastras* and small tin suitcases. Those who possessed tin suitcases also had one or two sets of modern clothes like trousers, shirts, etc. Along with these we also found painted mandibles of some deceased members of the family kept in the suitcase. They make a platform with cane and bamboo to serve as a bed. The couple and young children sleep in one platform. From the age of six or seven years, children start sleeping on separate beds.

Previously, the Onge were not accustomed to use any sort of metal utensils. Now these things have been introduced; sometimes these are given as gifts. Often, after cooking or eating, they leave the utensils unwashed, and the dogs lick those clean. Then they are again used. In the same manner, some of the Onge wear clothes without washing them for days together. We have seen many women wearing petticoats over their traditional tassel, which are very dirty. The upper portion of the body of the people remains uncovered. According to their concept of modesty, only the genital organs of both the sexes are to be covered. Even after introduction of modern dresses, women continue to wear tassels. A tassel is made of a special variety of grass. We have seen in many huts, the grass for making tassel being processed. With this tassel, women cover their private parts in a perfect manner. The Onge women are extra careful about the tassel; whenever they sit or do anything, they invariably put their left hand over the tassel. Similarly, men too cover their genitals in a cloth pouch in such a way that they do not look nude. In the absence of body hair, the Onge men look like children. Children of either sex usually start wearing the tassel or the pouch from a very early age. The young girls, even up to the age of thirteen, sometime use a piece of cloth on the waist tucked between the thighs instead of the tassel. However, when they go out of the settlement they never forget to wear the tassel. The Onge men wear shorts or trousers when they go to or pass through Hut Bay. They sometime put on shoes or sandals. Two men of the Dugong Creek settlement wear wristwatches. Nowadays, many Onge men wear some apparel not originally theirs, like T-shirts, briefs, etc. Even in the settlement we found men wearing briefs instead of putting their genitals within a pouch. The T-shirts or briefs are tight-fitting and they wear them without washing them properly. As a result, sometimes they suffer from fungal infections of the skin. Except a handful of people, most of the Onge did not look very healthy when we visited them, though they are very happy-go-lucky in their temperament.

DAILY ACTIVITIES OF THE ONGE WITHIN THE SETTLEMENT

We had an opportunity to observe the Onge camping at Hut Bay. It has already been mentioned that for visiting South Bay settlement from Dugong Creek, the Onge have to pass through Hut Bay. We met two Onge men of Dugong Creek at Hut Bay who were going to visit South Bay settlement. They could speak broken Hindi. One of them was called Tambolai and the other Totanange. Both of them were in clothes that were not their usual attire. One wore shorts and a sleeveless vest and the other trousers and a shirt with short sleeves. It was reported by Tambolai that he had been called upon by the *Raja* of South Bay. Totanange worked as an assistant in the health centre at Dugong Creek. He had come to Hut Bay to escort the doctor who was to return to the settlement. At Hut Bay they stayed in the resthouse meant for the Onge. It was a single-room wooden cottage. Inside the room there was a hearth. They made *parathas* and milk from Amul Milk Powder. We had tea and dinner in a hotel with them. There, they enjoyed rice and curry prepared in Bengali style. We were told by the hotel keeper that the Onge occasionally came there to eat. Payment for their food was made by a member of AAJVS posted at Hut Bay. Sometimes the Onge, too, paid for their meals, though they are not well-familiar with monetary transactions. We observed that the Onge were very fond of chewing *pan* (betel leaves). Often they bought *pan* from the nearby shop and their teeth were deeply stained with *pan* juice.

On our request both the Onge men agreed to accompany us to the Dugong Creek settlement. In the morning, before starting for Dugong Creek they again made *parathas*. After reaching Vivekanandapuram village, the Onge walked through the forest while we crossed the creek by a country boat. On reaching the other end of the creek (Chota Nala) they joined us. It was almost past midday when we reached the settlement. It may be mentioned here that we carried our luggage ourselves till we reached the settlement but the luggage of the local doctor was carried all the way by Totanange. On the bank of the creek we found six small huts made of wood, corrugated sheet and palm leaves. Men were absent from the settlement as this was the occasion of pig hunting in connection with the initiation ceremony of two young men. Women and children were relaxing in their huts. The surroundings of the settlement was littered with garbage. Unclean utensils were strewn everywhere. Only one boy aged about 14, wearing traditional dress, came up from the creek with some clean aluminium pots. During our stay for three days, we never found anybody cleaning utensils.

On the other bank of the creek, the establishment of AAJVS is located. We reached it on an outrigged canoe paddled by the two Onge men. It is a settlement complex with some good quarters meant for its staff, a powerhouse, a dispensary, a community centre, etc. At the end of the settlement there are 26 one-roomed wooden cottages on piles meant for the Onge. There are four lean-to type huts (*corale*) near these wooden cottages. Women there were relaxing outside the huts with their children. They were cheerful but looked rather sickly. The faces of most of the women were daubed with white clay but not with any particular design as used to be found in the 1950s. Many of the women wore a petticoat over the tassel. An elderly man came out wearing shorts and T-shirt as soon as he saw us, though those were not at all clean and not of his size either. They belonged to his young son. We met the same man in the evening in traditional attire carrying a jerrycan filled with drinking water. Another man was making a cane basket. A few were carrying coconuts in big gunny sacks from the plantation on their back. There was one piggery initially built by AAJVS. Now the same was used as a storehouse for coconuts. The pigs, however, roamed about like stray animals and often caused damage to the plantation. The Onge did not eat meat of domesticated pigs. In the evening, at about 7.30 p.m., the hunting party consisting of 16 adult men including the two young initiates returned from the forest. On that day, they had killed five full-grown pigs and two piglets (Figure 1.2).

On the following morning, I visited the settlement. The Onge in general are late risers. The sun rises very early in this part of the world, but the Onge settlement does not come to life before 6.30 a.m. As food supply was almost assured at that time, they were not required to observe a work schedule for the day as it had been in previous

Figure 1.2: Two initiates (in ceremonial red thread attire) with the hunting party as they returned from the forest (Photo: Anup Giri).

decades. They spent most of the day at leisure without doing much hard work. During day time we found many Onge busy in making baskets or making an *adze* or cot for sleeping, etc.

There were 11 huts in the midst of the plantation located very close to one another. While going to this settlement, we found a number of women weeding grass from the road. Some were carrying fire-wood. In the settlement, the Onge were mostly in their traditional attire covering the genitals only. Small boys and girls were without any clothes. Two little girls wore frocks. Very few were in non-traditional dress.

In the Onge hut, the hearth was always alive with a slow fire, mostly with an aluminium pot full of water with a few tea leaves simmering in it for hours. Whenever anyone felt like it, he/she consumed some of this concoction without milk or sugar. The Onge are yet to learn to offer tea to an outsider. Similarly, in some houses, pork was kept for boiling on the fire. We found a number of people eating pork, and surrounded by dogs. It was observed that people ate pork, taking the fat in the left hand and the meat in the right hand. This practice of eating fat and meat separately might have some significance from the dietary point of view. In the evening we saw some women cooking rice. They had adopted the method of cooking rice as they had been taught. They strained the gruel of rice and did not have it. Rice was taken with some kind of curry. These days they prepare the curry in oil or *vanaspati* and add spices which are supplied free to them.

It was observed that the two young initiates had been put into seclusion. In earlier days this sort of function was to be held in the communal hut. Now, in the absence of the communal hut, the cots on which the men used to sleep were placed together and the space enclosed by bed covers from four sides. During the day these young men lay inside while their wives sat outside the enclosure. No one was allowed inside the enclosure and they did not talk to anyone. It was pitch dark inside the enclosure. The initiation ceremony started from 26 May 1984 and was to be continued for 40 days. Except during the period of hunting, these two young men would remain in seclusion. In the settlement, one hut was used as the community kitchen.

We found nine baskets containing roasted pork hanging there. Thirteen pig skulls were arranged in a row on a bamboo pole hung horizontally from the kitchen wall. Altogether, 26 pigs had been hunted since 26 May in connection with the initiation ceremony. On that night many had a share of the meat. Those who could not come collected their share the next morning.

ANALYSIS OF THE OBSERVATION

Though our stay among the Onge was brief we could observe them from close quarters, which revealed some important facts.

The Onge have not yet learnt the art of cultivation or manufacturing. They do not need anything from outside for their livelihood. For that reason most of the people do not go beyond their own habitat. The women never go out of their settlement on their own. The AAJVS opened a consumer cooperative shop within the settlement to distribute free ration and other necessities like, garments, tobacco, etc. Nowadays, both Onge men and women get some wages in terms of money for working on the plantation. With that money they usually buy the following articles – areca nuts, biscuits, lozenges, torch cells, fishing hook, tobacco, lime, sieve for wheat flour, triangular file for preparing arrowhead, etc. Those who were considered to be leaders, having had some exposure to Port Blair, bought certain kind of luxury goods like talcum powder, perfume, sunglasses, pen, wrist watch, radio, etc. However, majority of them bought tobacco, lime and areca nuts. Very few of them understood the monetary transaction needed for any purchase, as almost none could count money.

The Onge have learnt to wear clothes different from their own, though not in the proper way. They cannot distinguish between undergarments and outer garments. Many Onge men were seen wearing only tight briefs. One man wore only two pockets of a pair of shorts instead of the complete shorts. Similarly, one woman was found wearing a brassiere. It was apparent that she did not know the purpose of wearing it. Previous enquiries in connection with the shopping habits of the Onge revealed that men sometime bought a bra for their wives and Onge considered that it was easier for a women to move about in the forest with this type of an upper garment.

The Onge also cannot distinguish between clothes for men and those for women. Sometimes, women could be seen wearing a man's bush shirt. Men interacted more with AAJVS people; they visited Hut Bay on some occasions and thus their exposure to outsiders was more. Perhaps for that reason the Onge men had better knowledge in this regard than their women. We never saw any Onge man wearing female attire. In general, notions about any kind of dress not their own was very vague among the Onge. They seldom wash their clothes. The AAJVS supplied soap as one of the items of free provision. When we visited Dugong Creek, the supply of ration had not reached there for about a month. The Onge did not feel the necessity of buying soap from the Consumer Cooperative stores though they had money. No attempt was made to interest them in washing their clothes. However, the use of clothes, though not familiar, made it clear that the Onge had became conscious, especially in front of outsiders. A young girl aged about sixteen wore a dirty petticoat over her tassel. When we wanted to photograph her, the Senior Social Executive requested her to remove the petticoat and keep only the tassel on. She did not like the suggestion and refused to comply. It seemed that such a request almost amounted to the violation of her modesty. The elderly women, however, still did not feel inhibited to be in their traditional attire.

It was observed that a sense of individual possession has increased though a sense of cooperation and sharing at the community level in certain activities like hunting, construction of huts, use of dugout-outrigger canoe, etc., still persists. A canoe is usually built by individual effort but any one in the community could use it at the time of need. The canoes are kept on the shore. Only if a canoe is to be taken for a longer voyage, formal permission of the owner is sought. However, due to the change of lifestyle, they did not need not go for a long voyage. The community kitchen has been replaced by the family kitchen. The former was symbolized by a small hut where surplus meat was stored in baskets along with skulls of pigs hunted on some ceremonial occasion like *tanagiru* (initiation ceremony).

The behaviour of the Onge couple towards each other appeared to be very affectionate. Often we found them sitting or eating together. The babies were well looked after. Except during night, I never found the babies being by themselves. They were always carried by their mother. At home, both the parents carried the baby. But as soon as they grew up and could fend for themselves, the responsibility of the parents towards them was almost over. A grown-up son or daughter was treated as a regular member of the community. Initiation or marriage of an individual was a community affair and the entire community took part in it. The initiation of the two young men was found to have been observed after their marriage.

A new word, *raja*, caught our attention at Hut Bay. In the settlement of Dugong Creek we heard the term a number of times. This word was perhaps introduced to the Onge by the AAJVS workers. *Raja* is used as a synonym for leader. It was not just a new word; it was altogether a new concept to them as the Onge never had any formal leader traditionally. It was the choice of the AAJVS people as to who were to be called *raja*, and they tried to emulate the pattern of leadership of mainstream society. According to that pattern, the leader would make his people work like a feudal lord while he himself would not do much work. He worked as a link between his own people and the welfare agency. Among the Onge, it had once been unthinkable that one could subsist on somebody else's labour. However, in the present situation they did not need to earn their own bread as they primarily subsisted on free ration. At present they are employed for carrying coconuts. For getting Onge men and women to work in the plantation AAJVS supervisors took the help of a few Onge men having leadership qualities, who were called *raja*.

It was observed that there *rajas* or leaders often worked as mates who collected hands for plantation work. We saw that already there were two such *rajas* in Dugong Creek. One is Tambolai and the other Nabekutte. It was also been reported by the AAJVS supervisors (senior social executive) that Tambolai did not do any work by himself but controlled his people who worked in the plantation, while Nabekutte himself worked and did not have much control over his people. Nabekutte was a member of the Tribal Council. He was considered the spokesman of his people. The AAJVS supervisors gave the impression that they had a major role in this process. Similarly, there was a *raja* in South Bay.

The Onge women appeared to be more obese than the men. Most of their time was spent on light domestic work and in the present situation there was hardly any scope for physical exertion. But somehow their typical feature of steatopygia has been reduced. This observation needs further probing. Though the Onge women are not as fit as they used to be, but they appear to be better adapted to the new situation as compared to their male counterparts. Women, in general, were found to be cheerful, whether relaxing or weeding. On the other hand, the men appeared lethargic. The job of carrying of coconuts in the plantation did not appeal to them in spite of the daily wage. It has been reported by the senior social executive that they hardly came to work in the plantation on their own. To an Onge man, life is very easy without any challenge because of assured and free food supply. When asked, the Onge said that earlier lifestyle in which food had to be procured through one's own labour was better than this sort of life. But this might not be the true feeling of the entire community. It is possible that a few who were sensitive reacted in this way. Some of the Onge complained about the prolonged delay in the arrival of the boat carrying rations for them. For years they had been leading this idle life. If food did not reach their door they felt distressed. It seems that their self-sufficiency is going to be replaced by the dependency on the welfare agency. Once all their activities had been centred on looking for food, now with an assured food supply, a sort of vacuum had been created. Due to their changed life pattern the Onge men appeared to be listless, as they suffered from a sort of purposelessness. However, they had not entirely lost their zeal. When there was no ready food supply from outside agency, they procured it from the forest or the sea. We noticed the earnestness and enthusiasm with which they went for crab collection or pig hunting, especially the women.

Once they were secure in their own eco-cultural niché the Onge never worry about food. As they were always sure that there was no dearth of food in the forest or sea they never thought of hoarding anything. Thus a sense of insecurity is altogether absent. From that perspective, the Onge could be called one of the 'original affluents' in the sense that Sahlin (1972) used the term. Hoarding comes from a sense of insecurity. To the Onge, every day was full of challenges as well as exultation. Whenever they wished to get food or anything, it was readily available, they only had to procure it with their strength and tenacity. But today the security, once ensured by nature's bounty, has been substituted by man's charity, which is often associated with uncertainty. As a result, the Onge now suffer from insecurity. It is a pertinent question as to whether development led to a better secured life or increased insecurity among Onge people. One can say the objectives of welfare or development agencies here are not that transparent.

When insecurity increases, suspicion grows. One of the Onge thought our team was of 'Madrasi' people, who are considered to be thieves. The exact term an Onge man used was *chor* (thief). It so happened that once he was sent to Vellore for his daughter's treatment. A man from Port Blair, appointed by the AAJVS, escorted him to Vellore, who, the Onge claimed, robbed him of his entire money. The life of the child was saved but the Onge returned to his place with the notion that all men from that linguistic group were thieves. This sort of contact with so-called civilized people had increased suspicion in the minds of the Onge people.

WELFARE PROGRAMME AND CHANGE

It has already been mentioned that the Andaman Adim Janjati Vikas Samiti, in short, AAJVS, had been established for taking appropriate care of the declining tribes. The ultimate goal of this sort of organization is to bring all the backward communities to the level of other general population of the country. The AAJVS has one of its operational centres at Dugong Creek. It executes the entire welfare and development programme for the Onge at the Dugong Creek and South Bay settlements. A social worker, relatively of junior rank, is posted at Hut Bay. A number of officials of AAJVS are also posted at Dugong Creek but none at South Bay. There is a Senior Social Executive, a powerhouse operator, a plantation-in-charge, and a messenger. There are two lady members of the staff: one Balwadi teacher-cum-social worker and one crafts teacher. Incidentally, these two women are wives of the Senior Social Executive and powerhouse operator, respectively. Besides, there is a doctor, a staff nurse and a ward boy for extending healthcare at Dugong Creek. They are appointed by the Andaman administration and the tenure of the stay of the doctor and nurse at Dugong Creek is one year. The doctor visits the South Bay settlement once a month. In Hut Bay there is a Primary Health Centre. The South Bay Onge can avail of the services of that centre at Hut Bay. The ward boy and some members at the health centre are the staff of AAJVS. Two Onge men work as assistants in the powerhouse and the health centre.

It is assumed that the Senior Social Executive is primarily responsible for the overall well being of the Onge. But his duty is confined mainly to looking after the plantations, which is of secondary importance to the Onge. No doubt, the profits derived from the plantations are meant only for the Onge. But the indigenous population, i.e. the Onge for whom the entire establishment of AAJVS at Dugong Creek is meant, are not much concerned about the plantations. Like the Nicobarese they do not have any cultural attachment to coconuts though nowadays they have developed a taste for them and have also learnt to make oil from it. On the other hand, it was matter of pride for the Senior Social Executive that he could increase the income from plantation from Rs. 1,500 to 7,500. On an average, 51-4 and 19-21 Onge of both sexes were on the master roll of the daily wage roster in the plantations at Dugong Creek and South Bay, respectively. It was reported by the Senior Social Executive that the women were better workers than the men. They were more regular in their attendance and did not have to be summoned to work like the men.

In Dugong Creek, the plantation was spread over two plots, one being of 25 acres and the other of 75 acres. The Onge men were employed for collecting fruits which drop to the ground. The Onge women do the work of weeding grass. Working time for both the sexes is eight hours. Men hardly worked for three hours a day while the women often worked for five hours. The Senior Social Executive calculated the average and paid them accordingly. Payment was made on a monthly basis. The officials made one or two Onge men mates. Previously, the Onge did not have any council on the basis of social rank or seniority. All members used to enjoy equal rank in society. Nowadays, the agency workers, according to their own sociocultural values, introduced certain concepts like 'leader' or 'mate', etc., among the Onge, which were once entirely alien to them. Due to this, two rudimentary factions emerged among the Onge of Dugong Creek. One group was represented by Tambolai and the other by Nabekate. The officials of AAJVS treated these two persons as if they were superior to other members. Naturally, they appeared as spokesmen of their society. Nabekate had been selected as a member in the Pradesh Tribal Council, for which he got an honorarium. With that money he bought a wristwatch and other luxury goods. Tamboali, too, aspired for this position. He too bought all these luxury goods. In this way, AAJVS attempted to introduce the notion of formal leadership among the Onge. The officials called them *raja*. For that reason, at Hut Bay, people referred to Tambolai as *raja*. The AAJVS people inculcated the idea that the leader should not do any manual labour. While returning from Dugong Creek, we could not arrange a boat. Tambolai and another Onge escorted us. The Senior Social Executive told us that Tambolai would not carry our luggage. But it was not possible for one individual to carry the load throughout the journey. We released the person after sometime. Then Tambolai himself volunteered to help us carry the load, but, of course, we were also carrying some pieces of the luggage ourselves. From this it was evident that the feeling of artificial superiority was only surface deep. The people did not consider manual labour derogatory. We entertained Tambolai, who accompanied us up to Hut Bay with food. Similarly, in the settlement when one of our party members asked for a pair of bow and arrow and a basket, they simply gave us what we had asked. A token payment was made for these things, as we knew that Onge baskets were sold in Port Blair market as an artifact at a fairly high price. The Onge did not understand the value of this sort of transaction. They did the work as guided by the officials posted there without realizing the implication or intricacies of sale of labour for money. In spite of their docile and peaceful nature, an unpleasant incident occurred when a young man (Endogage, son of Thilai) beat one of the officers and his wife on 16 May 1984. Even the doctor who tried to intervene was not spared. This kind of behaviour is extremely unusual on the part of an Onge when they do not even use any abusive language to refer to their children or beat them. These are rare incidences but have far reaching implications.

The Onge are employed as labourers in their own plantations but they have not been taught horticulture or kitchen gardening, formally. Most of the Onge men were exposed to Hut Bay market and know the uses of vegetables and fruits, especially banana. Besides, the agency people had kitchen gardens in their quarters. If taught, the Onge might have felt interested in growing vegetables. They did not rear pigs or poultry either, who often damaged the gardens. It was rather easy to introduce some kind of gardening. But they were not encouraged by the AAJVS people; rather their enthusiasm in this regard was dampened by not being paid wages for the work (Basu 1984). If they had been taught some gardening they could have perhaps experienced a breakthrough from a food-collecting to a food-producing economy.

CONSUMER COOPERATIVE STORE

Next to the care of plantations, the major activity of the AAJVS was to run a consumer cooperative store. The shop supplied necessities that a civilized man needed. The Onge did some shopping here but its main function was to distribute free rations supplied by the administration to the Onge. Usually, the supply reached Dugong Creek once a month. In South Bay there was no shop to distribute the ration. The provisions there were stored in one of the wooden cottages. According to their need, the Onge took different items from that stock. The list of articles distributed through the free ration system is furnished below.

LIST OF ITEMS DISTRIBUTED TO THE ONGE (PER HEAD PER MONTH) THROUGH FREE RATIONS

Rice		5 kg
Atta (flour of wheat)		9 kg
Dal (pulse)		½ kg
Dalda		½ kg
Groundnut oil		½ kg
Tea leaves		½ kg
Salt		½ kg
Milk powder		½ kg
Haldi	different items of spices	50 gm
Chilli		
Tamarind		100 gm
Onion		½ kg
Tobacco		250 gm, per adult only
Toilet soap		1
Washing soap		1
Matchbox		2
Candle		1 packet (per family)
Kerosene oil		2 ltr

Excepting milk powder and soap, children up to eight years got half of the above mentioned rations. However, the quantity of pulses and cereals appeared to be insufficient, while the quantity of cooking oil was on the higher side. In general, the supply of different food items show an imbalance from the dietary point of view.

No work has been done so far to evaluate the impact of change of food among the Onge. Apparently, from the old photographs and the film produced by the AnSI, it could be said that their general health was relatively better than what we found at present. During those days they looked very healthy with a streamlined, fatless physique. Now they looked depressed, if not melancholic, and either emaciated or obese. It could not be said for certain that this was due to introduction of new food or sedentary habits, though both the factors had a common origin as their movements were highly restricted. They could move up only till Hut Bay, i.e. they could not go beyond Little

Andaman. They had to obtain permission from the administration for going to Port Blair or another island. But in the past they had moved from island to island and even to Port Blair in their outrigged canoes. Now the uncertainty of food supply through hunting and gathering was taken care of by supplying them with free ration, but this was at the cost of their spontaneous joy and freedom. Sometimes rations did not reach in time and naturally the people felt distressed, something unknown to them earlier. Sometimes the consumer cooperative shop also ran short of provisions. However, though the shop could not supply provisions regularly, it maintained a stock of areca nut, lime and tobacco, along with various types of garments, fishing hooks, etc. In earlier days, the Onge used to consume a wild variety of areca nut from the forest along with betel leaves without lime. Now they chewed a tobacco leaf which was readily available in the shop. They bought briefs and vests for the men and petticoats for the women. It should be mentioned here that if dresses they were not used to were to be introduced to them, sufficient care should have been taken to teach them how to use them and clean them regularly. Except a few individuals, no one cared to clean their clothes. Besides, the motive behind a dress is to cover the body for protection and to look beautiful, according to the prevailing aesthetic code of a culture. The environment where the Onge lived is very warm and humid, and in that situation, their traditional dress seems more appropriate. Perhaps, these clothes had been introduced to them not for their own sake or benefit but for the benefit of the outsiders who stayed around them and the visitors who occasionally landed there. It is perhaps safer for the indigenous population not to be visited by outsiders who do not understand their culture in its proper perspective.

POWERHOUSE

The powerhouse was another facility to provide the Onge with modern amenities by the welfare agency. It worked on diesel and supplied electricity to the residential area of the AAJVS workers from 6 p.m. to 10 p.m. The cottages meant for the Onge also had electricity which they did not need. The bulk of the Onge population lived quite far from the AAJVS complex and without electricity. The only direct beneficiary from the powerhouse was an Onge man who worked as an assistant to the powerhouse operator. He could now operate the machine and earn a salary. Till date the Onge could very easily take care of their accommodation and other basic needs of life. With all these extraneous help, our enthusiasm might eventually transform a self-sufficient population to a parasitic people depending for everything on others.

SCHOOL

The next important area covered by AAJVS is education. A primary school had been set up in the community at Dugong Creek to impart modern education to the Onge. It had tables and chairs for the teachers, one sewing machine and a few pictorial charts for teaching alphabet, both in Hindi and English. There were two lady teachers, one a teacher-cum-social worker and the other a craft teacher. As reported by the teachers, the Onge children were not interested in attending school. These people, for generations, got their lessons of life from nature. They were never exposed to formal schooling. The Onge children enjoyed games imitating fishing, hunting, etc., with their miniature bows and arrows. Besides, learning the alphabet through rote, as in 'a' for apple, 'b' for ball, appeared incomprehensible to the Onge children. It did not belong to their cognitive world. Most of the pictures of animals or flowers in the chart were alien to them and beyond their comprehension. The teachers also agreed that this type of education had no social relevance in Onge culture. Hence, though schooling for the Onge started since 1976, there were no literate Onge boys or girls yet. On the other hand, it had been observed that the Onge children had a special aptitude for drawing. They could draw whatever they saw, almost instantly. In this school they drew helicopter or 'Milale', the small ship which visited their shore with rations. They could also interpret these things in their own language and gave an Onge term for such foreign objects. Some of the young boys could draw their names with the help of Hindi alphabet. The Onge are forgetting the beautiful designs they used to paint over their bodies. This could perhaps be revived through training in the school.

Whether it was a teacher or social worker, he/she did not have any special commitment for such work or love for the people. From the episode of 16 May 1984 of a scuffle between the senior social executive and one Onge boy, as narrated by the lady social worker-cum-teacher, it appeared that she did not have any concern for these 'uncivilized' people nor any hope for their future. The craft teacher felt equally frustrated. In the community centre we saw a number of embroidered tablecloths, sling bags, plastic cane bags, etc., partially prepared by the Onge and the crafts teacher. What was the value of embroidered table cloth or plastic bags for people who did not even understand the use of clothes? These were kept for sale, though the craftsmanship was not of superior quality. Of late, it had been realized that the Onge were expert in basketry and Onge baskets have a demand in the market, hence they are encouraged to make cane baskets which can be sold at Port Blair. Except two persons, no one could count money. They identified currency notes as *bara note* (big size) and *chota note* (small size). *Bara note* stood for Rs. 50 and all others below that denomination were *chota note*. It is very strange that in spite of having a school for so many years, the Onge have not learnt to count money.

DISPENSARY

A sub-centre was established at Dugong Creek for the health programme for the Onge. It had one doctor (MBBS) and one ward boy. Only the ward boy had been continuing there for nine years. Often, the doctor was a new recruit who had just passed the MBBS examination without any training about the people under his care. In such a case, for a doctor fresh from the medical college, the Dugong Creek Onge settlement was an alien world about which he knew nothing. He felt isolated and spent the time as if in exile. During this one-year tenure he took as much leave as possible to avoid staying at Dugong Creek. By the time he got acquainted with the land and the people his term was over.

The dispensary was not well equipped. In case of serious illnesses, the patients were to be shifted to Hut Bay or Port Blair and there were no facilities for removing the patient to these places instantly. Under such circumstances, the doctor could treat only minor ailments and injuries, something for which a qualified doctor was not really required.

From the register of the hospital it could be said that the Onge were not much used to modern medicine. They had their own herbal medicines and indigenous ways of healing. If the health department staff were enthusiastic they could test the efficacy of the indigenous medicines of the Onge.

From the hospital records and from the doctor, we came to know that a good number of Onge were suffering from pulmonary tuberculosis. Malarial fever cases was comparatively fewer. However, Onge were susceptible to cough and cold. The average body temperature of the Onge, as reported by the doctor, is high. Most of the Onge suffered from some kind of skin disease.

From our observation it can be said that the Onge took care of their health according to their cultural codes. They took bath regularly, and brushed their teeth with some twigs three times a day. Dental health of the Onge was good. One thing, however, needed mention here. Though the Onge were now victims of some diseases associated with the mainstream population, these could not become a psychosomatic problem to them. The diseases affected the Onge physique but could not affect their culture and psyche. Though their health status was deteriorating they were not aware of these diseases. Whether the disease was pulmonary tuberculosis or poliomyelitis, it did not make any difference to them. Due to various welfare and developmental programmes, changes that have taken place in different spheres of Onge culture is shown below through the following chart.

CHANGE IN ONGE CULTURE

Items of Culture	Pre-Development Stage	Development Stage
Material culture	Material belongings consist of cane basket, wooden bucket for honey collection, bows and arrows, *adze*, etc., *dao* (iron knife). All these articles are made by themselves.	Material possession increased

Items of Culture	Pre-Development Stage	Development Stage
Garments	Tassel made of grass worn by women and men to cover their genitals.	Petticoat made of cheap cloth is worn by women over the tassel. Men wear anything they like. In the settlement still they prefer traditional dress.
Personal decoration	Shell necklace, painting of body with different designs by red ochre and coloured clay. Decoration with different designs by red ochre and coloured clay.	Necklace of glass beads, beautiful designs of earlier days are not made today. Somehow daub the face with clay.
Crafts	Basket making, pottery, canoe making, making of wooden containers, bows and arrows and *adze*.	Forgot pottery. Basket and canoe making are still prevalent
Shelter	Lean-to type (*corale*) temporary hut and beehive communal hut (*beyra*) were constructed in such a way that rain or storm could not do any damage.	Lean-to type is built in a very casual manner. Community hut is not built.
Food	Primary food was meat aided with edible roots and honey.	Cereals, pulses, milk powder introduced.
Method of cooking	Roasting and boiling, no cooking oil and salt were used.	Learnt modern method of cooking, cooking medium is Vanaspati.
Provider of food economy	Nature (forest and sea) Self-sufficient	Primarily, welfare agency. Almost completely dependent on outside agency
Subsistence activities	Hunting and gathering	No specific subsistence. Activities, wage labour is being introduced.
Area of operation	Entire Little Andaman	Specified area
Mode of transaction	Barter	Transaction through money, though most of them cannot count money.

Items of Culture	Pre-Development Stage	Development Stage
Freedom of movement	Unrestricted	Restricted
Social structure	Based on local group, the community hut was the central pivot of the social structure. Structure of the society community-centred. No formal leader of tribal council.	Local group is completely defunct. Community hut is absent Community feeling is getting weak. Formal leadership is being introduced
Values of society	Egalitarian in principle Sense of cooperation and community sharing were strong. Nature was the basic donor.	Nothing specific. Sense of cooperation and sharing still prevails. Outside agency is the basic donor.

These were the very few elements of culture listed above which we could observe during our short stay at Dugong Creek. But from these also one could judge the extent and effect of outside contact among the Onge of Little Andaman.

The limitation of most of the welfare organizations in India is assumption of the role of self-styled saviour for the simple folks without proper assessment of their life and culture. The noble motive of the welfare agency is well taken. Welfare or development measures are no doubt for the benefit of the Onge.

With the infringement of the welfare agency on their lifestyle, when the role of nature as universal donor got replaced by human administration, the Onge began to feel the pinch of insecurity. If the ration did not reach on time they felt quite distressed. This means that they were losing their confidence in their own agency. They were also getting habituated to the kind of food that they had not learned to grow.

There might be some real necessity to rehabilitate the people in a limited area that is required to accommodate other populations in the Onge land. As Sinha observed in this connection, 'Their (aboriginals) economic self-sufficiency suffers from two very serious limitations:

(a) A very large tract can maintain only a small band.
(b) The productive skill is too poor to put them up with comparatively advanced civilized contact.

The amount of social integration of these aboriginals is very great. They have the deepest sentiment for their motherland and have no kinship or other bonds with people outside the islands' (Sinha, 1955: 28)

When a large tract of land was taken away for settlers from outside, some alternatives were required to be provided to Onge for their survival. In the changed circumstances, when we consider the subsistence activities of the present day Onge, it gives a dismal picture. Though the Onge live in this modern world, their cultural clock is more in tune with techno-economy of the Stone Age. The Onge have lived with their relatively archaic culture in geographic isolation. Measures have been taken to make them at par with other mainstream societies. Their subsistence economy is being discouraged without giving them any viable alternative. Wage labour, a product of the modern market economy, was introduced among them. The people, who never knew anything beyond their own world of sea and forest and numerous spirits, were suddenly exposed to a modern way of living. Under the circumstances it was very likely that this sort of sudden change would not lead to gradual transformation but a culture shock for which the people were not at all prepared. Thus they became victims of circumstances to which they could not adjust.

If changes are introduced in a pre-literate society which does not have any socio-economic specialization, the whole system is affected. Therefore, the changes introduced in the self-sufficient economy of the Onge, affected their entire culture quite drastically.

The entire social structure of the Onge was changed as a result. Earlier, as wanderers, they had the communal hut (*beyra*) which was the pivot of the Onge social structure. It was a big hut shaped like a beehive, very nicely built with shared labour of the entire band. The people were affiliated through *beyra*. It was the centre for all socio-ritual activities. Now they do not build any communal hut as it had lost its significance in the changed circumstances. They did not even use the communal hut made by AAJVS for any purpose. Old values were losing ground very fast but, for the Onge, it was too big a leap to catch up with the modern way of thinking and living.

It can be said that the Onge society does not show any sign of structural transformation, which manifested itself through the process of diversification. Often, diversification in society takes place through gradual change that needs must be from within and it follows a long process of social evolution. Induced changes cannot ordinarily transform a society without disturbing its given structure. Nor can they bring about structural changes without disturbing the harmony. Largely due to this, the Onge suffer from multiple maladies at present. In such a society it is necessary to introduce gradual changes within the given structural frame. According to Meena, development means, '(i) a change for better, (ii) never-ending change, (iii) gradual change, (iv) a combination of qualitative and quantitative change, (v) change in all spheres–political, social, economic and administrative and (vi) not necessarily a copy of Western countries' (quoted in Kabra 1984: 11). But the Onge experienced a sudden change, with the transformation of their traditional economy, which they could hardly comprehend properly. They were exposed to an entirely new way of life today as bewildered captives in their own land, who do not have the choice of living a life their own way.

REFERENCES

Basu, B.K., 'Problems of Contact and Welfare Among the Onge: A Hunter Gather Community of Andaman Islands' (unpublished), 1984.

Kabra, G.D., *Development of Weaker Sections: Organisational Alternatives*, New Delhi: Inter India Publications, 1984.

Sahlins, M., *Stone Age Economics*, Chicago and New York: Aldone Atherton, Inc., 1972.

Sinha, S.C., *Resettlement of East Pakistan Refugees in Andaman Islands*. Report on Survey of Further Possibilities of Resettlement, Government Press Alipore, West Bengal, 1955.

CHAPTER 2

Geo-historical Perspective of Little Andaman

GEOGRAPHICAL OVERVIEW

The Little Andaman Island is a part of the Indian archipelago of the Andaman and Nicobar Islands spread over the southeastern Bay of Bengal, forming a broken arc of landmasses containing 319 islands, besides many smaller rocky fragments having a total geographical area of 8,293 sq. km. From 6° north to 14° north latitude these islands cover about 700 km with the longitudinal extent between 92° and 94° east having an average width of 26 km. The distance of this archipelago is 1,800 to 2,400 km from the mainland of India. It is just 1,122 km away from Sumatra Island of Indonesia and 400 km from Cape Negrais of Myanmar. Incidentally, only 38 islands are inhabited, of which 26 are in the Andaman Group and twelve are in the Nicobar Group (Figure 2.1).

Geologically, the archipelago is connected to the origin of the Himalayan mountain system of the Tertiary period resulting out of tectonic collision between the Indo-Australian and Eurasian continental plates. In terms of plate tectonics, the archipelago is formed along the western edge of the Burma micro-plate with the Andaman Basin on its east. The great Sunda Subduction Trench along the western margin of the archipelago has been a tectonically active line for at least 55 million years in the late Palaeocene Epoch of the Tertiary period. In fact, the post-2004 earthquake and tsunami researches revealed that the Indian plate in the Bay of Bengal is thrusting under (i.e. subduction) the Burma micro-plate along the Sunda Trench in southern Bay of Bengal, northwestward, at an annual rate of 60-70 mm as reported by the USGS (http://walrus.wr.usgs.gov/tsunami/sumatraEQ/tectonic.htm).

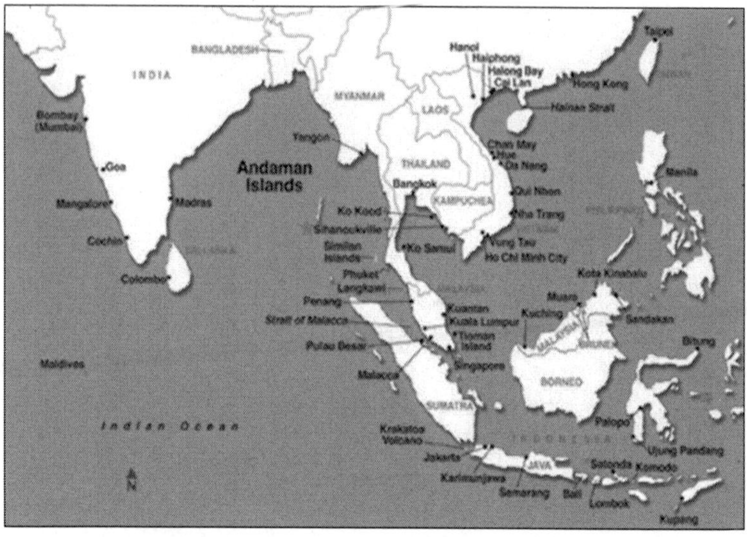

Source: www.vacationstogo.com/cruise_port/Hanoi_(Halong_Bay)__Vietnam.cfm

Figure 2.1: Location of Andaman and Nicobar Islands.

This tertiary fold mountain system, standing on the oceanic floor, has two sedimentary formations—the Port Blair Series and the Archipelago Series. In the Port Blair Series, the rock types are grey sandstone with inter-bedded shale (Oldham 1884). The Archipelago Series is a dominant rock group and consists of soft limestone formed of coral, shell, and soft calcareous sandstones and soft white clays with occasional bands of conglomerates. Of all the formations, the eocene rocks are most widely prevalent. They occupy the three main islands, i.e. North, Middle and South Andaman Islands. Conglomerate rock formation is common in North Andaman and in some parts of Middle Andaman, while sandstone is common in South Andaman.

ANDAMAN OROGENY

In the absence of any conclusive theory about the origin of these islands in the midst of the Bay of Bengal, there are three prominent hypotheses which constitute a partial discussion of the origin of the islands (Murthy, 2007). These are as follows:

1. *Sir Charles Darwin's Theory:* The English evolutionist Sir Charles Darwin's theory is the most accepted one. In 1842, he concluded that the subsidence of a volcanic island resulted in the formation of a fringing reef and the continual subsidence allowed complete submergence. Thus the atoll encircling the lagoon was formed. Then, with the action of wind, waves, currents and temperatures, etc., the coral islands were formed. Sandbanks are the first to be formed in an atoll. Soon they became the breeding ground for sea birds. Eventually, as a result of the fertilization of the soil by bird droppings, ground vegetation became possible. Thus, the island became suitable for human habitation. This is all that is known about the evolution of the islands that still holds good and is accepted by most of the people.

2. *The Continental Drift Theory*: Alfred Wagener's Continental Drift Theory (1915) tells us that the southern landmass of the earth called Gondwanaland, split to form India, Australia, Africa, South America, etc. The Indian landmass or Gondwanaland took millions of years to drift and compress the Tethys Sea to finally join Angaraland or mainland Asia and the collision of the two landmasses resulted in the formation of the mighty Himalayas. This hypothesis is aptly supported by the discovery of sea fossils at impossible heights of the Himalayas. The Eastern Himalayas extend right up to Burma as the Arakan Yoma range. The Andamans are nothing but the visible upper portions of the long mountain ranges, which primarily remained submerged in the sea of this region. In fact, this is considered as further extension of the Himalayan system to the Cape Negrais in Myanmar to Achin head in Sumatra Island of Indonesia. Hydrographic studies of the seabed around the islands confirm the tongue-like projection of the mountain range through Cape Negrais in Burma. Anthropological, botanical, zoological and geological lists of evidence also support this theory. Several researchers have postulated that these islands, at some stage, had physical contiguity with the landmass of Myanmar. This land connection, in fact, provided the migration route for the Negrito tribal groups from mainland Myanmar to the Andaman Islands. Later on, the mountain range subsided under the sea and got disconnected from the mainland due to geological movements. The present islands are thus nothing but the highest crests of the submerged mountain range.

3. *The Plate Tectonics Theory*: Arthur Holmes in 1929 provided a mechanism for plate movement of the earth's crust largely inspired by the Continental Drift Theory, which raised several unanswered questions. According to this theory, the Andaman and Nicobar Islands developed due to tectonic movements of the two continental plates under the seabed of the Andaman region. As a result of the subduction of the India plate below the Burma mini-plate, a long chain of islands formed from Myanmar in the north to Indonesia in the south. This also explains the presence of volcanoes in the region. Incidentally, the Andaman and Nicobar Islands fall under 'Seismic Zone V' as they are near the boundary of the Indian plate and the Burma plate. Earthquakes in and around these islands are due to the submarine subduction process.

The depth contours on the west show the existence of a lofty range of submarine mountains between Cape Negrais and Achin head in Sumatra. The works of Colonel Sewell (1840) proved the theory of connections with the mainland since the Triassic period. It was further opined by Kurz in 1866 and Oldham in 1884 that these were the residues above water of the submarine subsidence which was still continuing. Sir R. Temple supported this theory in the census report, 1901. Indeed, Boden Kloss, in *The Andaman and Nicobar* (1903), made a thorough study of the flora and fauna of the island and holds that there has never been any surface connection with the continent. About 150 million years ago, due to geological disturbances, the land near about these islands submerged into the sea and the summits of the mountain range and other elevated areas standing out of the sea became the islands of the present day, known as Andaman and Nicobar. R.D. Oldham also believes that the land now constituting the Andamans first appeared above the sea as an extension of Cape Negrais in the latter part of the Tertiary period and later became isolated by subsidence due to neighbouring volcanic action. Oldham's report of 1884 also confirmed the theory of continuing subsidence of the islands by Kurz (1866), though North Andaman and Nicobar are showing signs of recent upheaval. The subsidence seems to be of recent origin, and signs of its continuance, most markedly on the east coast, are found at several places: Port Mount, Rangachang on the east coast of

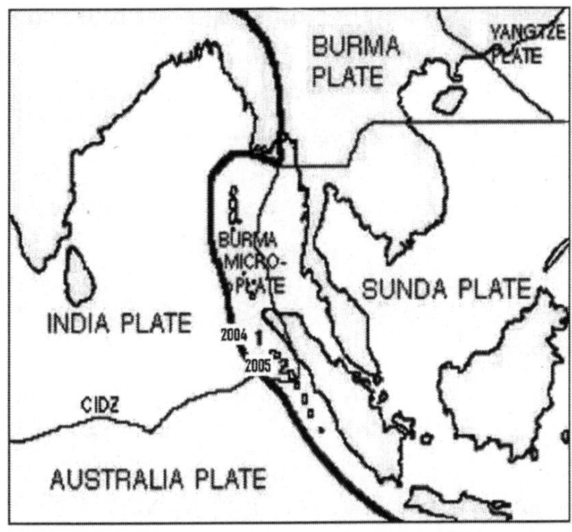

Source: www.sumatra-indonesia-earthquake.weebly.com

Figure 2.2: Layout of Plates around Andaman and Nicobar Islands.

South Andaman near Port Blair, Outram Harbour and Havelock Island in the archipelago, the northern ends of Little Andaman, North Sentinel and North Andaman. Again, the physiographic state of these islands has gone through a remarkable change from the impact of the 2004 earthquake and tsunami.

Though it is logical to presume a former land connection from Cape Negrais in the southern part of Burma to Achin Head (Cape Pedro) in Andalas (Sumatra), the flora and fauna of these islands indicate that this land connection, if it existed, would have been prior to the development of the present lifeforms inhabiting them.

Natural Resource Base of Little Andaman

The rocks of Little Andaman are chiefly limestone and sandstone, with widespread coral on the east and south coasts. Occasional igneous outcrops are also common (Kloss 1903). In the west, central and southern parts, the land is mostly around 75 m above the mean sea level. In the coastal belt, the maximum relief is attained near West Bay, which varies from 60 to 90 m above mean sea level while the whole of the northern and most of the eastern coasts are mainly flat. In between West Bay and Jackson Creek, the coast is totally rocky and has a higher gradient. Rock outcrops are seldom visible due to thick cover of tall trees in most parts of the island. There are numerous streams on this island flowing from the centre towards the coast in a radial pattern, only with the exception of one. This stream, second in length, flows parallel to the coast, originating near West Bay and falls in the Jackson Creek. The longest stream, commonly called Bara Nala, originates in the heart of the island and flows northeastward. There are four major creeks, namely, Jackson Creek, Bumila Creek, Egu-Belong, and Dugong Creek.

The island experiences both southwest and northeast monsoon owing to its location in the middle of the Bay of Bengal and closeness to the equator. In general, the climate is moderate owing to maritime influences. Despite its north-south elongation, no significant latitudinal variation is seen. Moreover, relief plays no role in controlling the climate, except minor local weather phenomena.

For obvious reasons, the vegetation of Little Andaman is very similar to that of the other islands of the Andamans. The tropical Andaman forest, distinctly Indo-Chinese and Malayan in character and akin to the Sunda biogeographical zone, can be broadly divided into littoral and non-littoral types of forests. The non-littoral coastal forest is characterized by an extensive growth of mangroves, pandanus, nipa palm, etc., which act as protector of shoreline and coast and also have economic value as firewood and alternate food. The coconut and pandanus are the characteristic littoral flora of Little Andaman. The main part of the Andaman forest comprises evergreen trees, climbers and patches of deciduous growth. Timber has been the main source of revenue. Nearly 41 per cent of the forest area is set aside as aboriginal tribal reserve and about 24 per cent, being the coastal belts, etc., is unsuitable for productive forests. Thus, hardly about 35 per cent of the forest area is available for commercial forestry operation. According to the revised Forest Survey Report (2012), the following types of forests have been recognized on these islands:

1A / C1	Giant Evergreen Forests
1A / C2	Andaman Tropical Evergreen Forests
1A / C3	Southern Tropical Evergreen Forests
El	Bamboo Brakes
2A / C1	Andaman Semi-Evergreen Forests
3A/ Cl	Andaman Moist Deciduous Forests
4A /LI	Littoral Forests
4B / TS2	Tide Swamp Forests (Mangrove)

There is no carnivorous animal on Little Andaman. Special mention may be made of the wild pig (*Sus andamanensis*), the wild cat (*Paradoxurus*) and the iguana. Important among the few poisonous snakes are the cobra, the hamadryade, the krait, several sea snakes and pit vipers. Besides, many varieties of fish, turtles, crocodiles and dugong (herbivorous sea mammals) constitute the important marine fauna of Little Andaman.

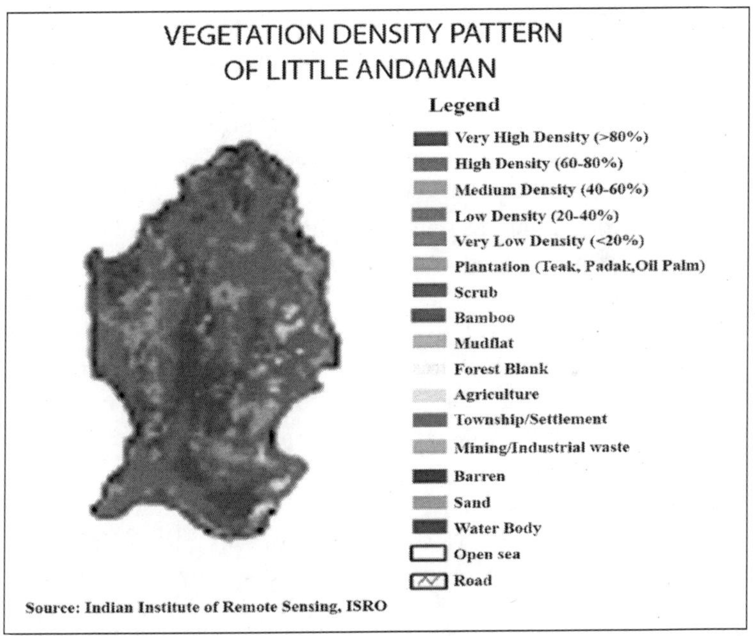

Figure 2.3: Vegetation Density and LULC map of Little Andaman Island.

Locational Aspects and Peopling

Little Andaman possesses a distinct geo-political and strategic character because of its distant location, diverse physiographic framework, ethnic diversity and economic slowness with disparity in levels of development. Moreover, the island region is flanked by three foreign countries, viz., Myanmar (315 km), Thailand (500 km) and Indonesia (90 km) and historically linked by sea routes through the Andaman Sea, Bay of Bengal, Arabian Sea, and Indian Ocean.

Little Andaman, the homeland of the Onges and the southernmost island of the Andaman Group, is located within the 10°30' N and 11° N latitudes. Its maximum length from north to south is about 44 km. The general elliptical shape of the island is disturbed to the south by the presence of four large bays, namely, West Bay, South Bay, Hut Bay and Butler Bay. On an average, the western shoreline is more rugged than the eastern, and the bays on the east are smaller in size than those on the west and south of which they are only two in number.

The locational uniqueness of the archipelago has been reflected in the historical diversity of this region. Indeed, during the first millennium AD, the Chinese and Japanese knew the region as Yang-t'amang and Andaban respectively. Nicole Conti, in an attempt to give the word Andaman a meaning, called it 'The Island of Gold'. In contrast, in the great Tanjore inscription of AD 1050, the islands appear to be mentioned under the translated name, Timaittivu, which means the islands of impurity, perhaps, because they were considered the abode of cannibals.

Since time immemorial, the Malays were using these islands. They would sail across the seas, capture some of the aborigines and sold them as slaves in trade. The Malays called them the islands of Handuman, because that is how they pronounced the name of Hanuman in the *Ramayana*. The Handuman became Andaman in course of time. Sir Henry Yule, who wrote a commentary on Marco Polo, suggested the term Angamanian, the name Marco Polo used, meaning dual in Arabic, indicating the two Andamans—the Great and the Little Andaman. Ptolemy described these islands as 'the islands' of good fortune. Arab merchants, on their way to the Strait of Sumatra, first reported the existence of these islands in the ninth century. The first Western visitor was Marco Polo, who called it 'the land of the head-hunters'. The Marathas annexed the islands in the late seventeenth century. In the early eighteenth century, the islands were the bases of Maratha admiral Kanhoji Angre, whose navy frequently captured British, Dutch, and Portuguese merchant ships.

The Nicobar Islands were annexed by Britain in 1869 and were joined with the Andaman Islands to form a single administrative unit in 1872, when the British established a penal colony for political prisoners here. Thus the Andaman Islands acquired the sinister name *Kala Pani* (Black Water). Since 1858, the British administration took up the reigns of development on these islands and started exploiting the natural resources here, and accordingly, formulated strategies to achieve their ends. Their stay lasted till Indian Independence in 1947. Today Cellular Jail, originally meant for political prisoners, is a major attraction along with the martyrs' memorial for tourists visiting the territory.

These islands were also under Japanese occupation during the Second World War from 21 March 1942, till 8 October 1945. In this war the Japanese had no difficulty in capturing the archipelago, from where their aircraft would bomb Calcutta and Madras. Indeed, the strategic importance of these islands to control Asia was realized by the Japanese. During the Indian Independence movement, Netaji Subhas Chandra Bose also paid a visit to these islands and named these islands 'Shahid and Swaraj'.

In Independent India these islands were opened to the people of all states for settlement. Bengalis from East Pakistan were the major population group who first came to these islands under the rehabilitation scheme of the Government of India. The permanent population now includes Indians, Bangladeshis, Sri Lankans and Karens from Myanmar. These islands were severely affected by the tsunami in December 2004.

The Andaman and Nicobar Islands have been inhabited for several thousand years. The earliest documented archaeological evidence goes back about 2,200 years; however, the indications from genetic, cultural, and linguistic isolation studies point to their peopling during the Middle Palaeolithic period. In the Andaman Islands, various

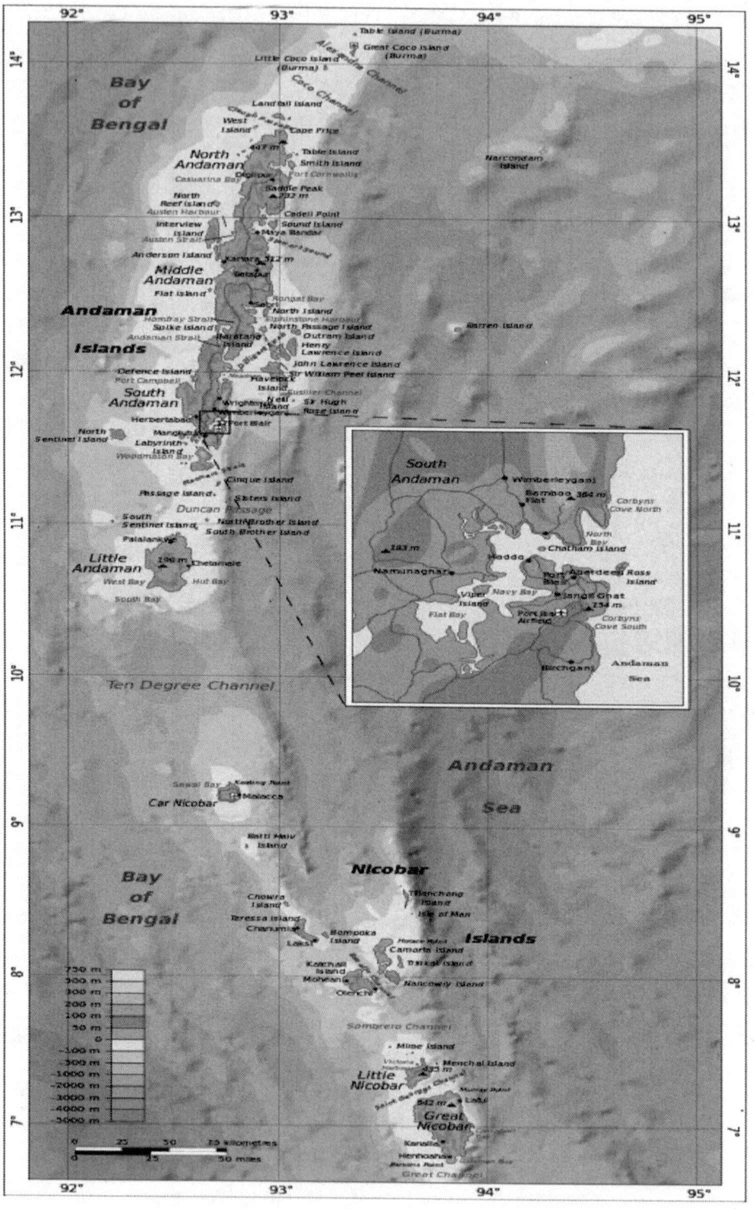

Source: http://www.maphill.com/india/andaman-nicobar/3d-maps/physical-map/

Figure 2.4: The Andaman and Nicobar archipelago.

Andamanese people maintained their separate identities through most of this time, diversifying themselves into distinct linguistic, cultural, and territorial groups. By the 1850s, when they first came into sustained contact with outside groups, the indigenous peoples of the Andamans were:

1. The Great Andamanese, who collectively represented at least ten distinct sub-groups and languages
2. The Jarawa
3. The Jangil (or Rutland Jarawa)
4. The Onge; and
5. The Sentinelese (the most isolated of all these groups).

At the time of the first encounters, these community groups numbered somewhere around 7,000, in all. As the number of settlers from the mainland increased (at first mostly prisoners and involuntary indentured labourers, later purposely recruited farmers), these indigenous peoples lost territory and numbers in the face of land encroachment and the effects of various epidemics. The Jangil and most of the Great Andamanese groups soon became extinct. Presently, there remain only about 400-500 indigenous Andamanese, the Jarawa, excepting a small group, and the Sentinelese, in particular, maintaining a persistent aloofness and refusing most attempts of contact.

The indigenous peoples of the Nicobars have a similarly isolated and lengthy association with the islands. There are two main groups:

1. The Nicobarese, or Nicobari, living throughout many of the islands; and
2. The Shompen, restricted to the interior of Great Nicobar.

The islands remained an abode for the aborigines prior to the colonization of these islands by the British, particularly after 1857. The aboriginal people belong to the Negrito stock and their way of life may be considered as the living form of the most ancient style of life. They are short in stature, their skin is black and their hair frizzy. There are some biological and cultural similarities of these tribes with the southeast Asiatic Negritos, like the Semangs of Malaya Peninsula and the Aeta of Philippines. Regarding the distribution of the four

Negrito tribes on three different islands of the Andaman and Nicobar, there are a number of assumptions, but all have a common proposition, that for their nomadic nature these tribes moved to different islands in their canoes.

At present, out of the 38 inhabited islands of Andaman and Nicobar archipelago, only four are inhabited by these aboriginal groups. Except the Shompen and Nicobarese, all other tribes belong to the Negrito stock and inhabit three islands of the Andaman Group. The Shompen belong to Mongoloid stock and are found on the Great Nicobar Island. The aborigines of the Andaman Islands have been experiencing a gradual shrinkage in their total command area because of the expansion of the area of influence by the new settlers. The Jarawa are today confined to the western part of the Middle and South Andaman Islands, the Onge to the Dugong Creek and South Bay areas of Little Andaman, the Great Andamanese to Strait Island and the Sentinelese to the North Sentinel Island. The relationship of the aborigines with the outsiders has been one of deep distrust and hostility, because of the unfriendly attitude of the outsiders. While the Great Andamanese and the Onge were coerced to be friendly during the colonial period, relations with the two other Negrito groups continued to be sour even during the post-Independence days. Decades of friendly gestures by the Andaman administration ultimately succeeded in the Jarawa being befriended in 1998, but this has not been the case with the Sentinelese. However, the acceptance of 'friendship' on the part of the aborigines has proved to be a bane for them as their numbers have drastically come down after the friendly contacts.

Contact and Conflict

Little Andaman has remained the homeland of the Onges from time immemorial. Prior to their rehabilitation in the lately provided government settlements, the movements of the Onge generally remained restricted within the bounds of the island. Only occasionally would they go to nearby islands, as far as Port Blair, in their dugout outrigger canoes.

In recognition of the significance of Portman's paper on the exploration and surveys of Little Andaman (1888), Professor Flower, Director of the Natural History Museum, remarked:

It was most remarkable that Little Andaman . . . was, till Mr Portman visited in 1880, as isolated from the civilized world as any region could be. The natives had lived there for thousands of years without any communication with the outside world except with the unfortunate shipwrecked crews that had been cast upon their shores, whom they appeared to have invariably murdered. One of the greatest privileges anthropologists could have at the present day was to be brought into peaceful contact with such a race and to be able to lift up the veil behind which they had been so long concealed. (Portman, 1888: 8-10)

For a considerable period, the Onges could evade all attempts of contact for conciliation by outsiders successfully through their hostility towards all strangers. In 1867 the captain and seven crew members of the ship *Assam Valley*, which landed in Little Andaman, never returned. A search party led by Mr Homfrey was sent for the missing persons, but the party failed in its mission due to the hostility of the Onges. Then the ship ICS *Aracan*, sent armed men on a punitive expedition to the island and they located the remains of the murdered men. The expedition resulted in severe fighting with the Onges, killing at least 70 of them (Census of India 1931).

THE EVER-SHRINKING ONGE RESERVE

As has already been stated, there had been a rapid increase in the non-Onge population in Little Andaman during the post-Independence period. The island was opened up for rehabilitation of refugees from East Pakistan in the year 1969 as a part of the colonization scheme of different islands, and the process continued with similar settlement of Tamil repatriates from Sri Lanka and Mynamar alongside the settlement of Nicobarese from Car Nicobar to reduce the population pressure on Car Nicobar Island. Some families of the Mopalah community from the South Andaman Islands were settled on Little Andaman (Table 2.1).

As usual, the rehabilitation of families required huge government

TABLE 2.1: SETTLEMENT OF REFUGEE FAMILIES

Community	No. of families	Year of settlement
Bengali	366	1969-79
Nicobarese	165	1973
Tamil (Sri Lanka)	25	1977
Tamil (Burma)	8	1977
Mopalah	83	1979

Source: Census of India 1981.

machinery and manpower for execution of programmes. So, apart from the rehabilitation department, there came up other departments like Andaman Harbour Works, Forest Department, Andaman Public Works Department, etc. Understandably, the presence of a considerable population attracted a large number of traders too. Over the years, the non-Onge population has grown very fast and has far outnumbered the Onge. In 1961, there were about 140 non-Onge on Little Andaman of whom 114 were labourers. This grew to 1911 in 1971. This increase in non-Onge population was due to opening up of the island for refugee rehabilitation. In successive decades, the non-Onge population has grown by leaps and bounds, mainly due to immigration. There were 18,722 non-Onge people against only 106 Onge during the 2011 census enumeration (Table 2.2).

With a view to preserving the habitat, tradition and life of the vulnerable tribes of these islands, the Andaman and Nicobar administration has renewed notification of different reserve areas for each during 2011 (Table 2.3).

Surprisingly, there exist certain variations in the reserve areas and the total geographical area and population of these tribes and the respective islands, even among different government departments. As per the Directorate of Economics and Statistics, Andaman and Nicobar Administration Little Andaman Tehsil, the island has a total population of 17,528, during 2010-11 of whom 1,223 belong to the Scheduled Tribes, including Onge, Nicobarese and others. The Islandwise Statistical Outline for 2016-17 shows the total area of the island to be 734.39 sq. km and area under forest 700.05 sq. km. On the other hand, latest figures revealed by the National Commission

TABLE 2.2: VARIATION OF THE ONGE AND NON-ONGE POPULATION

Year	Onge Population	Non-Onge Population
1901	672	0
1911	631	0
1921	346	0
1931	250	0
1941	0	0
1951	150	0
1961	129	140
1971	112	1,911
1981	97	7,214
1991	97	13,452
2001	96	16,500
2011	106	18,717

Source: Census of India 2011.

TABLE 2.3: RESERVED AREAS FOR SCHEDULED TRIBES IN ANDAMAN AND NICOBAR ISLANDS

S. No.	Name of Tribe	Area (in sq. km)
1.	Shompen	991.61
2.	Onge	731.60
3.	Great Andamanese	6.02
4.	Jarawa	1,028.00
5.	Sentinelese	59.67

Source: Annual Report of AAJVS 2010-11.

For Scheduled Tribes it shows only 403.37 sq. km as under the Onge Reserve (Table 2.4). The Forest and Plantation Development Corporation, A & N Island, has reported the total area of Little Andaman as 731.416 sq. km against 731.60 sq. km as per AAJVS. In volume *DCHB*, Part B, South Andaman, of Census of India 2011, the Onge population in the Dugong Creek settlement is shown as 101 where the community is settled after the tsunami of 2004. A total of 734.39 sq. km area is reported by the Forest Survey of India in 1981 in the Report on Forest Resource of Little Andaman.

TABLE 2.4: TOUR NOTE OF SECRETARY, NATIONAL COMMISSION FOR SCHEDULED TRIBES TO ANDAMAN & NICOBAR ISLANDS FROM 15-19 JUNE 2017

The demographic composition of the tribes of Andaman & Nicobar Islands is as follows:

Name of Tribe	Location	Population	Tribal Reserve (in sq. km)	Category
Andamanese	Strait Island	67 (actual)	6.01	PVTG
Onges	Little Andaman	118 (actual)	403.37	PVTG
Jarawas	Middle & South Andaman	480 (actual)	1,040.84	PVTG
Sentinelese	North Sentinel	50 (estimated)	59.67	
Shompens	Great Nicobar	238 (estimated)	853.19	PVTG
Nicobarese	Nicobar District	27,168 (as per 2011 census)	899.764	ST only
	Uninhabitated islands used by the STS		16.441	
Total	UT of A&N islands	28,077 (7.39%)	3,279.285 (32.79 %)	

Source: National Commission for Scheduled Tribes.

WELFARE MEASURES

At the Onge settlements, the Andaman Adim Janjati Vikas Samiti (AAJVS), the official tribal welfare body of the administration, introduced a range of foodstuff, such as rice, dal, oil and biscuits, to a community whose traditional food included the meat of wild boar and turtle, fish, tubers and honey. The agency even offered each adult 250 g of tobacco as a 'welfare' measure. This has partly contributed towards making them indolent.

In fact, the welfare scheme, in all practicality, was a blatant attempt to move the forestry operations deeper into the Onge reserve, by settling the nomadic Onge at Dugong Creek in the northeast of the island and at South Bay at its southern tip. During the settlement, the Onge of Jackson Creek joined the Onges of Dugong Creek while the Onge of South Bay preferred to stay back. A locational analysis of the Onge settlement suggests certain disadvantages, which are as follows:

1. The Dugong Creek location is nearer the settlement of the non-Onge and thus more prone to poaching. If at all the Onge were to be settled, the western coast would have been a better choice.
2. Settling the two territorial groups of the Onge together at Dugong Creek meant that more people were foraging in the same area, using similar resources.

Wooden houses on stilts, with asbestos roofing, were constructed for Onge at these places, which were naturally not suited for the hot and humid tropical environment of the islands. The Onge people preferred to live in their traditional huts in the forest nearby. The houses were certainly not suitable for the hot and humid climate of the island, as during daytime they become too hot to stay in. During the initial years, the Onge made a hole in the floor to defecate, especially during the night as they dared not go out at that time. Earlier, the Onge used to migrate to the forest during summer. Now this practice had been abandoned. Instead, they raised some temporary huts near the settlement to avoid the sultry summer weather.

Simultaneously, attempts were made to introduce a cash economy in a community which did not even have a barter system. Ill-conceived schemes, such as the raising of a coconut plantation (in which the Onge people were made workers), cattle-rearing (the community does not consume milk) and pig breeding, were introduced. All of them failed. During our long stay at those settlements, it was noted that the Onge people were found being used to do menial chores, such as fetching water, for welfare workers appointed by the administration.

The present land use pattern on Little Andaman shows that out of a total of 77,699.37 ha. of land available, 3,435.96 ha. is under revenue, 1,768.7 ha under plantation, 47,295.34 ha. under forest and 25,200 ha. under tribal reserve. On analysis of the land use pattern, one finds that there has been a two-third reduction in the territory of the Onge. Presently, the Onges have only 25,200 ha. under them. Though officially the Onge have never been prohibited from entering and using the resources of the reserved forest, regular extraction of timber by the Forest Department has greatly thinned the resources of the reserved forest. It is only in year 2000, due to a court case, extraction activities from the reserved forest came to a halt. Besides, the forestland adjacent to villages had been encroached upon for agricultural and settlement purposes. Recent study shows that the settlers' population regularly visit for resource extraction, forest areas falling in the radius of about 10 km. Thus, roughly 40 per cent of the entire territory is out of reach of the Onge. Though Little Andaman was the abode of the Onge, their habitat also encompassed North and South Brother Islands, Cinque Island and Rutland. They used to visit these islands for honey, turtle, turtle eggs and wild boar. Since late 1970s the Onge have stopped visiting them as these islands are visited more by outsiders (Sekhsaria 1999).

TSUNAMI AND AFTER

After the devastating effects of the tsunami in 2004, all the Onge from South Bay settlement were shifted to a new site near the old Dugong Creek settlement. It is really noteworthy that while the non-tribal population and even the Nicobarese people suffered a lot from the tsunami waves, the Negrito communities like the Onge, Jarawa, Sentinelese, and the Great Andamanese had not suffered any casualty. With their traditional knowledge of strong earthquakes, not uncommon in this seismically and tectonically active zone, they could foresee the disaster. The elderly Onge of the Dugong Creek settlement ran to the sea beach after the tremor, in anticipation, and then came back rushing to alert all fellow members. Then they ran towards the forest and reached a known high point to avoid the surge. Later they were shifted to a place southwestward near the Ramakrishnapuram village but after a few days they chose their new settlement site in the forest and settled there. The site, as narrated by them, was an old deserted settlement site named Tandalu (see box below).

EXCERPTS FROM *WHEN LAND BECAME WATER: TSUNAMI AND THE ONGE OF LITTLE ANDAMAN ISLAND* BY VISHVAJIT PANDYA

The population of Andaman islanders is made up of 43 Great Andamanese on Strait Island, 97 Onge of Little Andaman Island, the 240 Jarawa of South and Middle Andaman Islands, together with about 39 Sentinelese of North Sentinel Island, were all safe and well taken care of in the immediate aftermath of the tsunami. What was remarkable, however, is that in contrast to non-indigenous settlers, the indigenous tribal community of Onge on the morning of 26 December showed a greater resilience in response to the grave disaster. They have picked up the pieces of their lives and started rebuilding them without depending entirely on an evidently hard-pressed administration. Soon after the tremors, about 83 Onge packed up systematically and walked through the forest from Dugong Creek for about three hours to the southwest location of Ramakrishnapuram. Here, for a total of eight days, they stayed in a shelter set up by the administration where rations, water and medical care was provided. But by the 9th of January the Onge decided to move back into the jungle and set up their own campsite, using a minimum of the relief material made available in abundance by the administration. Nevertheless, the welfare agency and island administration continued to provide rations and resources on a regular basis to the Onge in a new location selected by the Onge themselves. Within the bounds of the reserve forest they have set up their own camp site at a location known to them as Tandalu. Instead of waiting for all the relief, the Onge have already resumed hunting and fishing and gathering from different parts of the forest.

The first impression I had on reaching the Tandalu campsite was that the Onge were happy that they had broken away from the administration-imposed-and-created settlement of Dugong Creek that was now badly damaged.

Though the Onge could escape the wrath of nature their island habitat was much affected due to the combined assault of the tsunami and anthropogenic pressure. The results of measurement of change through much reliable satellite imageries covering both pre- and post-tsunami land cover of the island depicts a clearer picture.

The 2003 and 2005 satellite data analysis indicates that the 60,091.47 ha. of reserved forest has shrunken to 59,854.34 ha. by 2005. Further in the year 2010, 443.87 ha. of thick vegetation and 206 ha. of sparse forest were cleared (Shankar et al. 2013). Approximately, 859 ha. of forest in total have been destroyed in just a span of eight years. Further, it is clearly evident that this deforestation is due to the expansion of human settlements (Table 2.5). Roughly, an increase of 859 ha. between 2003 and 2010 in settlement area is noticed. The

TABLE 2.5: LAND USE AND LAND COVER CHANGES IN LITTLE ANDAMAN ISLAND

Land Use	Area (ha.) 2003	Area (ha.) 2005	Area (ha.) 2010	Changes in Area (ha.) between 2003 and 2005	Changes in Area (ha.) between 2003 and 2005	Total Changes in Area (ha.) between 2003 and 2010
Settlement with vegetation	4,161.72	4,371.25	5,021.12	-209.52	-649.87	-859.4
Reef area	1,759.5	1,582.09	1,582.09	177.41	0	177.41
Sand over reef	0	177.06	177.06	-177.06	0	-177.06
Mangroves	5,295.45	71.1	3,187.38	5,224.35	-3,116.28	2,108.07
Degraded mangroves	142.18	147.13	494.15	-4.95	-347.02	-351.97
Submerged mangroves	0	3,463.3	0	-3,463.3	3,463.3	0
Damaged mangroves	0	1,756.1	1,756.1	-1,756.1	0	-1,756.1
Reserved forest	60,091.47	59,854.34	59,410.47	237.13	443.87	681
Sparse forest	1,184.3	1,206.29	10,00.29	-21.99	206	184.01
Plantation	48.11	48.11	48.11	0	0	0
Sandy beach	583.07	588.55	588.55	-5.48	0	-5.48
Tidal mudflat	151.2	151.68	151.68	-0.48	0	-0.48
				0		
Total Area	73,417	73,417	73,417			

Source: V. Shiva Shankar et al. (2013).

Note: The above figures confirm that the correct area of the island as 734.17 sq. km at the first instance and that there have been considerable changes in land use categories, Damages in mangrove, coral reef and forest cover are remarkable and vital to the Onge economy.

annual rate of expansion was found to be 107.42 ha., as observed. The deforestation is prominent around the existing settlements, as compared to an earlier period.

REFERENCES

Cooper, Z., 'The Origin of the Andaman Islanders: Local Myth and Archaeological Evidence', *Antiquity Journal*, 67: 394-9, June 1993.

——, *Archaeology and History: Early Settlements in the Andaman Islands*, New Delhi: Oxford University Press, 2002 http://www.andamanonline.in/about/Profile/History/index.html# sthash. r7839ema.dpuf

Hutton, J.H., *Census of India 1931*, vol. 1, pt. 1, 1933.

Klosse, C.B., *In the Andaman and Nicobars*, London: John Murray, 1903.

Kurz, S., 'Report on the Vegetation of the Andaman', in R.D. Oldham, *Records of the Geological Survey of India*, Calcutta, 1884, pt. II, p. 335.

Murthy, P.V.R., *Andaman and Nicobar Island: A Geo-political and Strategic Perspective*, New Delhi: Northern Book Centre, 2007.

Oldham. R.D., *Records of the Geological Survey of India*, Calcutta, pt. II, 1884, p. 474.

Portman, M., *The Exploration and Survey of the Little Andamans*, London: Royal Geographical Society, 1888.

Sewell, R.B.S., 'Geographic and Oceanographic Research in Indian Waters', in *Journal of Asiatic Society of Bengal*, vol. IX, no. 1, 1840.

Sekhsaria, 'A People in Peril', in *Frontline*, vol. 16, issue 9, 24 April-7 May 1999.

Shiva Shankar, V. et al., 'Pre and Post Tsunami Changes of Land Use and Land Cover in the Little Andaman Island, India: A Geospatial Approaach'. *International Journal of Earth Sciences and Engineering*, vol. 6, no. 1, February 2013.

CHAPTER 3

Ecology of Little Andaman: The Onge Perception

GEOGRAPHICAL SETUP OF LITTLE ANDAMAN

This southernmost island of the Andaman Group is located within 10° 30' N and 11° N latitudes. Its maximum length along north-south is about 44 km. The general elliptical shape of the island is disturbed to the south due to the presence of four large bays: West Bay, South Bay, Hut Bay and Butler Bay. On an average, the western shoreline is more rugged than the east and the bays on the east are smaller in size than those on the west and south.

The rocks of Little Andaman are chiefly limestone and sandstone, with a good deal of actual coral rock on the eastern and southern coasts; while occasionally some outcrops of igneous nature are present (Kloss 1903). In the western, central and southern parts, the land is mostly 75 m above the mean sea level. In the coastal belt, the maximum relief is attained near West Bay which varies in the range of 60-130 m. The whole of the northern and most of the eastern coasts are mainly flat. In between West Bay and Jackson Creek, the coast is totally rocky and has a high gradient.

Rock outcrops are seldom visible due to a thick cover of tall trees on most parts of the island. Rivers are numerous in this region. All rivers or streamlets flow from the centre towards the coast in a radial manner, with the exception of one. This river, second in length, flows parallel to the coast originating northward near Bara Nala West Bay to fall into Jackson Creek. The longest river, commonly called Bara Nala, has its source in the heart of the island and flows northeastward. After taking a sharp bend southeastward it falls into the Andaman Sea near the northeast coast.

Another most important feature here is a large number of tidal creeks near the mouth of these rivers. This makes human movement very difficult. Among those creeks, the major ones are Jackson Creek, Bumila Creek, Egu-belong Creek and Dugong Creek. They are distinctively different due to their short but wide extent and vast tracts of saline swamp near the mouth. These features, along with several other observations by the early European visitors, clearly indicate evidences of several coastal submergences of land. These submerged offshore areas have helped develop an intensive chain of coral reefs along the eastern coast, restricting the approach from sea. But the west coast has remained almost free from coral development due to higher gradient of the shore and strong wave action during the southwest monsoon. These creeks and coral reefs around the island offer uninterrupted supply of several marine species of different sizes and shapes.

By virtue of their location, the Andaman Group of Islands experience subtropical hot and humid weather conditions, which tend to be somewhat moderate due to the marine influence of the Bay of Bengal. Instead of its north-south elongation (10°30'-13°30' N) no significant latitudinal variation is seen. Moreover, relief plays no role in controlling the climate, except for minor local weather phenomena.

Primarily, these islands are very much on the route of the south-west monsoon. In fact, the Bay of Bengal monsoon, in all probability, originates from the warm sea water around these islands. The process starts from the middle of April and the first week of May is the expected time for the monsoon outburst. The rain continues till the end of September or even up to November. In the short course of its return journey in the form of the northeast monsoon, the wind also produces some rain here between October and December. Hence, the driest period of the year is between January and April, though in actuality no rainless month is recorded (Table 3.1).

At Port Blair, the mean maximum temperature is close to 30 °C while the mean minimum becomes 23 °C. The maximum daily range of highest temperatures is attained during the months of February, March and April. Similarly, the lowest daily range and mean temperatures occur during the period from June to September.

TABLE 3.1: MONTH WISE GENERAL WEATHER CONDITION AROUND BAY ISLANDS

Month	General Wind Direction	Rainfall	Sea Surface	Temperature Condition	Remarks
January	N & NE	Traces	Mostly calm	Fairly cool	–
February	N & NE	A few showers and dew	-Do-	Cool with strong sun	–
March	N & NE	Traces	Calm	Warm day cool night	–
April	N & NE Changing	Heavy if early monsoon	Calm to rough	Very hot sultry	–
May	SW & W	Heavy	Quite rough	Pleasant	Monsoon outburst on the first day
June	SW & W Squall	Incessant	-Do-	-Do-	–
July	-Do-	-Do-	-Do-	-Do-	–
August	-Do-	-Do-	-Do-	Fairly cool	–
September	-Do-	Heavy	-Do-	-Do-	–
October	SW & W Changing	Infrequent	Rough to calm	-Do-	–
November	NE Changing	Occasional	Gets rough	Fairly cool	Sea and weather uncertain
December	N & NE	-Do-	Rough	-Do-	–

Sources: Based on Nigam (1962) and Meteorological Statistics, A & N Islands (1984).

The mean monthly relative humidity curve reaches its peak during the southwest monsoon months from June to October, when the percentage reads between 80 and 90 per cent. But humidity never falls below 66 per cent, indicating a fairly high humid condition in these islands.

SEASONS

Generally, a year is divided into three main seasons, depending on the prevailing climate conditions in this region.

(i) *The southwest monsoon*: The longest and most prominent season in Andaman Island starts from the month of May with a sudden rise in humidity as well as rainfall. The temperature tends to be high (29 °C). The strong southwest and westerly winds blow continuously hitting the western coast. Sometimes trees are completely stripped of their leaves. The normal maximum wind speed recorded in June is 20 km per hour.

(ii) *The northeast monsoon*: The next season starts with the gradual withdrawal of the southwest monsoon leading to a complete reversal of the prevailing wind direction. Thus at the end of October or early November, the northeast monsoon currents come to the region with a lower velocity of wind and lower rainfall. As the temperature remains in the lower margin (25 °C) during this period, along with a decreasing trend of humidity, November and December are the two most pleasant months on the island. But this is also the season for destructive cyclones which cross the archipelago on a northwesterly path causing large damages in all respects.

(iii) *The dry season*: During the next four months, the Bay Islands mostly remain dry with only about 50 mm of mean monthly rainfall and a rising trend in the mean maximum temperature (Table 3.1).

CLIMATIC VARIATIONS IN LITTLE ANDAMAN

Situated in the heart of the archipelago, meteorologically, the island demands no separate treatment. However, our interest is in having an idea about how the original inhabitants of Little Andaman, the Onge, perceive the climate and the weather around them for their survival through a hunting-gathering economy; hence there has been an attempt to study the available data recorded at Hut Bay Meteorological Observatory on the island. The following features can be observed:

(i) According to the normal annual rainfall figures published in 1984, the Hut Bay Station receives the highest rainfall in the whole of Andaman and Nicobar Island, though the total annual rainfall for sixteen years (1970-86) shows a moderately high Coefficient of Variability (C.V.-12 per cent).

(ii) The normal monthly rainfall figure shows that the island receives maximum rainfall during June and July similar to other islands but in November-December, the retreating monsoon also gives a fair amount of rain similar to a few places in the Nicobar Group of Islands.

(iii) Utilizing the available data (1987-8), the monthly wind speed of Hut Bay is comparable with the normal wind speed of Port Blair, to note a few marked differences. It is peculiar that in Hut Bay, a very low velocity is recorded during the southwest monsoon months. This phenomenon can probably be related to the location of the observatory on the eastern coast. Moreover, the station is not well exposed to the normal path of the wind because of the high wall of dense tropical forest just 200 m on the western side. Hence, only the westerly (west and south-west) winds are wrongly recorded but the velocity of other winds do match well with the normal condition of the region (Table 3.2).

(iv) From our own records of daily temperature at the main camp at Dugong Creek, using a maximum-minimum thermometer, figures for the months of January-March 1986 and August-September 1988 are available (Table 3.3). In comparison with Port Blair, Dugong Creek shows a markedly lower range of temperature during the observed months, though the mean monthly temperature remains the same. The daily range is lower in August-September (about 1.75 °C) than in February-March (3.8 and 4.0 °C). Moreover, in the drier months (January-March), both the maximum and minimum daily temperature fluctuate more than those in the wet months (August-September).

(v) Both from the memories of the local settlers as well as witnessing several large uprooted tree trunks along the coast, one can easily

TABLE 3.2: COMPARISON OF WIND SPEED AT PORT BLAIR AND HUT BAY (km/h)

Station	Jan	Feb	Mar	Apr	May	June	July	Aug	Sep	Oct	Nov	Dec
Port Blair (Normal)	5.74	5.14	5.16	5.62	8.86	20.7	15.0	19.3	11.8	7.76	7.16	7.78
Hut Bay (1987-8)	5.35	5.20	5.10	5.60	6.50	4.50	4.20	4.8	4.5	5.35	5.12	7.20

Source: Meteorological Statistics, A&N Isands (1984).

TABLE 3.3: RECORDED TEMPERATURE AT DUGONG CREEK, LITTLE ANDAMAN (°C)

Month	Year	Mean maximum	Mean minimum	Mean monthly	Mean daily range
January	1986	29.05	26.90	28.25	2.56
February	1986	30.28	25.74	27.04	3.87
March	1986	31.20	27.00	27.61	4.10
August	1988	27.80	26.02	26.08	1.77
September	1988	26.80	26.75	26.05	1.61

Source: Recorded during field study.

assume the ravages of cyclonic storms along the eastern coast. Most mentioned cyclones are those that hit the island in November 1988. But data regarding the western coast is totally absent.

THE ONGE PERCEPTION OF THE ECOLOGY OF THE ISLAND

The Onge, in their endeavour to exploit the natural resources for survival, had developed a fairly good knowledge of their own habitat. This knowledge is the result of face-to-face interaction between man and nature through their hunting-gathering activities. Records show that till the middle of the seventies of the previous century, these expert sea-faring people used to visit several surrounding islands of Little Andaman such as, Rutland, Cinque, Brother and Sister Group of Islands, even going as far as Port Blair. Moreover, in spite of about two decades of interference of government welfare organizations and outsiders, these primitive hunter-gatherers have preserved their ability to survive on their own as they have been doing for centuries. The root cause of their success is perhaps their own expertise and adjustment with nature through traditional wisdom developed out of the study of knowledge of their own habitat.

TOPOGRAPHICAL FEATURE

The names of the old Onge settlements bear the significant physical features of the area. Though, at present, very few of the Onge can explain or recollect the traditional significance of those, still they use certain physiographic terms to indicate the topographical features and geographical regions of the island.

It is interesting to observe that in accordance with the common morphological divisions of several Andaman islands, the Onge have traditionally divided their own island into two regions, i.e. the coastal plains and the central forested upland area. Most expectedly, they developed this regionalization to signify the basic difference in the immediate habitats of the coast dwellers (*embelakwe*) and the forest dwellers (*engeakwe*). Thus the communal huts or (*beyra*) have been grouped according to their location on the coast or inland.

The term *engakwaleye* has been used to denote the group of huts located far from the coastal plains inside the inland forest. The remaining coastal rim of land has again been divided into north and east coast and south and west coast, which have been called *giremekaye* and *girerarátwaye*, repectively (Nigam 1962).

Based on the plotting of the communal huts on the map of Little Andaman by Cipriani (1953) and the names of such huts distributed under those three geographical regions provided by R.C. Nigam (1962), we have attempted to draw the regional boundaries on the map of Little Andaman as perceived by the Onge.

Taking 22 select huts scattered all over the island, the tentative line of demarcation between the regions has been interpolated, which brings out certain features of the Onge's conception of their own habitat, as described below:

1. The coastal region varies in width from 2 to 6 km, encircling the whole island. Though the boundary, in general, does not follow any physical aspect like relief, in general most areas of the interior forest region are above 75 m in contour height.
2. The coastal region is widest on the southwestern corner (about 10 km) formed by a tongue-shaped sandy flat land north of South Bay, described in Cipriani's map as Sandy Point. The boundary line between the coastal and inland regions comes closest to the sea near Hut Bay on southeast coast.
3. Neither the two coastal regions nor the inland region is divided according to any topographical feature like relief, etc. Moreover, the terrain itself has nothing to justify the question, as to why the north is linked with the eastern coast and the south with the west in respect of regionalization. Perhaps the answer lies with the most dominant physical factor in this region, the wind. Hence it may not be unwise to presume that these two coastal sub-divisions have been made as per the frontal zones of the two major winds, i.e. the southwest and northeast monsoons. Therefore, the south and west coast regions or *girerarátwaye* is the zone maximum affected by the strongest currents of southwest monsoon and hence wider than the *giremekaye*, the zone facing northeast milder monsoon. The central forest belt is a protected zone sandwiched between

two winds. It is thus obvious that the Onge of these three geographical zones experience different seasonal characters which have been reflected in their calendar of seasonal subsistence activities (Figure 3.1).

The Onge knowledge of their own habitat is further enriched by the way they identify the micro-topographical features around them. While staying with these people for a fairly long period, it was observed

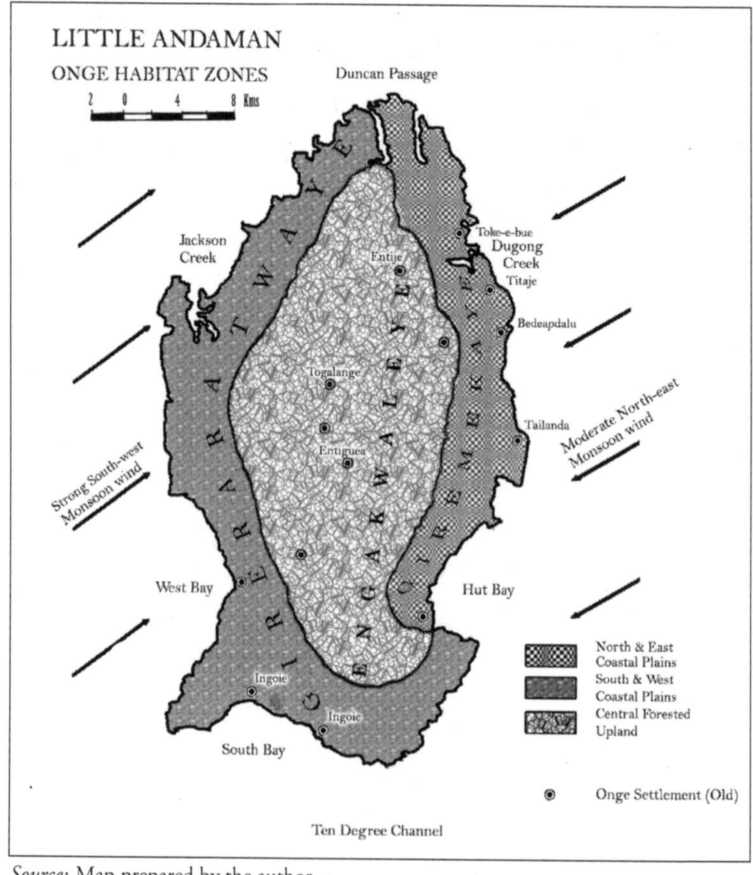

Source: Map prepared by the author.

Figure 3.1: Major old settlements or *beyra* shown in the Onge habitat zones.

that they used some terms to denote specific types of surface features. These probable physiographic terms are in fact related to their hunting and gathering activities in terms of accessibility to the forest or availability of certain games, etc.

Thus, *butu* is a type of forest where it is easy to chase a pig as it is a dry forest of tall trees with less undergrowth, and thus easily accessible for pig hunting. In South Bay, the Onge use another term, *kalo*, which is almost synonymous with *butu*, as described by the Dugong Creek Onge. It may be mentioned that it is a very common practice among the Onge to use different terms for a single item. It is mostly situational or related to speaker concern.

Tambojoko is a forest full of cane and bamboo, an ideal site for cane collection. This is less accessible for hunting. The intricate net of the breathing roots in the vast mangrove forest is the real barricade for these people, who describe the same as *kwakolodo*. This area is chosen by the Onge for collection of large crabs and small fish.

Another type of land surface around South Bay settlement which is highly broken with scattered rocks is called *enale*, a typical example of which is marked by the portion of land between the rivers Kwechenna and Chanaram Nang on the extreme southwest corner of the island. The *dembere* is a land just south of the *enale* where the surface is relatively less rocky.

The coral reef near the Dugong Creek shore suitable for group fishing during extreme low tide, is called *parene*. While the end point of such a reef zone is called *kimboi,* this is nothing but the head of the bay with bare rocks and corals.

KNOWLEDGE OF SKY, WEATHER AND CLIMATE

The Onge, being among the earliest settlers of this region, perceived the island weather and climate very well and developed a strong perception of their own. During our stay with them in different seasons, it had become evident that most of their daily activities were in one way or the other related to nature, particularly to the climate and weather condition. In fact, these people have acquired a regular meteorological observation and forecasting system completely indigenous to them. The elderly male members of each settlement acquired this knowledge from the previous generation and passed on the same to the next one. Thus they fixed up the days for hunting and gathering activities according to the weather, for example days of calm sea were selected for long sea voyages for turtle hunting or visiting other islands as practised in earlier days.

In order to have an idea about the Onge perception of meteorology we interviewed them in two ways. First, the adult males of different age groups were asked about their conception of a calendar, if any, and seasonal variations in weather, and secondly, we tried to establish a relationship between different subsistence activities with seasons or periods of a year.

THE ONGE CALENDAR

A calendar is something used to fix time in terms of days, months and year which is necessary for any people regulating their life cycle activities. Being hunter-gatherers, the Onge traditionally had no activities other than for subsistence, which were primarily hunting, fishing and gathering. Day in and day out, their life used to revolve around these activities only, with some intervals in between. As they could not count beyond three, no concept of week or month developed among them. Only day and night were perceived with the appearance or disappearance of celestial bodies like the sun, the moon and the stars. Their subsistence activities were, however, very much related to the varying weather and climatic conditions of the region. Phenomena like wind, rain and tide had a direct bearing on their subsistence activities. It was expected that they must have some knowledge to synchronize their activities with such natural phenomena, especially the tide which has a direct relationship with the waning and waxing of the moon. So, though they could not count beyond three, they had some sort of a lunar almanac to observe the tide for regulating their activities in the sea. Without any knowledge about tides and the character of waves, no people can venture to sail on the sea. Depending on the fact that, in the Onge vocabulary, natural objects like the sun, moon, ocean, wind, cloud, etc., are so meticulously described, we decided to explore the relevance of those in the Onge way of life. With great difficulty, we could make them understand enough to describe the changing phases of the moon, as observed at night.

During our field visit in 1988 the Onge could utter a few words to signify the different phases of the moon. We explained the thing by showing a simple chart depicting the shapes of the moon, both in the waning and waxing phases during one lunar month. They identified some of those and the terms thus obtained were checked and cross-verified repeatedly from several Onge individuals. Eventually, we could make a tentative Onge lunar calendar. As their present state of knowledge did not permit the Onge to make any numerical calculations, they demarcated the phases of moon on the basis of qualitative observation, i.e., the shape and size of the moon for a particular period of days. On that basis they described a long cycle of the moon, dividing it into several phases at two to three day intervals.

It was observed that the Onge used the moon to correlate the tidal conditions of the sea and other weather conditions. Hence several names were given to the full and new moon when extreme tidal levels occurred and, accordingly, they planned their activities in the sea. In fact, two days before and after the full and new moon are the most important period to the Onge for crab collection and turtle hunting. They also identified the period of the lowest tidal effects with minimum fluctuation of sea level in a day. Hence the full moon, new moon and half moon have been denoted by some specific terms or names. Similarly, there are names of the other phases of the moon according to their importance and associated phenomena. These names may be compared with the *tithi* of the Hindu almanac.

Ikutueme is the most widely used term for the full moon while in the general Onge vocabulary, the word is related to anything big or large or full grown. It means that the moon has attained its maximum size. *Gakoegambutebe* or *gobumamebe* is also used to refer to this phase of the moon which starts from two-three days before the full moon. These two terms are also used for the waxing phase of the moon. The following three days are named as the *gakoearalabe*. During the five to seven days around full moon, the Onge observed that high tides occurred during the early part of the day and accordingly planned community fishing on coral reef at midday and afternoon during low

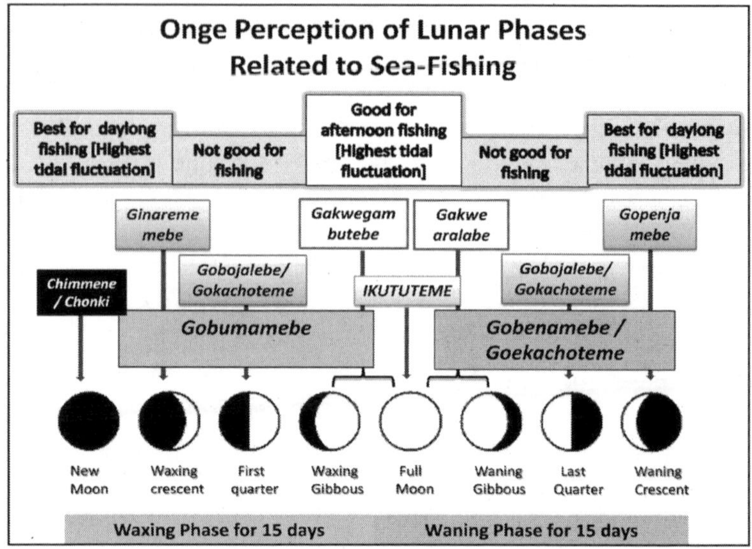

Source: Prepared by the authors.

Figure 3.2: Onge perception of lunar phases and related fishing activities.

tidal levels. This period is considered most suitable for such activities. However, the tide does not fall enough to expose the coral reef during the middle of the lunar fortnightly phase (between the full and new moons). Hence, the few days around the 7th or 8th day after the full or the new moon are not suitable for fishing or turtle hunting and the Onge call this phase *gobojalebe* or *gokachoteme* or *gokacholegube*. Again, the new moon or the dark phase is expressed by several terms, such as *chimmene* or *chonki*. The Onge have also marked the slim crescent shape of the moon which appears immediately before and after the new moon. These relics of moon are called *ginarememebe* or *gopenjamebe* (*genjamebe*). This phase of the moon is also equally important to them as the maximum tidal fluctuation occurs during this period and fishing activities are common as during full moon. There might be some minute distinction signified by different terms which we could not decipher. Sometimes it also happened that the terms varied according to the sex and civil condition of a person referred to. To cite an example there are two different terms or words for the moon itself, one term for the person who passed through the initiation ceremony and the other term for young boys, whose initiation was yet to take place. All this signifies the importance of the moon in Onge culture. This is particularly so as no such variation is observed in case of the sun or other celestial bodies. However, the Onge divide a whole day on the basis of the sun's location above the horizon.

Though the Onge cannot make finer (astronomical) distinctions within a particular phase of moon they are quite aware of the time of appearance and disappearance of the moon in the night sky without looking at the moon and measure the level of the sea water without going to the sea. Not only that, the Onge can also identify the two fortnightly phases, i.e. the waxing and waning periods between two successive full moons. We noted that *gobumamebe* denotes the period of waxing and *gobenjamebe* (*goekachoteme* after Ganguly) to that of waning. Moreover, some of the expert sky watchers among the Onge can read relative positions of certain stars to identify the phases of the moon. They pointed out one bright star as 'Acha Baruera' which can be observed around the moon. This star rises ahead of the moon during the waning or decreasing phase and appears after the moon in the phase of waxing. Hence, when this star is seen very close or on the same line with the moon it must be a period around full moon. So by observing this single star they can easily identify the *ikututeme* phase (full moon) and also almost correctly answer the number of days left before or after full moon, which is very important to them.

WEATHER AND SEASON

To the Onge people, wind is the most important element of climate and they have given different names for winds blowing from different directions. In fact, depending on the major prevailing wind currents they have marked four seasons having different weather conditions which cover almost one year as per the modern concept of calendar. Thus names of winds are synonymous with the names of seasons. We did not find any Onge term denoting directions but they always indicate the direction with the help of certain names or simply by pointing towards the intended direction. Nevertheless, their conception of direction is mostly proved perfect.

In fact, in general, there are two well-defined seasons in the

Andamans—the rainy season or southwest monsoon and the dry season or northeast monsoon. The rainy season extends from mid-May to October and the span of dry season is from mid-November to March or April and for much of this period the wind blows from the northeast. The Onge believe that special categories of spirits are responsible for sending the winds from their respective places. In the northeast quarter of Little Andaman, far across the sea, is the land of *Mekange* who send the northeast wind. In the southwest quarter of Little Andaman lies the land of *Kwalokange* and a little southward from it is the land of *Dare*. These two kinds of spirits sent southwest winds which bring rain. All these lands of spirits have their special characteristic features in terms of natural phenomena like tree and animals. These two seasons are primarily based on wind types. As the Onge are wholly dependent on nature for subsistence, availability of certain food articles also forms one of the characteristic features of a particular season. They are perfectly aware of things like what fruits or plants are edible or the season in which pigs are available and when they have maximum fat on their bodies.

Thus, on the basis of the wind and other weather conditions like rainfall or cyclone and availability of food materials, the Onge have divided a year into four seasons. It should be mentioned here that they do not have any term related to a complete year and thus never have the conception of the solar cycle, excepting the day. As they do not have any seasonal festival to be observed at any particular point of time, they cannot mention which season marks the beginning of a year but they do explain the sequence or the cyclic order of these four seasons. For our convenience we chose the southwest monsoon season or *dahre* as the first season due to its longest duration and importance to these people.

The Onge identify the onset of a season mainly by a change in wind direction and certain related changes in weather conditions as well as the growth of certain plants or fruits in the forest. To mark a season, they also studied types of clouds that were formed during different periods of the year and recognized the main characteristic clouds of different seasons as well. Thus *enakoe* means a rain-bearing cloud mainly seen during *dahre* or the southwest monsoon. But *beyja* is a common term meaning a heavy dark cloud full of rains; e.g. cumulus or cumulonimbus clouds. They pointed out one cloud type in early *mekange* (end of September) as *onibototagulum* which they saw only in the evening. Likewise, during the hot sunny days of *torale,* the white high cloud termed in Onge language as *bamboage* and the cloud (also a high one) which declared the start of honey collection, was named *uerele* (cirrus or cirrostratus).

Other than clouds they also identified certain birds as the indicator of a season. During mid-September at Dugong Creek some of the Onge men showed us an insect-eating bird walking swiftly on the sandy soil near the settlement with a continuous flip of its tail. They call it *mekende* and believed that its appearance signalled the onset of the season *mekange*, or the end of rainy season. Moreover, they never hunted or hurt the bird as they believed that this might result in severe chest pain and also stormy weather. In Bengal, the bird is known as the *khanjana.*

The Onge predicted rainfall almost correctly by observing clouds. There were certain beliefs regarding some categories of cloud formation among them. When on a moonlit night, a halo was formed around the moon (as a result of a cirrostratus cloud cover), they described the phenomenon as *abatotaeku* and believed that a celestial person named Chendalui had cleaned the moon with soap, so foams had accumulated around it. They expected a few showers with wind in the near future when such phenomena occurred. Through repeated interviews with most of the adult Onge males (some elderly Onge women also provided information in this regard), we collected a series of general views regarding seasons from which a tentative seasonal calendar could be prepared.

It is important to remember that the above attempt to divide the year according to the Onge seasons cannot be absolute or correct as these seasons are related to the effects of certain weather conditions and would vary from year to year. For example, the Onge can include the month of May into *Torale* if there is an abnormal delay in southwest monsoon outburst.

In an attempt to compare the four seasons identified by the Onge, with the system of three seasons adopted by meteorologists of today,

TABLE 3.4: SEASONAL CYCLE AS PERCEIVED BY THE ONGE

Name of the Season	Wind and Wind Direction	Weather Condition and other Related Phenomena	Duration of Period	Availability of Subsistence	Any Other Information
Dahre	Early part of southwest monsoon, wind from west coast or southwest.	Heavy rainfall, sky full of dark clouds, rough sea	May to mid-August	Fish available near sea shore, pigs accumulate maximum fat.	*Tanagiru* (initiation ceremony of young boys observed).
Kolokwange	Later part of south-west monsoon, wind from Car Nicobar i.e. south or southeast	Maximum velocity of wind with occasional heavy rain and cyclonic storms (*bigobakulla*) high waves in the sea (*ingatinge*)	Mid-August to mid-October	Fish, turtle, (dugong in early times) available maximum in the sea and wild potatoes in the forest.	
Mekange	Northeast monsoon north wind from north and northeast, wind from Port Blair.	Little rain with lower temperatures, mostly clear sky.	Mid-October to December of wild potatoes.	Maximum availability	Arrival of the *mekande* bird indicates the onset of this season. It is observed that this particular bird starts coming by the end of September and is seen till early October.
Torale	Northeast monsoon north wind continues as in Mekange	Totally dry and sunny hot weather.	January to April	Honey collection in the forest.	Appearance of white high clouds *uerele* marks the beginning of this season. When honey will be finished the Torale season will also be over.

Source: Authors.

we find the great relevance of Onge perception. Most expectedly, the basis of seasonal divisions followed by these hunter-gatherers are their subsistence activities rather than the simple expression of climatic parameters. Hence the wind directions and its velocity are related to the factor of availability of fish and turtle. According to the Onge, the rainy season (southwest monsoon) is important because pigs get fat and are also easy to hunt due to water-logged forests. Hence they usually fix up the date of *Tanagiru* or the initiation ceremony during *Dahre* (May-July), as it necessitates regular availability of pigs in the nearby forests. Likewise, *Kolokwange* is a season of sorrow and hunger because the sea becomes rough and the forest becomes inaccessible and risky due to high-speed winds and cyclonic weather. They said that they usually become weak during this season. The *Mekange* brings to them a mixed fortune, as they start fishing and turtling regularly and collect large quantities of wild potato and fruits from the forest. *Torale* is the driest period of the year and it is enjoyed by them most when movements in the forest and on sea become the easiest to carry out for their hunting and gathering pursuits. The Onge likes the season of *Torale* most when life seems to be enjoyable also due to less rain and availability of various kinds of food. Moreover, this is the season they welcome warmly, as honey, their most favourite delicacy, becomes available. The appearance of *uerele*, the white high cloud, marks the beginning of both honey collection and the *Torale* season, though there is a marked change in wind direction from that in *Mekange*.

In the course of studying the geographical perception of this steadily declining population, it was realized that not much scientific investigation has been made in this direction. The main reasons behind this may be similar to the problems faced by us in finding out the latent knowledge of these people, for instance: (i) only the elderly persons (mostly senile) still possess the complete knowledge but can hardly communicate even with their own youngsters; (ii) most of the Onge are not well conversant with any language other than their own and it is difficult to find a suitable interpreter; (iii) the younger generation is confronting forces of acculturation by contact with the nearby 'civilized' settlers; (iv) the basic need and usage of their traditional perception are getting unimportant gradually, due to the interference by welfare agencies; and (v) consequently, the Onge are leaving behind their nomadic habits and restricting their movements within a very limited area around their permanent settlements.

Moreover, perhaps not much time is left before these people become totally extinct, both culturally and otherwise.

REFERENCES

Cipriani, Lidio, 'Report of a Survey of the Little Andaman During 1951-53', *Bulletin of Department of Anthropology* 2 (1): 61-82, 1953.

——, *The Andaman Islànders*, London: Weiden Feed and Nicolson, 1966.

Nigam, R.C., 'The Onge of Little Andaman: Their Settlements and Population', *Vanyajati*, 10 (3): 44-53, 1963.

——, 'The Onge of Little Andaman Factors of Habit', *Vanyajati* 11: 55-67, 1962.

CHAPTER 4

The Onge Population

The declining trend of the Negrito populations the world over has created an alarm among anthropologists as well as demographers. Friendly contact was established with the Onge in 1886-7. Since then their population is steadily decreasing. In 1858, they numbered 700. During earlier days, due to their nomadic habit, it was very difficult to get the correct estimation of the Onge population. Thus the estimated figures of their population given in the decennial census are not of much value. However, the Anthropological Survey of India (AnSI) started conducting systematic research among the Onge of Little Andaman since 1948. In that year, a short visit was paid by Dr B.S. Guha, the then director of the AnSI, and following his visit, a number of officers of the Survey started planned anthropological investigations. Data on population could be ascertained from the study of Nigam (1953-5), De (1960) and Agarwal (1963-4). We have ourselves recorded the data on population representing the years 1984, 1986, and 1988. Fortunately, the major bulk of the then Onge population had been recorded in the studies of Nigam and De. From De, we obtained the pedigrees which we updated in 1988. These pedigrees helped us reconstruct the reproductive history of the women of complete sibships. Otherwise, owing to their superstitious belief, it would have been very difficult to elicit the names of the photographs from the AnSI collection and the published book by Cipriani. The Onge people felt very happy to see the old photographs of the dead persons. The photographs were identified by them. It is a general belief that with the utterance of the name of a dead person, one's face will be deformed on one side. But one or two progressive Onge after seeing the old photographs overcame that fear. These people helped us in eliciting the genuine information, especially from the women who could remember all the people either dead or alive.

Though the decennial figures do not represent the picture of the Onge population through the ages, it gives the reader an idea about the trend of population growth (Figure 4.1).

The sharp fall in the Onge population is evident from Table 4.1. It should be mentioned here that the decennial figures up to 1951, do not represent the correct picture as the figures were mostly estimated ones. Since 1955 (the figures based on actual enumeration at regular intervals), the rate of decrease is maintaining a lower gradient. The general trend shows a declining residual population similar to a negative exponential growth.

A similar trend is observed in the decadal percentage variation of the population (Figure 4.2). The general negative variation is in a lower tone after 1951. The average decadal variation since 1955 is 12.23 per cent negative. If the present trend persists, the population may face an absolute stagnant condition within a few decades.

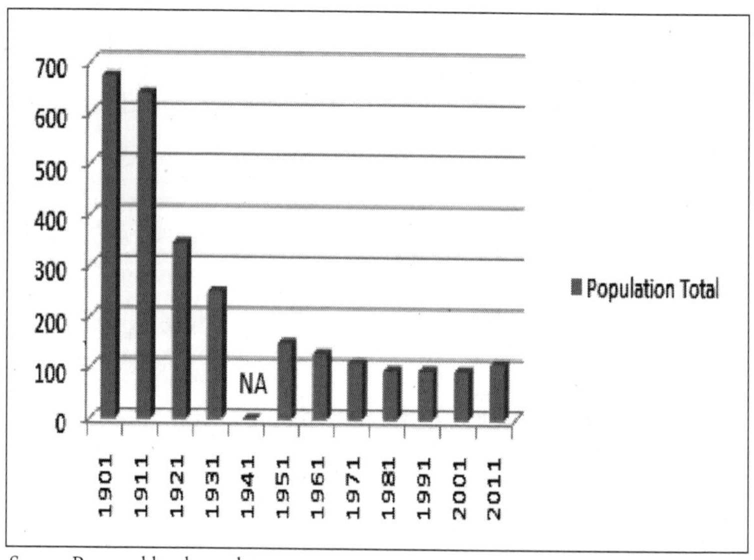

Source: Prepared by the authors.

Figure 4.1: Trend of Onge population during 1901-2011.

TABLE 4.1: POPULATION OF THE ONGE IN VARIOUS DECENNIAL CENSUSES AND IN SURVEYED YEARS

Year	Population			Source
	Male	Female	Total	
1901	531	341	872	Census 1901
1911	301	330	631	Census 1911
1921	204	142	346	Census 1921
1931	147	103	250	Census 1931
1941	–	–	–	Not recorded
1951	–	–	150	Census 1951
1955	76	85	161	AnSI *
1961	–	–	129	Census 1961
1969	61	60	121	AnSI
1971	59	53	112	Census 1971
1977	48	49	97	AnSI
1984	51	51	102	AnSI
1986	55	44	99	AnSI
1988	53	43	96	AnSI
1991	–	–	97	Census 1991
2001	–	–	96	Census 2001
2011	–	–	101	Census 2011

Source: Prepared by the authors.

Note: AnSI = Anthropological Survey of India.

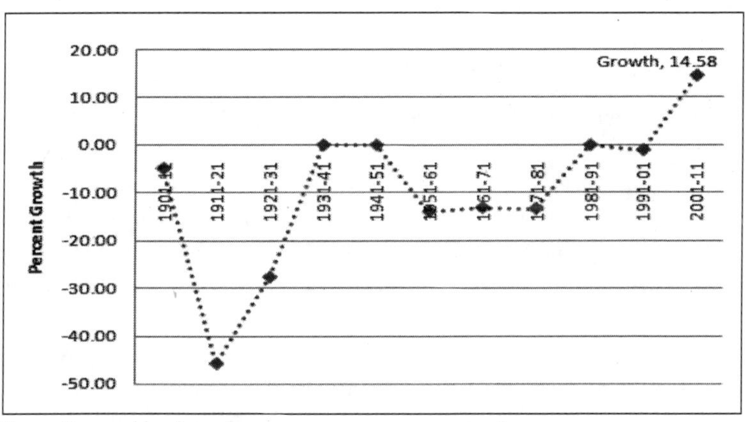

Source: Prepared by the authors.

Figure 4.2: Decadal growth rate of Onge population during 1901-2011.

TERRITORIAL DISTRIBUTION

Traditionally the Onge habitat of the Little Andaman Island was divided into three geographical regions and the population was categorized on the basis of ecology as coast dwellers (*embelakwe*) and forest dwellers (*engeakwe*) (Nigam 1960). Each region was inhabited by a number of local groups (*beyra*). In fact, *beyra* is the term for the beehive type of communal huts where a number of affiliated families used to live. So residential affiliation acts as a social institution in the life of the Onge, as they do not have any clan like organization. As an institution, the communal hut performs the function of a clan, especially regulating the cultural aspect of sexual life of the people, i.e., it determines the degree of incest. The communal huts were often named after the characteristic physiographical features of the immediate surroundings. In summer months, the Onge used to move into the interiors of the forest, partially to avoid heat and to save botheration of traversing a long way for hunting purposes when the pig population also moved further inside. The Onge used to camp in the communal huts during the peak of the rainy season.

In earlier days, the communal huts were located almost all over the island without any particular pattern of distribution. From the report based on field studies made during 1955-6, it was learnt that an Onge population not exceeding 200 souls were spread out in about 30 *beyra*. On the basis of their geographical location these communal huts were of the two native categories of the population which have already been mentioned. Three geographical regions, according to the cognition of the Onge, were as follows: (i) *Giremekaye*, which included the *beyras* and their inhabitants of the northern and eastern coast; (ii) *Girerarattwaye,* formed by the huts on the southern and western coast of the island, and (iii) the *Engakwaleye* region, which was the thickly forested interior of the island (Figure 3.1).

Cipriani plotted the communal huts for the first time by trekking the island. It is believed that there were some discrepancies in his mode of enumeration. However, it is a fact that since the 1950s, the number of communal huts is constantly getting lesser. Some of the huts from the very early time were inhabited by a very small number of people.

It seems that with the death of this handful of persons, these communal huts would get lost. In this way, many communal huts mentioned in Cipriani's work got lost. With a first hand population record, we have tried to show the year-wise variation of population since 1955 (Table 4.2).

Before going into the analysis of the table showing variation of population by communal huts, we should make one thing clear about its role in the past as well as in the present. In Table 4.2 we have incorporated the data collected by the officers from Anthropological Survey of India. In the report of 1955-69, the inmates of communal huts, irrespective of their kin affiliation, were branded as members of that and only that hut. In that situation, married women who came from other huts as wives and widowed sisters who came back to their parental communal huts were considered at par with respect to hut affiliation. Thus the hut was more a residential than a structural unit though it had an important role in regulating marriage in Onge society. With drastic change induced in their habitat, the communal hut as residential unit no longer exists. The Onge people nowadays live in their individual family huts. However, they are very much conscious about their communal hut affiliation. It may be said that in the earlier days, communal huts determined the spatial organization of the group while now it holds the structure of the Onge society in general. Hence, for this very practical reason, in the present study, the women have been considered members of their parental communal huts.

For studying the variation of Onge population in different geographical regions, 22 major communal huts were taken into account. Comparison is made within four sets of population figures enumerated within a span of thirty years (1955, 1964, 1969 and 1988). It has already been mentioned that this data was collected by different teams of the Anthropological Survey of India during the aforementioned years. It should be noted that in earlier periods due to the location of Onge communal huts in relatively more inaccessible areas and their wandering habits, it is not unlikely that there might have been some data gap especially in terms of total enumeration. Some references are there regarding the presence of Onge population in Rutland Island up to 1921. But no Onge was reported from there in the Census of

TABLE 4.2: VARIATION OF POPULATION BY MAJOR COMMUNAL HUTS IN GEOGRAPHICAL REGIONS SINCE 1955

Geographical Regions	Sl. No.	Name of Communal Hut	Year				Total % Variation in 33 Years
			1955	1964	1969	1988	
A.	1.	Tokebuea	7	8	7	7	0.000
GIREMEKAYE	2.	Tambebuea	3	3	3	2	-33.3
(North and	3.	Titaje	6	9	11	8	+33.3
East Coastal)	4.	Badiabdalu	7	15	6	6	-14.3
	5.	Tailanda	5	3	–	1	-80.00
	6.	Kwatetu Kwage	7	6	6	3	-57.14
		Total	35	44	33	27	-22.86 %
% Variation per year			+2.8	-5.0	-0.9	–	-0.7
B.							
GIREMEKAYE	7.	Ingoi	13	6	4	3	-77.0
(South and	8.	Totibuea	–	12	13	6	-44.0 (in 24 yrs)
West Coastal)	9.	Koname	14	7	5	4	-71.4
	10.	Tagulemme	–	10	5	2	-80.0 (in 24 yrs)
	11.	Tulah	9	11	12	7	-22.2
	12.	Gaje	12	5	6	2	-83.3
	13.	Tochedda	–	3	–	2	-33.3 (in 24 yrs)
	14.	Genyadange	11	–	–	–	-100.00
		Total	59	54	45	26	-44 %
% Variation per year			-0.94	-3.3	-2.2	-1.34	

C.	15.	Togalange	15	15	11	19	+26.7
ENGAKWALEYE	16.	Entiji	8	3	2	1	-12.5
(Forested	17.	Entiguea	10	2	4	1	-90.0
Interior)	18.	Chemale	4	9	10	9	+125.0
	19.	Cheruge	5	–	–	3	-40.0 (incomplete)
	20.	Torabe	6	2	–	3	-50.0
	21.	Luijabokale	6	0	5	2	-66.60
	22.	Tebobe	2	–	5	4	+100.00
		Total	56	31	37	42	-30.36 %
% Variation per year			-4.9	+3.9	+0.3	-0.92	

Source: Based on L. Cipriani and field study.

1931 (Sarkar 1960). However, the available data which encompassed the major bulk of the then Onge population, highlighted the general trend of population at best up to 70-80 per cent correctness. In recent days there is no communal hut, and the *beyra* affiliation of each individual Onge is shown as reported by themselves.

From Table 4.2 the following features about the variations in Onge population over time become conspicuous.

(i) About 77 per cent of the population were concentrated in two geographical regions, viz., 'B', South and West coast, and 'C', the forested interior area, leaving 23 per cent in the north and east coastal area (the 'A' region). In 1988, around 42 per cent of people were from the 'C' region and the other two regions contributed equally to the remaining percentage (see Fig. 4.2).

(ii) There has been a remarkably high percentage of decrease in population (44 per cent) in the South and West coastal huts. North and East coastal people have suffered the minimum decline (-23 per cent) and the interior experienced a moderately high decline (-31 per cent) during the span of 33 years.

This phenomenon may be due to the occurrence of greater natural calamities like cyclonic storms during southwest monsoon and related phenomena in the southern and western coastal zones. The north and east coasts, being on the leeward side of the prevailing southwest monsoon, are naturally well-sheltered.

(iii) During the nine years between 1955 and 1964, the annual average variation of population shows a very high loss of lives in 'C' (-4.9) while population in 'B' remained almost constant (6.94) and the population of 'A' increased by 2.8 per cent. The next five years i.e. 1964-9, proved to be the worst for 'A' and 'B' while 'C' witnessed a gain of 3.9 per cent. This fact suggests a hazardous life for all the coastal Onge. The last phase of 19 years (1969-88) indicates a slow trend of stability in the population with the exception of 'B' which experienced a 2.2 per cent negative variation. It should be kept in mind that as the span is quite long, the per year rates have shown lower figures such as -0.7, -1.34 and -0.92, respectively, for 'A', 'B' and 'C' over the last 33 years.

(iv) In studying the rates of variation regarding the individual communal hut over 33 years, certain unusual things came into notice. The very high rates of negative variation in the communal huts in Genyadange (100 per cent), Gaje (83 per cent) Tailanda (80 per cent) Tagulemme (90 per cent) are difficult to explain due to a lack of detailed reports, though causes like boat capsize for a whole *beyra* group, desertion of a particular *beyra* for unknown causes or a greater number of marriage of women in any particular *beyra* and migration to other new huts may not be ruled out entirely. On the other hand, high increase of population, as in the *beyra* of Chemale (125 per cent), Tebobe (100 per cent), etc., can similarly be linked with marriage or migration or presence of a fertile couple at the time of enumeration.

Though the traditional communal hut is non-existent, the affiliation of the Onge to it is very strong. Marriage relations are prohibited among the members of the same communal hut.

In the olden days, marriage by capture was the conventional mode of acquiring a wife. Mates were often captured from another communal hut as there was no blood relationship. The present-day Onge population is 96, distributed over 22 communal huts (Table 4.3). In earlier records, too, we had almost the same number of communal huts.

The present settlement of Dugong Creek is the earlier site of the Tokebue communal hut. In fact, members of the communal huts located in the northern and eastern coasts and interior forests, i.e. the Onge of 'A' and 'C' regions are settled here. It has already been mentioned that 'C' has suffered the minimum loss of population during the last 30 years. In Dugong Creek, the members of the Togalange communal hut are the most numerous among all the groups, having a population of 19. In South Bay, out of 19 persons, 7 belong to the Tulah communal hut. The other important groups are Chemale, Titaje, Tokebuea and Bediabdalu. When the child population is taken into account, Togalange and Tokebuea stand a better chance of survival. Most of the huts are represented by one or two adult members which indicate that these communal huts would be extinct with the death of their present set of adults.

TABLE 4.3: DISTRIBUTION OF POPULATION BY COMMUNAL HUT (*BEYRA*) AFFILIATION (1988)

Name of communal hut	Adult		Children		Total		
	Male	Female	Male	Female	Male	Female	Total
Bediabdalu	2	1	2	1	4	2	6
Chemale	3	4	2	–	5	4	9
Cheruge	1	1	–	1	1	2	3
Entiguea	–	1	–	–	–	1	1
Entije	–	1	–	–	–	1	1
Gaje	1	1	1	–	1	1	2
Ingoi	2	–	–	–	3	–	3
Koname	2	2	–	–	2	2	4
Kwa-te-tu-kwage	2	1	–	–	2	1	3
Luijabokale	1	1	–	–	1	1	2
Tagulemme	1	2	–	–	1	2	3
Tailanda	–	1	–	–	–	1	1
Tambebuea	–	2	–	–	–	2	2
Tebobe	1	2	1	–	2	2	4
Titaje	4	1	2	1	6	2	8
Tochedda	2	-	–	–	2	–	2
Togalange	5	5	4	5	9	10	19
Tokebuea	3	–	1	5	4	3	7
Torakeange	–	1	–	–	–	1	1
Totibuea	4	2	–	1	4	3	7
Totamadalu	1	–	–	–	1	–	1
Tulah	4	1	1	1	5	2	7
	39	30	14	13	53	43	96

Source: Field study.

AGE-SEX STRUCTURE

The present-day Onge population, being a very small one, shows a haphazard variation in age groups. The age structure of the population is shown in Table 4.4.

From the table it is evident that children (0-14) form 27.10 per cent of the total population. The bulk of population is concentrated in the 15-49 age group. The sex ratio is 811 females per thousand males. In all age groups, males outnumber the females. However, certain broad general characteristics of the population appear evident.

Primarily, the age structure of the Onge population shows a slim

TABLE 4.4: AGE-SEX STRUCTURE OF ONGE POPULATION (1988)

Age Group	Male	Female	Total	Remarks
0-4	6	4	10	Male-14
5-9	4	6	10	Female-12
10-14	4	2	6	Total (0-14 yrs.) = 26
				Percentage to total = 27.10
				Sex Ratio = 857
15-19	1	1	2	Male = 27
20-24	2	2	4	Female = 19
25-29	5	3	8	Total (15-49 yrs.)= 46
30-34	4	3	7	Percentage to total = 48.0
35-39	5	4	9	
40-44	3	3	6	Sex Ratio = 704
45-49	7	3	10	
50-54	7	5	12	Male = 12
55-59	2	4	6	Female = 12
60+	3	3	6	Total (50-60+yrs.)=24
				Percentage to total= 25.00
				Sex Ratio = 100
All ages	53	43	96	Sex ratio = 811

Source: Based on data collected by D.C. De.

and moderately broad base tapering abruptly in the 15-19 age group, which indicates that in spite of a moderate rate of birth, child mortality is very high and most of the children die before the age of 15 years. Incidentally, child mortality is also quite high in the age group of 10-14 years.

The sex ratio of children is balanced till 9 years and after that the female population starts decreasing. So within the 0-14 age groups, the ratio becomes 897 females per 1,000 males. The least number of people is found in the 15-19 age group. After that, the age structure starts increasing steadily but slowly. In both the sexes this increase continues and reaches the maximum in the age group of 50-4. Thus it is apparent that almost half of the population is concentrated in the middle age group of 15-49 years, though in the true sense the concentration is remarkably higher towards the end of the reproductive age. The sex ratio also falls to 704 in this group.

The older people (50-60+) form 25 per cent of the total population, which is almost equal to the child population. The sex ratio in this group is perfectly balanced, but for obvious reasons, without any impact on the growth of population. It should be noted that adult mortality has increased abruptly after the 55-9 group, indicating 54 as the critical limit of average longevity.

To have an idea about the growth of population, the present data may be compared with that of 1969. It may be mentioned here that till then the Onge lived mostly on their own, without much interference from any outside agency. They used to live a traditional way of life. The then age-sex structure has been prepared on the basis of data from 1969 (Table 4.5).

It is evident from the table that the sex ratio being 952 females per 1,000 males, there was not much scarcity of females among the Onge in 1969.

The age structure of the Onge population takes a cylindrical shape, with a slightly tapering top, indicating an almost equal distribution in the age group of 0-49. The narrow base of the age structure points towards low childbirth in the last few years. The most prominent bulging is evident in the 25-34 age group for both the sexes which shows an excess of young working force capable of running subsistence activities and hopeful reproductive performance. But a sharp fall of figures in the following upper age groups probably depicts a number of early deaths. The very low percentage of population in the upper age groups (55 years and above) indicates lower longevity among the Onge. There was no female beyond the age of 59 years (Figure 4.3).

As a whole, the structure shows a healthy trend for a dwindling population. The reproductive group shares about 63 per cent of the total population having a balanced sex ratio of 949 females per thousand males. But only 28 per cent children with a sex ratio of 888 hints that there will be a crisis of suitable brides for the boys when they attain adulthood.

When the age structure of the Onge populations of 1969 and 1988 were compared, the following differences were observed (Tables 4.4 and 4.5).

First, it can be said that child mortality was not so high in 1969 as

TABLE 4.5: AGE-SEX STRUCTURE (1969)

Age Group	Male	Female	Total	Remarks
0-4	5	4	9	Male-18
5-9	8	4	12	Female-16
10-14	5	8	13	Total (0-14) = 34
				Percentage to total = 28.1
				Sex ratio = 888
15-19	5	6	11	Male-39
20-4	5	3	8	Female = 37
25-9	9	5	14	Total (15-49 yrs.)=7630-4
	8	8	16	Percentage to total = 62.8
35-9	4	5	9	Sex ratio = 949
40-4	4	6	10	
45-9	4	4	8	
50-4	3	3	6	Male = 5
55-9	–	3	3	Female = 6
60+	2	–	2	Total (50-60) = 11
				Percentage to total = 9.1
				Sex ratio = 1200
All ages	62	59	121	Sex ratio = 952

Source: Based on data collected by D.C. De.

it is at present. However, the children's group had an almost equal share in the total population in both the years. The reproductive group suffered a decrease of 25 per cent from 1969 to 1988, a real threat to the Onge population. Moreover, the sex ratio has also dropped considerably at present. On the other hand, the top of the age pyramid has swelled up from 9 to 25 per cent during these 19 years.

MARRIAGE PATTERN

The Onge are monogamous. As a nuclear family is the traditional norm, man and wife are considered to be the best companions in Onge society. No one wants to remain unmarried. Due to scarcity of marriageable mates the widow gets married at the earliest, sometimes with a young man who marries for the first time. It means no choice is left to him. The situation was not so critical in the earlier days.

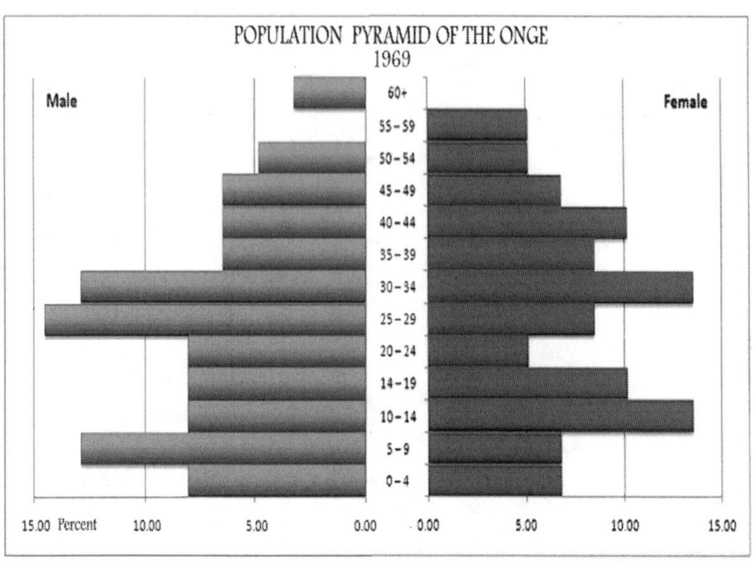

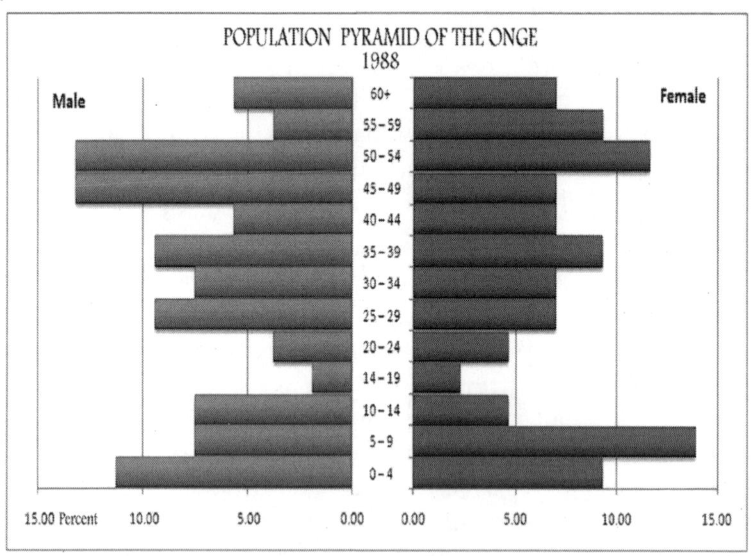

Source: Prepared by the authors.

Figure 4.3: Population pyramid of Onge of the 1969 and 1988.

AGE AT MARRIAGE

Today there is no standard age of marriage in the Onge society. Traditionally, the boys and girls were to be married after the initiation ceremony (*tanagiru*) and puberty rites, respectively. Nobody used to marry without becoming an adult. However, in contemporary society, the demographic position has reached such a state that no traditional order is maintained in this respect. The marital status of the Onge population is presented in Table 4.6.

An interesting feature is that 25 per cent of the female children are married. In this group two girls below ten have been married to men 22 and 30 years old. Such child marriage is a new addition to Onge society. It has its effect on residence rules. As the girls are too young to move out, they continue to live with their parents. Their husbands visit them in their parents' house. Sometimes the reverse also happens. Young men are married to elderly menopausal women who restrict the population growth to some extent. More men (32.1 per cent) remain unmarried than women. All this suggest that there is a shortage of marriageable women among the Onge. For the same reason two men of South Bay in their late twenties are still unmarried. There is a preponderance of widowed males over widowed females. Among the Onge, divorce is not practised much. In the present study only one case of divorce has been observed where the woman married another man. One couple, however, is found to be separated as the man is a deviant type and lives more often in Port Blair.

When we compared the 1988 situation of the Onge in terms of marital status with that in 1969 (Table 4.7), some significant changes came to our notice.

In 1969, the marital situation was more ideal. The important differences are as follow: (i) There was no unmarried person above the age of 24 years. (ii) No early marriage occurred before the age of 15. (iii) No Onge married before the initiation ceremony though that was the beginning of the period of bridal shortage in the Onge society. Nowadays, a marriage takes place without observing this traditional norm. (iv) A number of young boys and girls were found to be unmarried. (v) Not a single marriage was performed with incompatibility of age in that period.

TABLE 4.6: MARTIAL STATUS OF ONGE (1988)

	Unmarried			Married			Widow			Divorced			Total			Remarks
Age Group	M	F	T	M	F	T	M	F	T	M	F	T	M	F	T	
0-4	6	4	10	0	0	0	0	0	0	0	0	0	6	4	10	
5-9	4	4	8	0	2	2	0	0	0	0	0	0	4	6	10	
10-14	4	1	5	0	1	1	0	0	0	0	0	0	4	2	6	
15-19	1	0	1	0	1	1	0	0	0	0	0	0	1	1	2	In age-group 15-49
20-24	0	0	0	2	2	4	0	0	0	0	0	0	2	2	4	there are 22 males
25-29	2	0	2	3	3	6	0	0	0	0	0	0	5	3	8	and 18 females
30-4	0	0	0	4*	3*	7	0	0	0	0	0	0	4	3	7	married, i.e.
35-9	0	0	0	5	4	9	0	0	0	0	0	0	5	4	9	Male=81.5 % and
40-4	0	0	0	3	3	6	0	0	0	0	0	0	3	3	6	F=94.7 % & 2
44-9	0	0	0	5	2	7	2	1	3	0	0	0	7	3	10	unmarried males
50-4	0	0	0	6	5	11	0	0	0	1	0	1	7	5	12	
55-9	0	0	0	1	4	5	1	0	1	0	0	0	2	4	6	
60+	0	0	0	3	3	6	0	0	0	0	0	0	3	3	6	
All	17	9	26	32	33	65	3	1	4	1	0	1	53	43	96	

Source: Field study.

Note: *One man and one woman got separated.

TABLE 4.7: COMPARED MARITAL STATUS OF ONGE, 1969 AND 1988

Year	% Unmarried						% Married						% Widowed		% Divorced	
	Child		Adult		Total		Child		Adult		Total					
	M	F	M	F	M	F	M	F	M	F	M	F	M	F	M	F
1969	100	100	18.2	11.6	40.9	35.6	0	0	79.5	81.4	57.4	59.3	0	3.4	1.6	1.7
1988	100	75	7.7	0	32.1	20.9	0	25.0	82.1	96.8	60.4	76.7	5.7	2.3	1.9	0

Sources: D.C. Dey (1969) and field study (1988).

FAMILY SIZE

Family among the Onge means a nuclear family. Husband, wife and their dependent children live in one household. As a widowed person are married soon after their spouse's deaths, the question of a widowed mother or father living with their children does not arise. Family size is shown in Table 4.8.

Out of a total of 28 families, 12 were composed of two members each, i.e. husband and wife only. Couples with wives below 10 years of age or yet to reach puberty have not been considered as family as they do not live together. The two-member families constitute more than 50 per cent of total Onge families. Such families are often represented by childless couples who never had any child in the long span of their married life. In South Bay one family is formed by a childless couple. On an average, an Onge family consists of 2.90 persons, i.e. less than three persons. This means not even a single child per family (0.89). In fact, there are eight childless families out of the 28 families, seven in Dugong Creek and one in South Bay. In Dugong Creek, two young couples are yet to have a child. The distribution of adults and children within families is shown in Table 4.9.

In this table we incorporated data available from previous studies. As it appears, the structure of the family remains almost the same over time. With shrinkage of population, the size of family decreases considerably. This reduction appears more conspicuous when the number of children per family is taken into account. During the period 1955-6, all families had at least one child on an average, which had come down to 0.77 in 1963-5. There were 53.33 children per hundred adults (Nigam 1962) which decreased to 38.75, as shown

TABLE 4.8: FAMILY SIZE (1988)

Name of Settlement	No. of members per family					Total no. of family	Total person	Average persons family
	2	3	4	5	6			
Dugong Creek	12	7	1	2	1	23	68	2.96
South Bay	3	1	1	0	0	5	13	2.6
Total	15	8	2	2	1	28	81	2.90

Source: Field study.

TABLE 4.9: DISTRIBUTION OF ADULTS AND CHILDREN

Year	Total Familes	Total Population	Adult			Children			Total Persons per Family	No. of Person per Family	No. of Children per Family	No. of Unattached Individuals			% of Unattached Individuals
			M	F	T	M	F	T				M	F	T	
1955-6	45	161	4	4	9	2	2	4	138	3.07	1.07	5	18	2	14.25
				5	5	0	6	2	8						3
1963-5	40	129	4	4	8	1	1	3	111	2.07	0.77	–	–	1	13.95
		0	0	0	8	3	1						8		
1967	35	121	3	3	7	1	1	3	101	2.88	0.89	9	11	2	16.05
			5	5	0	8	3	1							
1988	28	96	2	2	5	1	1	2	81	2.09	0.89	1	4	1	15.06
			8	8	6	4	1	5				4		5	

Sources: Nigam (1962), Agarwal (1967) and field study (1988).

by Agrawal. Thus there was a sharp decline in child population in the course of only nine years. It showed a little improvement in 1969. From this time onward the situation remained almost static. Now an average Onge family does not even have one child.

Widowed and grown-up unmarried persons live separately, forming a cluster in a single household. However, people of different sexes never live in the same household. People of the same sex only form such households. In earlier days, young boys and girls before the initiation and puberty ceremonies, used to live in separate households other than that of their parents. That tradition is still continuing. These persons are designated as 'unattached persons'. There are fifteen such unattached persons in the present population of the Onge, including a married female child.

REPRODUCTIVE PERFORMANCE

The reproductive performance of a group is directly related to the natural growth of its population. The study of reproductive performance of the Onge is even more important as the population shows a declining trend. This can be studied in terms of both parents but our data is restricted only to the mother.

Before going into the details of demographic features like fertility, mortality and survival, etc., it is important to say a few words about the reproductive age of the Onge. Ordinarily, reproductive or child-bearing age ranges from 15 to 49 years in case of women. But among the Onge it has been observed that the girls attain menarche not before 16, sometimes even later. This is evident from the case histories of young girls whose exact age can be verified through records. Otherwise, it is difficult to assess the age of Onge men and women. The women, however, reach menopause by the age of 49 or even earlier.

The Onge ordinarily do not count beyond three and neither do they utter the name of dead persons, thus it is difficult to get the maternity history of an Onge woman. The pedigree prepared by De in 1969 and interviews of old people helped us a good deal in reconstructing the histories of individual mothers. With the available past records and old photographs, we interviewed all the adult women and procured details of the maternity history of each married Onge woman from which a fairly complete account of demographic features could be reconstructed for all the living mothers at the time of our study. It may be mentioned here that all the birth cases presented here are offspring born of married couples, thus indicating only martial fertility. The offspring born of a woman are not always of a single husband, as the Onge practice serial monogamy. This, however, does not affect the reproductive performance of a woman as the subsequent marriage takes place a short while after the death of the previous husband.

Altogether, 31 married women were there in the Onge population. Some characteristic features of these women have been presented in Table 4.10.

Table 4.10 describes the present state of the Onge women in terms of the pregnancy, birth and survival of the children. It may be mentioned here that in the table only those married women were considered who were above the age of fourteen years. Two married girls aged eight and thirteen years had not been included here as they had not attained the age of child-bearing and did not live with their husbands. Out of 31 married women, 20 had children. Eleven women were found to have never been pregnant. Out of them, seven women were above the age of 45. It was learnt from the 1969 record that, except one, none of these women had borne any child with any of their husbands, even though the record shows that sometimes the husbands had children by their previous wives. A couple got married after 1969 but till date, no child has been born out of wedlock. Thus

TABLE 4.10: DEMOGRAPHIC FEATURES OF MARRIED WOMEN BY AGE-GROUP (1988)

Categories	Age-group of women							
	15-19	20-4	25-9	30-4	35-9	40-4	45+	Total
Ever married	1	2	3	3	4	3	15	31
Ever pregnant	–	1	3	2	3	3	8	20
Never pregnant	1	1	–	1	1	–	7	11
Children born	–	2	9	4	18	17	28	78
Children died	–	1	3	4	9	9	17	43
Children survived	–	1	6	0	9	8	11	35

Source: Field study.

we have detailed information regarding the reproductive performance. of the Onge. Table 4.11 presents the information in this regard.

The table reveals the following facts:

(i) Total number of mothers: 20
(ii) Total number of pregnancies: 79
(iii) Pregnancy per mother: 3.95
(iv) Total number of births: 78 (one miscarriage)
(v) Average number of births per mother: 3.9
(vi) Number of living children: 35
(vii) Number of children dead: 43

TABLE 4.11: REPRODUCTIVE PERFORMANCE OF 20 MOTHERS TILL 1988

Mother (age)	No. of pregnancies	Children					
		Born		Died		Survived	
		M	F	M	F	M	F
Bebai (28)	3	1	2	–	2	1	–
Betibegi (51)	4	1	3	1	1	–	2
Botalei (48)	3	–	3	–	1	–	2
Choiboi (43)	6	5	1	2	1	3	–
Dambodai (75)	4	2	2	2	–	–	2
Dankalanka (35)	7	2	5	1	3	1	2
Lilai (36), D.C.	7	3	4	2	2	1	2
Lelai (23). S.B.	2	1	1	–	1	1	–
Malai (50)	4	–	4	–	3	–	–
Maya (40)	2	1	1	–	–	1	1
Melambebe (55)	6	5	1	4	–	1	1
Minai (40)	9	6	3	4	2	2	1
Minakshi (30)	1	–	1	–	1	–	–
Nabemboi (60)	1	–	1	–	1	–	–
Naborolegi (35)	4	2	2	–	1	2	1
Pagili (53)	4	2	1	1	1	1	–
Shila (27)	4	1	3	–	–	1	3
Sitai (32)	3	2	1	2	1	–	–
Tolato Begi (52)	3	3	–	2	–	1	–
Tonkitai (28)	2	1	1	–	1	1	–
Total	79	43	35	24	19	19	16

Source: Field study.

(viii) Percentage of children dead: 55 per cent (M-55.38; F-54.3)
(ix) Number of living children per mother: 1.75
(x) Child-woman ratio: 5: 2.6

It may be mentioned here that for working out the child-woman ratio, women in the 15-49 years age group have been taken into account. Considering the reproductive span of the Onge women have, it could been done with the women of the 20-9 years age group. Though no preference for the male child is noticed among the Onge, nevertheless the proportion of male children born is relatively high. Ultimately almost an equal number of children of either sex survive. This suggests that the girl child is not discriminated against in Onge society. The number of children born to Onge women by age group is given in Table 4.12.

It may be mentioned here that the record presented in the table relates to all the married women alive (31 in number) during the time of investigation (1988). But all of them are not at present in child-bearing age, which may be seen from Table 4.11. From Table 4.12 it appears that of the 35.5 per cent of married women seven were found to be childless. It is expected that the maximum number of children would be born to women belonging to the age group of 25-45 years. No children were born to women in the 15-19 age group, which means that the Onge ordinarily had children after the age of twenty. Ten women bore 3 to 4 children. But the chance of survival of the children is not very encouraging. Tables 4.13 and 4.14 depict the exact picture in this regard.

To 45 per cent of the mothers no child survived. About 20 per cent had only one living child. There were 16 per cent having two living children each and another 16 per cent mothers having three living children each. Four surviving children have been recorded among 3 per cent of mothers (Table 4.13). From Table 4.14 it is evident that in the case of 10 per cent of mothers there is no incidence of child death. Among the 20 mothers there were only 10 with completed sibship (Table 4.15)

The average number of live births per mother was 3.6 which was much lower than that of other tribes. More than a half (55.6 per cent) of the offspring born to them died, thus having an average of

TABLE 4.12: NUMBER OF CHILDREN BORN TO MARRIED WOMEN BY AGE GROUP

No. of children	Age-group of women							Total	per cent
(living + dead)	15-19	20-4	25-9	30-4	35-9	40-4	45+		
0	1	1	–	1	1	–	7	11	35.5
1	–	–	–	1	–	–	1	2	6.5
2	–	1	1	–	–	1	–	3	9.7
3	–	–	1	1	–	–	3	5	16.1
4	–	–	1	–	1	–	3	5	16.1
5	–	–	–	–	–	–	–	–	–
6	–	–	–	–	–	1	1	2	6.5
7	–	–	–	–	–	1	–	3	9.6
Total	1	2	3	3	4	3	15	31	100

Source: Field study.

TABLE 4.13: NUMBER OF LIVING CHILDREN TO MARRIED WOMEN

No. of Children (Living + Dead)	Age Group of Women							Total	per cent
	15-19	20-4	25-9	30-4	35-9	40-4	45+		
0	1	1	–	3	1	–	8	14	45.2
1	–	1	2	–	–	–	3	6	19.4
2	–	1	–	–	–	1	4	5	16.1
3	–	–	–	–	3	2	–	5	16.1
4	–	–	1	–	–	–	–	1	3.2
Total	1	3	3	3	4	3	15	31	100

Source: Field study.

TABLE 4.14: NUMBER OF DEAD CHILDREN TO MARRIED WOMEN

No. of Children (Living + Dead)	Age Group of Women							Total	per cent
	15-19	20-4	25-9	30-4	35-9	40-4	45+		
0	–	–	1	–	–	1	0	2	10
1	–	1	1	1	1	0	2	6	30
2	–	–	1	–	–	–	4	5	25
3	–	–	–	1	–	1	3	3	15
4+	–	–	–	–	2	1	4	4	20
Total	0	1	3	2	3	3	8	20	100

Source: Field study.

TABLE 4.15: REPRODUCTIVE PERFORMANCE OF THE MOTHERS WITH COMPLETED SIBSHIP

No. of Mothers with Completed Sibship (40 years)	Live Birth				
	Living	Dead	Total	Average No. of Live Births per Mother	Average No. of Surviving Off-spring per Mother
10	16	20	36	3.6	1.6

Source: Field study.

1.6 surviving offspring per mother. All this information indicated that child mortality is very high among the Onge.

MORTALITY

So far we have discussed the reproductive performance of Onge women. With this meagre amount of data, it is difficult to make an attempt to calculate the crude birth and death rates of the Onge population. However, certain couples were identified there who could have children. So if most of them had children in a particular year, the following year remained almost unproductive for the entire population.

These two rates could have been calculated on the basis of data on birth and death and mid-year population for five consecutive years as the population is extremely small. Unfortunately, we do not have all the relevant data for the last five years uninterrupted. However, birth and death records since 1977 have been procured (Table 4.16). From the monthwise frequency of childbirths some interesting observations have been made through Table 4.17.

The maximum number of deliveries (26 or 66.67 per cent) occurred during the January to June period, which means the maximum number of conceptions took place during the months of heavy rains, i.e. April through September.

It may be noted here that the rainy season is the most difficult period for the Onge when they cannot go to the forest for pig hunting or to the sea for turtle hunting. In terms of food supply it is the lean

TABLE 4.16: BIRTH AND DEATH RECORDS 1977-1988

Year	Birth			Death		
	M	F	T	M	F	T
1977	1	2	3	2	7	9
1978	2	2	4	3	2	5
1979	0	2	2	3	2	5
1980	1	4	5	2	1	3
1981	2	1	3	0	0	0
1982	0	2	1	1	1	2
1983	2	2	4	1	0	1
1984	1	5	6	0	1	1
1985	1	2	3	1	5	6
1986	3	2	5	0	1	1
1987	1	0	1	0	2	2
1988	2	1	3	1	3	4
Total	16	25	41	17	21	38

Source: Records of the Health Centre of Dugong Creek.

TABLE 4.17: MONTH-WISE CHILD BIRTH SINCE 1977

Month	No of Births	Month	No. of Births
January	4	July	2
February	5	August	2
March	4	September	2
April	4	October	3
May	4	November	3
June	5	December	1
		Month not stated	1
Total	26	Total	14 = 40

Source: Records of the Health Centre of Dugong Creek.

period but it is the period of leisure, primarily for the menfolk, when they relax in the settlement. Hence, it is observed that among the Onge the period of recreation is also the period of procreation.

An attempt has been made here to examine the general pattern of mortality among the Onge in different age groups. For doing so we treated the age-sex structure of 1969 as the base and compared the 1988 population with that. The 1969 population was extrapolated to get the assumed population of 1988, i.e. to get size, what could have been the present age groupwise distribution if there was no death during the last 19 years. Thus the population of the 0-4 years age group in 1969 could have reached the 20-4 age group. In this way, the relative mortality between males, females, and the total population in each age group was worked out. It is evident that: (1) a large number of deaths occurred before reaching the age group of 20-34 years and again beyond 59 years. High mortality is, however, natural in higher age group due to old age morbidity, but middle age mortality suggests a declining trend of the population concerned. In fact the incidences of mortality was high among the children (0-14 years) of 1969; (2) the rate of death among the youth (15-24 years) was lowest, which indicates that once persons reached puberty they had a fair chance of surviving; (3) another alarming fact was that female mortality is comparatively higher with only 50 per cent survival in 19 years.

It has already been mentioned that child mortality was high even in 1969. The record of birth and child mortality in the last five years from 1984 to 1988 (Table 4.18) shows that high child mortality is directly related to the declining trend of the population (Figure 4.3).

It appears from the table that infant mortality is very high. Eighteen children were born during the last five years out of whom 14 died in infancy and early childhood. It is quite likely that a population cannot prosper with such a bleak chance (22 per cent) of survival of its child population. After scrutinizing the record of Dugong Creek Health Centre since 1977 one can make a tentative idea about the causes of death among the Onge. Ordinarily old people die due to general

TABLE 4.18: FIVE YEARS RECORD OF CHILD BIRTH AND DEATH

Year	Children born	Infants died	Children died	Total died	Total survived
1984	6	3	1	4	2
1985	3	1	3	4	-1
1986	5	1	0	1	4
1987	1	0	2	2	-1
1988	3	2	1	3	0
Total	18	7	7	14	4

Source: Records of the Health Centre of Dugong Creek.

debility, often leading to anaemia and respiratory complications. It is important to notice that before 1980, incidence of death due to enteric trouble was insignificant. Most of the deaths occurred on account of bronchopneumonia. Since 1980, increase of enteric disease is noticeable. Accidental death (falling from a tree, drowning, etc.) in case of children was quite common in the past as well as in the present. Among other causes of infant and child mortality, respiratory trouble, gastroenteritis and protein energy malnutrition are important and common.

Scientific research so far conducted could not throw much light on the causes of the decline of the Onge population. Various developmental and welfare activities could not do much to save the population either. It is now almost universally accepted that the Onge are a threatened population. For long, it has been on the verge of decline and since the mid-fifties it has been declining rapidly (Ganguly 1975). With the exception of the Jarawa and Sentinelese, the Onge seem to be the most highly inbred human population in the sub-continent. How far the inbreeding for countless centuries has affected the fertility of the Onge is not known. Their fertility is quite low when compared to that of other people. Basu's work may be recalled in this context (1972). According to the present study, 22 per cent women appeared to be infertile. Incompatibility of age among Onge couples is another factor added in recent years which has some bearing on their fertility performance. The present study, however, suggests that high infant mortality is the real threat to the Onge population. If this could be checked, Onge society could be saved from a number of anomalies and the total extinction of these people could be stalled.

Long ago, Cipriani (1953) recommended an 'Onge Reserve' in Little Andaman and minimum interference for their protection. Many ameliorative measures have been taken in order to protect the Onge but nothing hopeful has come out as yet. However, perhaps due to such efforts there is an increase of people in the older age groups. In earlier days, people did not often survive beyond the age of 50 years.

Now with assured food supply and semi-sedentary habits, the old people show a trend of having a longer life. Moreover, old men get preference over the young ones while selecting a mate, which has an implication on the growth of population and on society as a whole.

The ameliorative measures could not make any dent on the rate of child mortality. In spite of earnest efforts of health personnel, the state of child health has not shown much improvement. The recent medical report says that more than 50 per cent children below 13 years of age at Dugong Creek showed some degree of growth retardation, including pot belly and knock knees. Their chest X-ray showed mild to moderate cardiomegaly. At South Bay, out of three children, two were found having these symptoms. Medical specialists think that this might be caused due to dietary factors. It needs further investigations by experts (communication with medical specialists, 1988).

Considering the structural arrangement and reproductive performance of the people we cannot hope for a brighter prospect for the Onge people in the near future. Under such circumstances, emphasis should be put upon and utmost efforts devoted to the sphere of child development and healthcare, so that they do not die young and the Onge population is saved from having a top-heavy structure.

REFERENCES

Agrawal, H.N., 'Reproductive life of Onge Women', *Vanyajati* 15, 1967, pp. 139-49.

Basu. Arabinda, 1972, 'A Demographic Study of the Kota of Nilgiri Hills', *Journal of Indian Arthropological Society*, 7, 1972, pp. 29-45.

Barclay, G.W., *Technique of Popuation Analysis*, New York: John Wiley and Sons, 1958.

Cipriani, Lidio, 'Report of a Survey of the Little Andaman During 1951-3', *Bulletin of Department of Anthropology* 2 (1), 1953, pp. 61-82.

De, D.C., 'A Demographic Study of the Onge of Little Andaman', *Bulletin of Department of Anthropology*, 19 (2), 1970, pp. 1-16.

Ganguly, P., 'The Negritos of Little Andaman', *Museum Bulletin* 10 (1), 1975.

Nigam, R.C., 'The Onge of Little Andaman–Their Settlements and Population', *Vanyajati*, 10 (3), 1962, pp. 44-53.

——, 'The Onge of Little Andaman Factors of Habit', *Vanyajati* 11, pp. 55-67.

Sarkar, S.S., 'Onge Population and Settlements', *Anthropos*, 55, 1960, pp. 561-3.

Sinha, V.C. and E. Zacharia, *Elements of Demographic Profile of India and the World*, Calcutta: Allied Publishing House, 1984.

CHAPTER 5

Children of the Onge

Children are the most valued asset in an Onge family and society. The elderly Onge believe that the birth and survival of their offspring are the key factors for the perpetuation of their people and culture. A considerably high infant and child mortality, coupled with low birth rate, is making the Onge population extremely vulnerable. Hence, the birth of a baby stirs the entire community. People pour in from even distant settlements to greet the newborn.

There was an incident of childbirth during our field study at Dugong Creek. It had been observed that the staff of the subsidiary health centre, especially the lady staff-nurse-cum-midwife (ANM), kept the pregnant Onge woman under regular observation and took care of her, as and when necessary. With the onset of labour pain the ANM was informed by the husband of the expectant mother.

In earlier days, the delivery used to take place in the hut. Now all deliveries take place in the health centre. The Onge have demonstrated some change in their behaviour by altering the venue of delivery from hut to health centre. But the degree of their attitudinal change seems very marginal. They make use of modern medical facilities in their own way and according to convenience. They do not use the regular labour room of the health centre, instead one of the big rooms is converted into a labour room so that all people, irrespective of age and sex, accompanying the expectant mother may be accommodated there, as if childbirth is a community affair. Like the olden days, the husband makes the bed for delivery with *bataga* leaves. Women around apply a compress on the abdomen and waist of the expectant mother with the leaves. The husband massages the upper abdomen. No one else is allowed to do this job except the husband. In the earlier days, massage was given to the feet. When the pain is acute and the delivery imminent, all male members, except the husband, leave the place. The husband remains throughout the labour right until the baby is born. Delivery takes place in a squatting position which is considered in medical science to be the safest position for childbirth.

In the case of childbirth observed by the woman author, it was noticed that after delivery the abdomen of the mother was tied up by the attending women so that the placenta could not move upward. With the second wave of conversions, the placenta was discharged. The newborn baby was given breast milk even before the discharge of the placenta. Immediately after delivery, all the Onge women around took the baby on their lap by turn but the ANM present was not allowed to hold the baby or to give a bath to it. She would administer medicine or an injection to the mother but nothing to the newborn. It shows that the Onge are extra-careful about their newborn. They prefer to take care of the baby in their own way.

Some elderly women smeared a paste of white clay all over the body of the baby and on the face and abdomen of the mother. It acts as an insect and evil spirit repellent. The senior social executive deputed there for development of the people, presented some gifts to Bairogegy, the father of the baby, like a towel, a feeding bottle, and Rs. 200.

Source: Photo taken by the author.

Figure 5.1: Children posing for a photograph on the veranda of a cottage provided by the agency.

Bairogegy happily accepted the gifts and celebrated the occasion by distributing lozenges among the people present there.

It was observed that just the day following the delivery, the couple got ready to go back to their home. However, the doctor did not allow them to do so and they stayed on in the health centre for another day. No food was given to the mother immediately after delivery. She was given a normal diet, including *roti* and pork, after two days of delivery. The Onge never give a bath to the baby. It is cleaned with a piece of cloth when it soils itself.

Teeth generally appear at the age of five months on the baby. Supporting food like biscuits, tinned milk and so on are given to the baby from the third month. Solid food like *roti*, pork, etc., is given to the baby when he or she is about one year old. When the children become three years old, they are also given betel nuts and chewed *pan* leaves.

It has been reported by the ANM that most of the couples are willing to come to the health centre for childbirth. Very few refuse to take any medical aid. In such cases, delivery takes place in the respective huts and the ANM attends to the mother there. Sometimes delivery takes place in the hut without the attendance of the ANM. In such a case, the husband and other women attend to the expecting mother. Whether delivery takes place in the hut or in the Health Centre, the medical staff makes their services available almost instantly, though their direction are never fully honoured by the Onge. So far, no case of difficult labour has been reported from among the Onge.

The following general observations can be made with respect to childbirth on the basis of our observations during field investigation at Dugong Creek.

For the Onge, childbirth is a phenomenon that involves the community as a whole. Though the labour pain is borne only by the mother, anxiety related to it is shared by all. Under the circumstances, all community members follow the expecting mother to the hospital and wait there till the baby is born. Childbirth is perceived as a natural phenomenon. So no extra care is taken for the delivery of the baby. The expecting mother walks to the hospital herself and has her usual food. The sense of privacy of the Onge does not prevent the male members from gathering there. No significant change is observed in the mode of delivery and related habits and customs.

Though the Onge come to the health centre for childbirth, they do not entirely rely on the so-called experts, viz., the ANM or doctor, for the care of the newborn. For childbirth, they allow the doctor or nurse to apply some medical aids to the expecting mother, but do not like their interference in case of the care of the newborn. The baby is a very precious thing to them, so it is not given to the ANM for post-delivery care. It is observed that during the honey collecting season, couples move out to the forest with newborn babies along with others without consulting the doctor or even ignoring his advice.

The Onge come to the hospital or health centre which shows that they want to cooperate with the welfare agency without disturbing their own system and traditions. They adjust with the situation for a very practical reason. Nowadays they bury the placenta, etc., outside instead of burying those on the spot where the birth has taken place.

In short, it can be said that with respect to childbirth, the Onge do not show any awareness of or interest in modern medical practices. They like to fall back upon their traditional system. Community and kinship come to the surface and become much conspicuous in moments of anxiety like childbirth. The Onge way of childbirth suggests that the emotional bonding between husband and wife is very strong. The husband empathizes with the wife in all possible ways in a situation like childbirth.

INFANCY AND CHILDHOOD

The different stages of life of an individual are denoted by different terms. In Onge society, a small child is called *echele*. When the child starts moving in a group at about 5/6 years of age, the boy is called *daya* and the girl *ebare*. In the post-puberty phase, the unmarried boy is referred to as *entoge* and an unmarried girl as *borangabe*.

The Onge children are treated with great care and fondness not only by their parents but also by other elders. Up to the age of three months, the Onge parents scarcely put the baby on the bed. The baby is always carried on the lap, except during night when it is put on the cot. Even when a bit grown up, the child is never left alone, and is habitually carried by the mother on her back or on her side. A circular tumpline made of a broad strip of bark is used for supporting the child. It is placed across the forehead of the mother when the baby is carried on the back and placed cross-wise on her shoulder when it is carried on the side. Only while answering nature's call, a mother passes on the baby to its father or to any elderly woman. The child is rarely found crying of hunger or any discomfort as most often they are found sleeping on the mother's back. The mother's movement makes a child sleepy.

The babies are cared by the parents themselves and seldom passed on to any adolescent boys or girl. Onge girls thus do not get any practical training for childcare as is commonly seen among other tribal folk. Perhaps for this reason, when a baby is born, all adult women are there to help the mother, even by breast-feeding.

The baby grows almost in constant skin-to-skin contact with the mother up to the age of two to three years. They are never allowed to play, crawl, or toddle. We never saw a toddler among the Onge children. It is said that in earlier days they had to move from place to place, so it was not safe to put the baby down alone to play or walk. The growth of a child at this stage gets affected as the child remains in the same position for long hours of the day. The movement of limbs is minimum. Though physical growth is initially a bit restricted due to the constant clinging position of the baby, the growth of mental faculties does not suffer as it can observe the mother in all situations.

The period of lactation is quite long. Weaning is enforced when the child is three years old. In fact, an infant sucks his mother's milk till the birth of the next baby, which is often born at an interval of two to three years. Only then is the child given regular food in little amounts, such as rice, *paratha,* tuber, meat and small fish after removing the bones. Honey is, however, given to small babies as per availability.

As already stated, an Onge child gets detached from its mother with the birth of another child. Children start walking around at the age of four years. They start moving or playing within the settlement on their own at the age of around five. Boys in 5-12 years range form a group and play together. It is important to note that the girl children usually do not play or mix with the boys. The ANM of the health centre sometime made them play together in some games. But left to themselves, they did not do it. Segregation of sexes among the Onge is noticed from a very early age.

Children of both the sexes go naked up to the age of seven/eight years. Boys wear shorts beyond that age while girls wear nothing up to the age of ten. Children of either sex are seen to put on costly synthetic garments during any ceremonial occasion like flag hoisting or visit of the dignitaries. Otherwise, the Onge are rather indifferent about children's dress.

Children are supplied with some clothes by the development agency, Andaman Adim Janjati Vikas Samiti (AAJVS). Besides, the Onge people also buy some clothes for them. During our stay at Dugong Creek we counted the dress items of children. There were 26 shirts and 19 shorts for 12 boys while for 10 girls there were 21 frocks and seven knickers. On an average each boy and girl had two pieces of shirts or frocks but the number of lower garments was somewhat fewer. It is not due to insufficiency of clothes that children go naked but due to relative erosion of traditional values of physical modesty, the parents do not pay attention in this regard. They have not yet imbibed the habit of dressing the children at an early age. During inclement cyclonic weather, too, the children, including small babies, were found without any clothes. As the boys moved out of the settlement frequently, they wore shorts for going out and thus got used to clothes. Girls, in comparison, remained restricted mostly to the settlement. Therefore, they were found to pick up the dressing habit later. But in earlier days, it is reported, 'physical modesty is enjoined on them after that age (5/6 years) and they (the boys) are taught to wear strips of cloth around the loins. The girls start wearing tassels a little earlier' (Ganguly, unpublished report).

A CHILD AT PLAY

Children start playing on their own not before two to three years of age, when they are allowed to do so by their parents. Initially, parents keep a watch on them from a distance. Fathers are generally seen playing with or cuddling their young kids, after returning home from hunting or fishing ventures. In fact, it has been observed that the Onge hold the young ones as soon as they return from any place, whether the forest or Hut Bay or Port Blair. If they visit a town, they never forget to bring something for the kids. From their behaviour it appears that they overcome exertion or tiredness by taking the children in their arms. In comparison, the Onge women do not show such warmth or expression of joy in the company of children. Perhaps prolonged contact with the children makes them somewhat passive to this emotion. However, we never saw an Onge mother annoyed or irritated with her children.

The most common playing materials of Onge children are sand, wooden sticks and coconut leaves, which change with age to small bows and arrows, cane baskets or any other toys and articles available to them. Afterwards, they start imitating their elders in every activity. Small boys aged between four and ten years roam about in the settlement with bows and arrows, which are made by the elderly. They practise shooting. Sometimes they shoot a bird and play with it, but they never eat the flesh. Most of the boys shoot with remarkable accuracy and the elders feel proud of it. They try to make iron arrowheads by filing. Some of them make a toy canoe or small baskets for the young boys.

Source: Photo taken by the author.

Figure 5.2: Children learning the use of bow and arrow while playing.

The female children copy their mothers by making small chapattis when the mother is away at work. This way, by playing they learn household work. Boys never accompany their parents to the forest or plantation. On the other hand, small girls generally move around with their mothers or other female relations, no matter whether they are in the settlement or in the forest.

Innovation or creativity is observed among many Onge children. On their own, they make toy carts with plastic containers or other articles that have drifted in from the sea. Sometimes they try to make models of helicopters, ships, etc., which nowadays they observe from close quarters. Toys with wheels attract Onge children a lot. Older boys (10-12 years) are found interested in cycling too.

ILL CHILDREN

Ailing children make their parents very depressed even when the ailment is minor. Any expression of pain or suffering of the child is unbearable to Onge parents. They try to comfort the child or share his/her ailment by lying with him or her as long as the illness persists. During illness, a child often refuses food. In such cases the parents, too, do not feel like eating. They administer their indigenous medicine and become eager to make the child feel better as fast as possible through application of modern medicine as well. Often, they do not allow the doctor or nurse to administer an injection or medicine apparently disliked by the child. It had once been observed during our stay at Dugong Creek that Madan, the son of Kogegele, was reluctant to swallow the medicine. At this, the doctor compelled the child to have medicine, an act which his parents did not appreciate at all.

PARENT-CHILDREN RELATION

In bringing up children, parents do not show any preferential treatment based on sex. Boys and girls, however, soon come to recognize the division of labour between the sexes. Onge parents are very permissive. As there is no overall authoritative figurehead in the society, the tradition to obey any senior has not developed among the

Onge children. The parents never dictate terms to their children. In this respect they are close to nature. They nurse and nurture the baby. The infants learn the norms of society on their own. They grow up as per the rules of nature and the parents make no effort towards their socialization. Starting from toilet training, an Onge mother follows nature's laws. Children learn only by seeing. During our stay among the Onge, we did not come across a single case of child beating. There were, however, instances when they were mildly rebuked.

Onge children, when they are somewhat grown, behave in a rather nagging manner. It is often found that parents and other elders obey their children as if the children are their masters. Elders hardly refuse any demand of their nagging children. When the Onge visit the cooperative store, children are found to demand costly and fancy items, like a torch or a purse. We observed that on one occasion, a small boy, whose parents stayed in another settlement, made a demand for a costly object from the cooperative store. Someone present there bought the thing for him for Rs. 30. From this it becomes clear that the wishes of Onge children ordinarily do not go unfulfilled. Children are not considered personal possessions, they belong to the community. Hence it is the responsibility of the entire community to take care of the children. This may be a characteristic feature of any primitive society as described by Evans-Pritchard,

> For the primitive, society is largely an extension of the family relationship. In most primitive societies each home spreads into another and the households intermingle in a communal life and without privacy, or the desire for it. There is not, therefore, the same emotional concentration on a tiny circle of persons. This is most clearly to be seen when a person dies. The primitive son or daughter may suffer the loss acutely but it is not the disaster as it is to us. (1965: 51)

The boy under reference is well looked after by his community members who are not even his near kin. He is called to accompany them on fishing expeditions. Any elderly man makes toy bows and arrows for him. In this way, he never feels the absence of parental care.

From about the age of ten, boys cease to lie with their parents on the same sleeping platform. Separate platforms are made for them when they reach adolescence, even when Onge children start living with widowed or unmarried persons. Adolescent girls are no exceptions. Post puberty, they are no longer considered to belong to their parents' family. They share food with those with whom they live and contribute their earnings in the form of fishing or collection as the case might be. Regular ration items, too, are stored there and cooked jointly. Girl children are nowadays married at a very young age, sometimes even before ten. At that age they live neither with the husband nor with widowed persons. They prefer to live with their parents. In such cases the husbands are much senior to them in age and they visit their wives in the evening in their parents' home.

GROWING UP INTO ADULTHOOD

Child marriage plays a very important role in the process of Onge personality development. The Onge have different terms of reference for young children, young men and women, middle aged persons and old people, but there are no terms for adolescents. In fact, among the Onge children, adolescence does not appear so conspicuous. When a bit grown, Onge children start participating in adult activity.

Puberty rites are there for both the sexes. Young women are called *borangabe* and the female puberty rite bears the same name. The male puberty rite is called *tanagiru*. *Borangabe* is observed when a girl attains her menarche, usually at the age of 16 or 17 year. During this period the girl abstains from eating pork, fish, or turtle. The male puberty rite is so important that it is the major ceremony in the life of an Onge man. Observance of this initiation ceremony signifies a breakthrough in one's life. It ensures for him the status of an adult in society. A man is not eligible to go for pig hunting if he is not initiated. In earlier days the Onge used to practise adult marriage and no one was allowed to marry before the observance of *tanagiru* or the initiation ceremony.

Now, with the change of time and dearth of suitable mates, the Onge do not wait for attaining adulthood. As already stated, girls are married at the age of 8 or 10 years. During our stay in Dugong Creek, we observed two cases of marriage where there was a lot of difference in age between the spouses. In one case, the man was 30 years of age and the bride was 10 years old and in another, the bridegroom was about 22 years old and the girl was only eight. At such an early age, girls do not understand the implications of marriage much and no physical relation with husband is developed before puberty. Hence the question of the couple living together does not arise. But it has often been observed that the husband regularly visits the bride at her parents' home after the day's work. A separate cot is prepared for him where he relaxes. The bride plays with him for some time in that cot. In one case, the boy was found to live there after marriage.

When we spoke to the girl about her husband, she blushed. Though every evening she spent some time with her husband in a playful mood she used to sleep with her parents only. This arrangement would continue till she became 10 or 12 years old. After that she might join the other girls who lived under the custody of an elderly woman (most often widowed), forming a separate household. This household acted almost like a dormitory for older girls, either unmarried or married (but not having attained puberty).

Onge parents think that if couple with a big age difference live closely, the girl would develop an emotional attachment to the man and also helps the girl to attain maturity. One such girl was married to a young man about two years back. Now she is about 13 years old but has not yet attained puberty. Since she is grown up by Onge standards, she lives in the household meant for such girls, as already mentioned. However, she visits her mother every day. It is interesting to observe that this particular girl does not show any sign of adolescence (i.e., growth of secondary sexual characteristics), rather, physically, she looks like a small girl. Nevertheless, she behaves like a grown up woman with a serious look on her face and she does not mix with other small girls. When her husband visits their settlement, she spends most of her time with him though she does not live with him.

From such observations it can be said that transformation of the Onge children from childhood to adulthood depends more on cultural factors than on the physical growth of the individual. As stated earlier, in case of young girls who are just kids, certain behavioural changes are noticed in their day-to-day life with marriage as if suddenly they have got entry into the world of adults. In Onge society, as the children have no other preoccupations of their own, their aim is to follow the lifestyle of their elders. So without experiencing the fact of marriage, they try to emulate the behaviour of adults. In fact, in the olden days, among the Onge, a girl and a boy were to be married only after attaining puberty and the observance of initiation ceremony. Thus the childhood was prolonged and it was preparatory to adulthood. Today, marriage, which is always an adult affair, is thrust upon the Onge children without their consent and, accordingly, their life is patterned in that way. Similarly, when a young man, 18 or 20 years old, is married before his initiation ceremony, he is not considered to be an adult as he has not achieved or proved his adulthood by hunting a pig by himself, which is the main thrust of the initiation ceremony. This means that then onwards the man is capable of providing food for himself and his family and so is eligible for marriage.

From the study of the Onge children the following facts emerge:

- Children are the most valued possessions of the Onge.
- They are equally looked after by the family as well as by the community at large.
- Children never miss parental care, rather they are often pampered.
- The Onge children are quite intelligent and innovative.
- No stress and strain or competition in the world of the children is perceptible.
- Childhood is short. They do not pass through the adolescent phase.
- Transformation from childhood to adulthood is abrupt.
- Cultural sequences are more important in transforming a child into a person than the physical maturity of the person.

CHAPTER 6

Subsistence Activities

Subsistence economy and activities of any group of people depends primarily on the ecological niche they inhabit. It has been observed that '... the contemporary hunter-gatherers in the world today live in such marginal areas as the Tundra, tropical rain forests and deserts—unsuitable for agriculture and pastoralism. These people have survived by much specialized adaptation to the harsh environment in these habitats' (Tanaka, 1976). The Onge have lived for countless centuries in the tropical rainforest of Little Andaman. Hunting-gathering is

Source: Photo taken by the author.

Figure 6.1: The happiest moment of an accomplished Onge hunter after he returned with two large pigs killed on the same day. He used two different techniques—trapping and direct chasing.

their basic economy. Till the early part of the last century, the Onge were the only inhabitants on this island. Except occasional encounters, which were not often friendly, they had no connection with so-called civilization.

The entire forest and the vast sea was their resource base. They never faced food scarcity in this set-up. For obvious reasons these people never felt the need for growing food or domesticating any animal except dogs, which have been used as a hunting aid. Under such circumstances, when food is readily available in the forest or the sea, they do not need to possess any knowledge for growing any food item. Some futile attempts had been made by the administration to introduce the art of domestication of pigs and cattle to them. But the Onge did not show any interest.

Generally, the Onge cannot count beyond three and cannot keep an exact record of days either. Their subsistence activities and dietary habits are attuned to the seasonal cycle. The current season is important while the past and the coming seasons are mainly phases of the continuum of the present. Tanaka (1976) pointed out that due to isolation, present-day hunter-gatherers could not internalize developed means of production. The particular habitat they live in is not suitable for such activities. Even otherwise, the abundance of natural resources around them never induced them to go for an improved technology. They feel happy, confident, and relaxed in their given situation.

For the Onge, this relaxed situation changed when the island was opened up for all and many people from the mainland were rehabilitated here. No estimate was made about the carrying capacity of the land, which might have been needed for the Onge to subsist on their traditional hunting-gathering economy. It is, nevertheless, common knowledge that the carrying capacity of land to sustain hunting-gathering as a means of livelihood is of too low an order. Being devoid of such preparedness, efforts were made to dissociate the Onge from their age-old way of life and make them habituated to a settled way of life. Strangely enough, in a hurry to promote transformation, new food in the form of cereals, pulses, oil, etc., have been introduced to these people through free supply of rations by welfare agencies. With such free food supply and continuous goading, the Onge have got habituated to such food. As food reaches them without any effort they do not feel the urge to produce them. In fact, Onge society is not yet at the stage of adopting a food producing economy.

The forest and sea form the resource base for hunting, fishing and gathering which have been the major subsistence activities of the Onge through the ages. They can procure food from these sources according to their needs and capability. As has already been mentioned, till the early part of the 1970s, these people were totally dependent on such activities for their primary needs, like food, dress, adornment as in body painting and shelter. Since the 1970s, they have been exposed to free supply of rationed articles and modern huts. At present, their main food consists of wheat, rice, pork, fish and coconut. Out of these, wheat and rice are supplied to them free of cost and coconuts are a free 'gift of nature' in the real sense of the term, as they do very little plantation work by themselves, though officially all adult Onge are shown as workers on the master roll for coconut plantation. In Dugong Creek, coconuts are picked up by women for their daily consumption. A soup-like preparation is made from coconut milk. The Ongle never eat the coconut kernel raw, though they often eat the soft pulp of green coconut and drink the water. South Bay Onges have not included the coconut in any form in their daily diet yet.

From time immemorial, animal food in the form of pork and fish has been the major subsistence base of the Onge, vegetable food being of secondary importance. Bose (1963) observed that if pork was available, they were not interested in gathering. But in other parts of the world, such communities depend primarily on plant food. For the Onge, dependence on animal food has been sustained due to its abundance in the forest and sea. Even today, the Onge, by and large, practise hunting and fishing, despite an assured and regular food supply. Nowadays, the womenfolk, especially of Dugong Creek, are not interested in regular gathering of roots, tubers, and shellfish. However, when it is the season for these activities, they do go out for collection in groups or with their husbands, mostly to break the monotony of their sedentary way of life in the settlement where they do not have much work to do.

As food is the primary concern of communities such as the Onge, demand and availability of food determine the course of their activities.

It has been observed that the cereals supplied as rations have only substituted their vegetable food in the form of their roots, tubers, and seasonal fruits collected from the forest, which were the primary source of carbohydrates in their diet. But all of animal food, the main source of protein, is still acquired through hunting and fishing. In December 1963, Bose observed that animal food accounted for over 75 per cent of the average daily food of the Onge. The present study also suggests that their dependence on animal food has remained almost the same and thus hunting still forms an important part of the Onge way of life (see Annexure II). We can say that there is no marked change in the subsistence activities of the Onge other than relative dependence on a wider range of food substances for subsistence. There is a general misconception that with the introduction of free rations, the Onge have abandoned their age-old habit of hunting and got well-adjusted with the sedentary way of life which has been designed for them by others. This may appear so from a brief visit or short stay among them. However, a long stay among the Onge and a deeper probe will make one revise one's opinion.

PIG-HUNTING TECHNIQUE

Nowadays, the Onge practise hunting primarily with the help of dogs. Most Onge families have a number of dogs. The dogs are loved by the Onge (Cipriani 1966, Danda 1989) who go to the forest with them. If someone does not have dogs of his own, he might borrow some from others. The Onge do not give any special training to the dogs for hunting. The dogs have a natural ability of chasing. To make them more active in the forest they are kept underfed before the expedition.

When in the forest with their masters, these apparently friendly animals become quite efficient in spotting and chasing pigs with a special signal. While moving with the Onge in the deep forest, we observed that the men sometimes make a short hissing sound pointing to a direction of the trail of hoof marks of pigs and the dogs at once start running in that direction. The hunter, too, follows the dog, holding the bow and arrow in shooting position. When the dogs chase the pig or pigs from different directions, the animals take shelter in the undergrowth. The dogs start circling around the undergrowth barking all the while so that the game cannot escape. By that time, the hunter reaches the spot and shoots the arrow at the game. The Onge hunters try to shoot at the neck of the game or at the base of its front legs. But the pigs do not die instantly as they have very thick layers of skin and fat. Hence the Onge generally use a special pig arrow with a detachable head. The arrowhead is tied up to the middle shaft to act as an obstruction, which gets entangled in the thicket as the pig tries to run away. Then it becomes easy to kill the game with the detachable steelhead spear or by an arrow. Piercing the chest below the left front leg makes for a swift killing. Immediately after killing the breast, the abdomen is opened and the intestines, liver, heart, etc., are taken out and offered to the dogs. Then the body cavity is filled up with green leaves to keep the shape of pig intact for uniform singeing.

In the process of chasing a large male pig with tusks, the dogs often get injured, sometimes fatally. However, the Onge take care of their dogs and give them a reasonable share of pork after each hunt in the form of intestines, heart, lungs and about four inch long pieces of leg above the hoof, aside from the tail, rectum, etc.

Nowadays, the Onge hunt pigs, mostly by setting a trap in the forest. They have learnt the use of the trap from Thai and Myanmarese people who visit the island frequently to collect various costly seashells. The Onge have modified the traps in their own way and use them quite effectively. They set the trap along the probable route of pigs in the forest. When an animal is trapped, it is killed in the same way as already described. The evolution of hunting technology is discussed exclusively in Chapter 7.

RECORD OF HUNTING

During nearly six months of our field study, for about two months, we kept records of the activities of either sex. The rainy season is not very suitable for outdoor activities. Despite inclement weather, it has been observed that the Onge love to go out hunting and fishing. While we were there, a good number of them went to the forest almost every day with or without dogs for hunting. They rarely returned empty-handed. Whosoever killed the game shared the meat with everyone. Relevant information on hunting has been presented in Tables 6.1 and 6.2.

TABLE 6.1: SUCCESSFUL HUNTERS OF DUGONG CREEK
(22 August 1988 to 2 October 1988)

Name of the Hunter	Age (Years)	Frequency of Successful Hunting
Nabekutte	55	5
Timai	52	5
Chota Raju	40	4
Otalate	55	3
Bada Raju	47	2
Billoi	46	2
Bairogegi	32	2
Longoti	30	1
Balla	40	1
Tejai	50	1
Chota Okaley	50	1
Kogegeli	38	1
Tai	49	1
Totanange	45	1
Bada Okaley	52	1
Moroi	54	1

Source: Field study.

TABLE 6.1a: AGE GROUPWISE HUNTING PARTICIPATION RATE AT DUGONG CREEK

Age Group	Total Male Pop.	No. of Hunters	Participation Rate %
25-34	5	3	60
35-44	4	4	100
45-54	12	8	66
55+	4	2	50
All	25	17	68

Source: Field study.

TABLE 6.2: RECORD OF PIG HUNTING AT DUGONG CREEK

(22 August 1988 to 2 October 1988)

Date	No. of Hunters	No. of Games	Amount of Pork (kg.)
22.08.1988	1	1	08.700
23.08.1988	2	2	17.000
31.08.1988	2	2	30.750
02.09.1988	2	2	33.550
03.09.1988	2	2	29.450
07.09.1988	4	5	78.600
09.09.1988	2	2	25.000
10.09.1988	1	2	22.000
13.09.1989	3	3	46.000
14.09.1988	1	1	22.450
17.09.1988	3	3	62.500
19.09.1988	1	1	09.000
20.09.1988	1	1	18.000
21.09.1988	1	1	12.000
23.09.1988	1	1	12.000
24.09.1988	1	1	10.000
26.09.1988	1	1	10.000
27.09.1988	1	1	25.000
01.10.1988	1	1	12.000
02.10.1988	2	2	53.000
Total	33	35	537.000

Source: Field study.

Table 6.1 lists 16 hunters out of 29 adult males at Dugong Creek, though this does not mean that the others did not go out for hunting. During the period of observation, we were able to extract complete information on hunting from these 16 persons who were considered accomplished hunters. With the exception of a few who were engaged in some form of regular duty at the powerhouse or elsewhere, all adult men went out for hunting. It may be mentioned that besides young men whose initiation ceremony was yet to take place and the very old, all adult men loved to participate in hunting. In total, 68 per cent of the male population participated in hunting and all four males in the 35-44 years age group participated regularly (Table 6.1a).

In Table 6.2, we have recorded hunting activities of the Dugong Creek Onge for the period between 22 August 1988 and 2 October

1988 with successful hunting ventures for 20 days. The hunting was done mostly by individual effort, either with spears aided by dogs or with an arrow or even using a trap. For keeping a record of daily hunting, arrangements were made so that we were instantly informed by someone as soon as the hunters or hunting party reached the settlement. The Onge always cooperated in this regard and the pork was never distributed to any member of the community until we measured the dressed whole pig with our weighing machine kept at the settlement.

From the record, it has been observed that out of 42 days they had met with success in hunting on 20 days (47.62 per cent successful days). Usually every day, one or several persons went for hunting. Before going they never consulted each other. Rather, all the hunters went individually, according to their own convenience. However, we could not keep track of other days when the hunters had met with no success in their hunting venture except the case of those hunters with whom we had close personal contacts. On an average, a person killed at least one pig on a hunting day. They got a supply of pork almost every alternate day. From the amount of pork consumed it can be said that on an average each family got a share of 500 grams per day (Figure 6.2).

Pork gets first preference in the diet of the Onge. It may be mentioned here that the Onge do not hunt any other animals except fish and turtle for sustenance. At times they shoot monitor lizards just for fun. The situation has not changed much if we compare the present set of data with that of 1963 when the Onge were entirely dependent on food procured through hunting and gathering and no cereals were introduced to them. A comparative statement is given in Table 6.3.

It should be mentioned here that the 1963 data was collected during the dry season (December 1963 and January 1964) while the present set of data represents the rainy season, which is less favourable for hunting activities. A greater success in hunting during previous occasions may be partially due to the difference in season and the availability of pig on the island. During that period there was no other competitor of the Onge in the whole island when it came to pig hunting. Today, there are many people who practise poaching in the territory of the Onge, which has a negative impact on their hunting

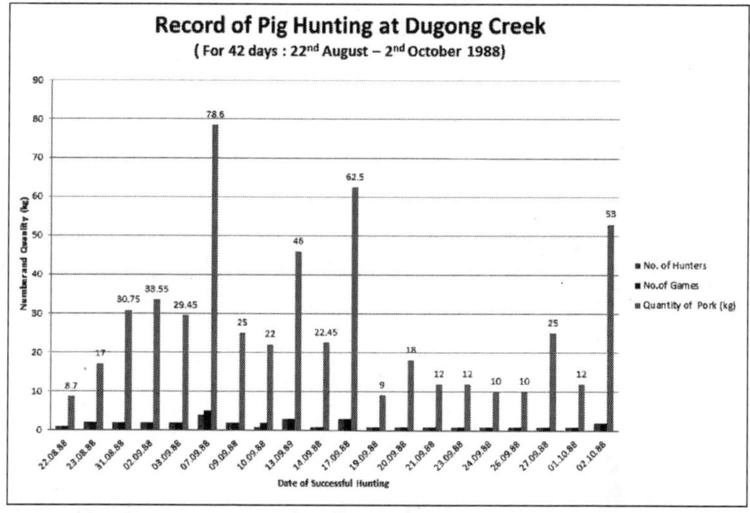

Source: Field study.

Figure 6.2: Day wise Record of Hunter, Game and Pork at Dugong Creek.

TABLE 6.3: COMPARATIVE STATEMENT OF PIG HUNTING AT DUGONG CREEK

	1963 (Bose)	1988
Percentage of days with successful hunting to total days observed	67	48
Average interval between two successful pig hunting	1 day	1 day
Amount of pork per hunting day	28.83 kg	27.35 kg
Amount of pork per day	19.22 kg	13.02 kg

Sources: Bose (1963) and field study (1988).

success. When the amount of pork per hunting day is considered, it can be said that no significant change has been noticed in the ability of the Onge men in terms of pig hunting. Rather, over the period, due to exposure to other people, they have adopted many new, labour-saving hunting devices. But the interval between hunting days and quantity of pork per day has changed to a great extent from 1963 to 1988. During the earlier period, the Onge had to hunt everyday as that was their main source of subsistence and concomitantly per day supply was more. However, in the present day despite having other sources of food, dependence on pig hunting is no less significant. But there is a marked change in the size of the game (Table 6.4).

It has been reported that in earlier days the Onge never killed young pigs as they preferred pork with lots of fat. Therefore, during those days they chose full-grown pigs instead of the young ones. Table 6.4 reveals the following possibilities:

(i) Now they do not spare young pigs.
(ii) Now they prefer medium-sized pigs, which are easy to carry
(iii) Large-sized pigs are not much available in the vicinity, which suggests that the animals might have moved away into the deep forest or have already got killed by poachers.

As there are many competitors around them, the Onge are not left with much choice. Besides the size of the pigs hunted, there is a direct relationship with some other factors such as change in their nomadic habit and community lifestyle. To hunt a large-sized pig of over 40 kg, more manpower is needed for stalking and carrying it to the settlement. In earlier days, the community huts were located in the midst of the forest and life was more community-centred. Pig hunting was more of a group activity for which larger game was the target. Nowadays, the Onge are settled in two areas. Therefore, after hunting, they have to return to their respective settlements before sunset. They cannot go too far a distance to trail a pig. Usually they do not go beyond a radius of approximately 6-8 km for hunting and do not make an overnight halt during the expedition. The changes that are being introduced have affected their lifestyle but not changed the ethos or the basis of their culture. The spirit of community life still

TABLE 6.4: SIZE OF THE PIGS HUNTED

Size of Pig (Weight after Dressing)	Category	No. of Pigs	% Pig in Each Group (kg)	Average Weight (kg)
5-10 kg	small	6	27.27	8.08
10-20 kg	medium	11	50.00	15.00
20 kg	large	5	22.72	24.87

persists in the form of sharing. Even today whosoever hunts any game, everybody in the settlement gets a share of pork.

TIME SPENT AND DISTANCE COVERED FOR PIG HUNTING

From our observations made during August-September 1988, it has been found that the total manhours spent for hunting pig with the aid of dog is more than those with the use of trap. The hunters ordinarily start for the forest around 9-10 a.m. in the morning after taking a light meal, mainly comprising *rotis*. But the hunters using traps return successfully within three to four hours with the game, while those hunting with dogs return around 5.00-5.30 p.m. Less time is involved in the actual process of hunting with the help of traps. The hunters spend more time in the forest for other activities like canoe making and collection of minor forest products, etc., after finishing with the hunting. In fact, hunting by trap does not mean a whole-time exclusive job, rather a secondary activity in the forest. On the other hand, the entire process for the traditional type of hunting from stalking to killing the game is a lengthy and strenuous one. When it is over, the hunter gets so exhausted that he cannot attend to any other job in the forest and no time is left, as he has to return home before dusk. In a few cases, it has been observed that the trappers ventured to the forest as late as 1.30 to 2.30 p.m. and returned with the game before dusk. In such cases, they only required the time to reach the spot to find if any game has been trapped (the trap had been laid earlier), kill the animal and bring it back to the settlement. At present, the Onge usually do not go beyond the limit of a 2-3 hours trek in the forest. It has been found that they generally follow a fixed route or path whenever they enter the forest.

Often, people are not aware how many people have ventured out for hunting on a particular day. But they always come to know when the hunter returns. It is mostly the children who bring the message, on seeing the dogs that precede the hunter. Howsoever tired the hunter may be, his face glows as soon as he enters the settlement. It has already been mentioned that the hunter does not show any interest in the share of the game but a sense of pride is always there that he is able

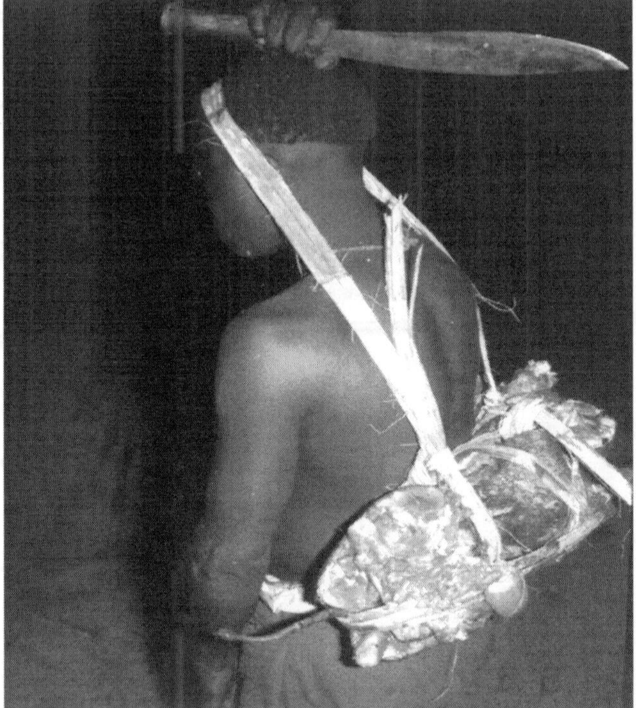

Source: Photo taken by the author.

Figure 6.3: This mode of carrying pork from the forest signifies a great distance covered. The Onge carry only the consumable part and feed the rest to the dogs who helped the hunter.

to provide pork for his community. As the Onge society has an egalitarian base, no one is ranked higher or enjoys any special privilege for one's hunting prowess or acumen. It is natural for an accomplished hunter to provide a share of the spoils to all. So the question of extra prestige or privilege of the hunter does not arise.

PIG CARVING

Pig carving is an art and the Onge do it so efficiently that observing an Onge man carving a pig is almost like observing an experienced butcher at work. All the Onge follow a particular style for doing the work. After singeing (the hair) they first clean the whole pig by scraping the skin with a knife and sometimes washing it with water. The head is first severed. Each leg is cut at 2"-3" above the hoof which is offered to the dogs. Then they start carving the pig from the top of the neck by laying it upside down with the legs pointing upward. Next, the four legs are separated from the trunk. Then the thick layer of skin and fat are taken out carefully from the white trunk. Lastly, the main body is separated in 4-5 chunks, according to the main muscles.

The pig is so important to the Onge that they can distinguish and identify the pork of different parts of the pig according to its taste and quality. The Onge have given different names to these parts (as shown in Figure 6.4).

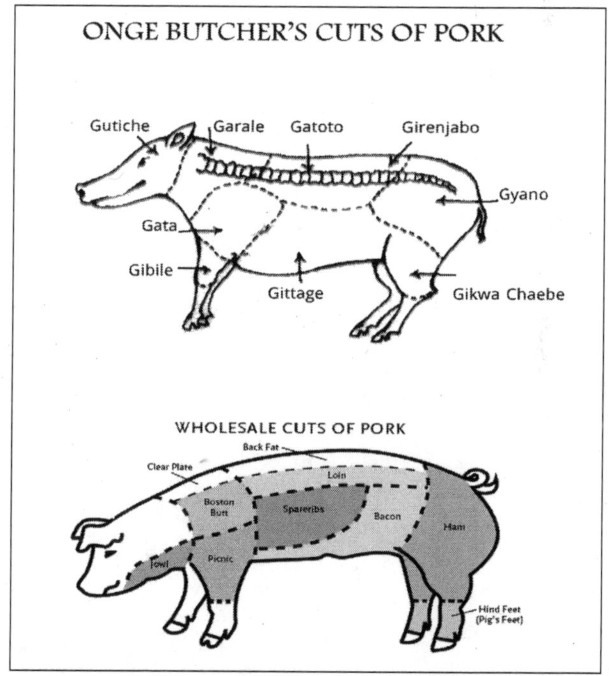

Source: Drawn by the author.

Figure 6.4: Onge pig carving. An Onge butcher's cuts of pork with names compared with the international cuts.

The most liked part of a pig are the hip and thigh muscles of the hind legs, called *gyano*, because this has the thickest layer of flesh with the least bone. As per taste and quality of flesh, the *garale* or neck comes next. *Gotato* is the fat and flesh on the spinal cord. The spinal cord itself is called *girenjabo*. The upper muscle of the front legs is called *gata* and ribs, chest cavity, and stomach are known as *gittage*. The calf muscles of the legs are called *gibile* and *gikwachabi*, respectively.

Among the Onge, the hunter's responsibility is over after killing the game and preliminary dressing. As the hunter feels tired after hunting; he gives the killed game to someone on his way back or after carrying it to the settlement. Then it becomes the latter's responsibility to dress the pig and distribute pork among his fellow community members. For doing this, he takes the game to his or the hunter's house. A fire is made for singeing the hair from the body of the pig. The man cuts slices from the whole pig and gives them to people (mostly women) who gather there to collect their share. It has been observed that it is almost obligatory to give some pork to the hunter's

Source: Photo taken by the author.

Figure 6.5: An Onge man carving and distributing pork among fellow families in Dugong Creek. Each share was weighed to measure consumption pattern.

nearest of kin like sister, mother, mother-in-law, daughter and those women who are widows or whose husbands are away. It has also been observed that skull of the pig is given to people who have small children. If it is a big one, the skull is distributed to a number of such families and if small, to a single family. After boiling it well, it is given to the children. Perhaps, according to the Onge perception, pig's brain is considered particularly nutritious for children.

DISTRIBUTION OF PORK

When pig carving is done the people show their preference for the meat of different parts of the pig and they get their favoured portions. Generally, the hunter or the next of his kin (especially sisters) are offered the best pieces, along with a piece of skin and fat. The Ongle are very fond of the fat, which is soft and tastes sweet. Generally, the Onge do not eat the intestine, heart, lungs, liver, etc. When we suggested to them that those were also edible, they reluctantly tasted them once but did not relish it.

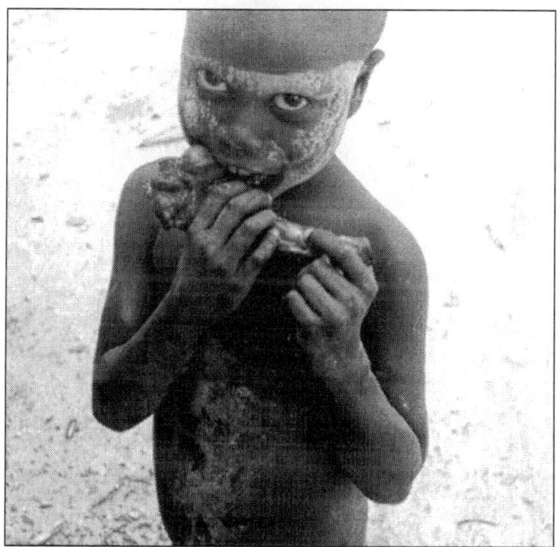

Source: Photo taken by the author.

Figure 6.6: A child enjoying his share of boiled pork after his mother smeared white clay on his face and body to repel flies and other insects.

FISHING

Traditionally, both Onge men and women are adept in the art of fishing. The style of fishing is always gender-specific. Women never go for sea fishing and never use the bow and arrow for this purpose. In earlier days, women used to do fishing with a hand-net (*chickwe*) which they made themselves from either plant fibre or nylon thread. Net making is purely a woman's job. Men do not know the art of net weaving. On the other hand, women cannot make a bow and arrow and do not use them either. With the help of the hand-net, women's groups used to fish in shallow waters or creeks. Men love to fish in groups, but sometimes singly too, primarily with a bow and arrow. Hook and line have also been introduced quite lately and fishing has become a popular pastime for the Onge. Though the Onge are fond of fish it is neither considered a staple nor is fishing a full time job. More often than not it is a hobby pursued to add variety to the Onge.

It has already been mentioned that most Onge go hunting almost regularly, but there are some who do not feel like doing any arduous job. They are often found fishing along the shoreline with a hook and line or the bow and arrow. At any time of the day they roam about the shoreline or on the creek and spend long hours in search of fish. Hook and line fishing is also quite popular now as the materials are easily available in the cooperative store in the settlement and very easy to carry. The Onge use hermit crab or small fish as bait. They generally select the spot near the mouth of the creek where fish gather at the beginning of high tide. As this simple set of tools ensures moderate success with less effort, it has become quite popular among the Onge who always carry the same while on the shore or during a journey by canoe.

Some innovations have been observed with respect to fishing. One day, Tai, an Onge man, demonstrated a peculiar method of fishing at the jetty of Dugong Creek. He killed a small fish, about 10" long, by piercing it from the top, standing on the jetty. The implement used was simple, a 2.5 ft long iron rod sharpened at one end and tied with a nylon string of about 4-5 ft length at the other. The free end of the string was tied around the right wrist and the iron rod thrown by the same hand like a spear directly on the fish. It requires a tremendous

Source: Photo taken by the author.

Figure 6.7: Line and hook used by the present day the Onge men and boys.

concentration, accuracy, and power to hit the slim moving target with a width of about one inch or even less. In South Bay, Ugule, the leader (*raja*) of that settlement, adopted an improvised spring harpoon for fishing. A 4.5 ft long aluminium pipe was fitted with a steel barbed arrowhead at one end and a strip of rubber (cut out from cycle tube) on the other. A rubber strip was fixed around the wrist of the right hand. Covering the eyes and nose with a diver's mask (collected from the sea) Ugule jumped into the shallow clear water of the reef holding the weapon with his right hand. After spotting a fish he released the harpoon handle with accurate aim, using the highly elastic rubber tape as a strong spring. Though one has to complete the action holding his breath, the technique proved effective as Ugule returned with 12 medium-sized fish within an hour and a half. On enquiry, he said that he had learned this technique from the Nicobarese of the neighbouring settlement of Harmindar Bay. The Onge also know the Nicobarese way of fishing by using the poisonous seed of a particular mangrove, named *chingototo* (Nicobarese call the fruit *kindiao*). The Onge, however, do not like this particular technique as there is no thrill in taking out fish which is numb due to the effect of the mild poison.

GROUP FISHING: TIME AND SPOT

Occasionally, the Onge go for fishing in groups. To the Onge, fishing is a pastime as well as a subsistence activity. Group hunting is seldom practised; fishing is the only major community activity still practised.

Usually, during the three-four days around the new or full moon, the Onge move to the coral reefs (at the mouth of the creek) for fishing with the bow and arrow. As the sea water reaches its lowest level during low tide around midday, they reach the shallow water encircled by coral reefs where an assorted variety of large fish are already trapped. During our stay at Dugong Creek, the Onge males often went for such fishing. Once we accompanied them on such a venture. The following description would give an idea about how the Onge enjoy such activity.

A group consisting of seven adults and four boys set out from the settlement at 12.30 p.m., each adult carrying a medium-sized bow and five fishing arrows (having a long nail head with a barb) and a fish storing cane basket (*tole*) tied at the waist. They crossed the creek in trips by canoe to reach the southern bank. Then they walked about 1.5 km to reach the actual fishing spot. All of them were dressed minimally with a short brief or a strip of cloth as a genital cover. It has been observed that on almost every trip two adolescent boys accompany the group as apprentices and they usually serve the elders by rowing the canoes and collecting pierced fishes. The boys keenly watched the entire fishing operation. All participants looked extremely jubilant as soon as they started for the fishing trip. They expressed their ecstasy by singing and laughing loudly and throwing arrows across the creek.

After reaching the seaward margin of the shallow waterbed, the Onge started combing the water in a row facing the beach. They held all the arrows and the bow by the hand positioned to shoot instantly. In the knee-deep transparent sea water each and every fish became visible as the Onge beat the water and the coral cavities. At the sight of a fish of their choice, an Onge instantly started shooting arrows. When the first person had exhausted all his arrows without success or the fish passed beyond his shooting range he made a vocal signal to the person next to him closer to the fish. An Onge can manage to hit the target in the fourth or fifth chance if the fish remains visible within a range of 12 to 15 m. It was observed that one fish was shot by the fourth person in a sequence of relay chasing after using six arrows successively along the path of the fish, which took 18-20 seconds. On an average an Onge took 3-4 seconds between two successive shootings. Immediately he started gathering all his arrows and got ready for spotting the next. As they were searching for fish inside the water about 2 to 3 ft. deep, their eyeballs bulged out indicating deep concentration and use of eyesight at its best. It was a very exciting game which they played with elated shouts expressing pristine joy. The choreography of their jubilant movements created visual images, which one would remember for a long time. With lots of thrill and excitement the entire fishing ground got transformed to a silhouetted dramatic scene against the background of the vast sea and glowing sun.

After an hour or so the Onge finished tracking their fishing trail, reaching the other end of the shallow waterbed near the beach. Towards the end, they enjoyed themselves by catching a few other fish which they do not eat. As the young boys usually fail to catch any, the elders gift those fish as encouraging gestures. On an average, each of the elders caught five to six large fish.

It is amazing to observe that an Onge can shoot three to four arrows in eight to ten seconds leaving them practically no time for aiming which is almost automatic. The maximum range of shooting a fish with arrows is about 10-15 ft, varying slightly from person to person. With that speed they also remain cautious to avoid hitting fellow hunters who are also busy fishing around them. Not a single arrow gets lost in the process. Suprisingly, we observed that in this fishing spree, their feet were not at all scratched by the sharp corals and other shells whereas it was difficult for us to move barefoot there.

From the group behaviour during community fishing, the following observations can be made:

1. This type of activity gives them the taste and flavour of their primordial life.
2. It is more a pastime and recreation than a mere subsistence activity. It involves more time and physical stress but people enjoy it highly.
3. It is a kind of training programme for the youngsters.

4. Such fishing needs deep knowledge about the tide and availability of fish and their behaviour.
5. It needs a high degree of precision in archery and highly synchronized group behaviour.

RECORD OF FISHING

Fishing activities pursued either by individual or groups have been recorded during our stay in Dugong Creek. However, we could not always keep the track of fishing by an individual member, though we never failed to record the cases of group fishing. The record presented in Table 6.5 shows that instances of group fishing are more than that of individual fishing.

From Table 6.5, the following information can be extracted:

Total catch of fish in 13 fishing days = 91.5 kg
Catch per fishing day = 7.04 kg
Average persons involved per fishing day = 5.85
Average hours spent fishing per day = 4 hrs
Per person yield = 1.2 kg for four hours.
23.4 manhours have yielded 7.04 kg of fish per fishing day.

TABLE 6.5: RECORD OF FISHING AT DUGONG CREEK
(22 August 1988 to 1 October 1988)

Date	No. of Persons	No. of Catches	Amount of Catches (kg)	Nature of Fishing
22.8.1988	1	10	2.200	Individual
24.8.1988	7	32	11.000	Group
27.8.1988	10	12	8.000	Group
12.9.1988	2	3	0.600	Individual
13.9.1988	6	14	10.000	Group
16.9.1988	12	–	14.250	Group
22.9.1988	5	–	6.000	Group
24.9.1988	4	–	1.400	Group
26.9.1988	9	25	15.000	Group
27.9.1988	4	4	4.500	Group
29.9.1988	3	12	8.250	Group
30.9.1988	1	2	0.800	Individual
1.10.1988	12	15	9.500	Group

Source: Field study.

It is evident from the record of fishing (Table 6.5) that people love to go for fishing in the sea at a suitable time depending on tides, especially around the full moon or the new moon. In the table, the number of persons exceeding three indicates events of group fishing. We have a record of fishing for 13 days. The average catches weigh 7 kg and per-person catch amounts to 1.2 kg.

It may be mentioned that there is a marked difference between the yields of hunting and fishing. Pig hunting is mostly an individual effort but the yield is shared by the community while fishing is mostly a community affair but the yield is shared among only the participants. Perhaps it depends on the volume of the catch, in case of pig the bulk of pork is often more than a family requirement and cannot be preserved for long due to weather. In olden times, fish was treated more as a fast food due to its easy availability and preparation. Now, of course, fish is something to be taken with rice.

Though fish is not shared on a community basis, the entire catch is not consumed by those involved in fishing. In Dugong Creek, a good number of officials are posted, most of whom expect that the Onge would give them some fish when they return from fishing. The individual fisherman cannot always be traced by them, besides the catch is also insignificant in such cases. But everybody comes to know when they return from group fishing. On their way back home, they are stopped and large fish are taken away by the officials. The Onge undoubtedly feel bad about it but cannot refuse because it is against their culture to decline anything when asked.

With respect to subsistence activities, especially in the case of hunting and fishing, the Onge have made various adaptations in keeping with the changing times and habitat. Due to this, certain differences in fishing techniques are noticeable between the Dugong Creek Onge and the South Bay Onge. In South Bay, men generally do not practise group fishing even on the coral reef. Like the Dugong Creek Onge, they, too, prefer the same timing of fishing, i.e. a few days around the full moon or the new moon and they mostly use the bow and arrow, but fishing is done individually.

There is a beautiful example of the ability of the Onge to adapt to a slightly different habitat and apply the most effective measures to get maximum returns. In South Bay, the most dominating coral in the process of reef making is an umbrella shaped one with a flat and broad canopy (*Acropora armata*). Moreover, various corals, e.g. *Staghora acropora* grow in a circle leaving a deep pool of water within a radius varying between 6 and 20 ft. Hence, at a particular time of low tide, the top canopy of the coral reef becomes exposed over the water level, thus trapping the fish within the pool. The Onge start fishing at the time when it becomes easy to spot them and shoot the targets from within a close proximity. This type of reef fishing ends as soon as the water level rises submerging the reef again. The Onge of South Bay, as mentioned earlier, adopted the technique of fishing by using the spring harpoon which is perhaps the most suitable for this type of reef. In Dugong Creek area fish are trapped during low tide but in a large shallow bed. Hence group fishing is needed. The preferred fish in South Bay is *ina,* a reddish medium-size fish (*lal bhetki*) instead of *pharsa,* the estuarine fish in Dugong Creek.

TURTLING

The turtle is the largest catch from the sea. Two large species are mainly available in the sea around Little Andaman. The famous green turtle—*Chelonia vigata*, and the *Caretta imbricata*, with large decorated scales over the shell, both attain very large sizes and produce about 25-40 kg flesh or more when mature. The Onge prefer the second variety, *Torangulu kutu* in Onge vernacular, for its taste. Turtles are plenty around the Onge habitat, mainly available in the breeding season when they come ashore for laying eggs in the sandy beach during the southwest monsoon months, i.e. July-August. However, the maximum number of turtle hunting expeditions occurs during the dry season of January-March (*Torale*) when the sea becomes clear and calm. It is learnt from the Onge that the turtle prefer the eastern coast of this island, i.e. the leeward side of southwest monsoon wind for laying eggs.

Like pig hunting and fishing, the Onge have innovated their own techniques for catching or hunting turtles which may be termed as 'turtling'. The essential equipment in turtling is the canoe, harpoon, *bone* (an indigenous torch made of palm leaves and natural resin), chopper, and a few baskets which are all made by the Onge.

At present, though turtling is a part of the subsistence activities of the Onge, the people look upon it more as an adventure which needs a lot of preparation and planning. In terms of yield, turtle hunting is not encouraging but the people feel very thrilled by the atmosphere created for turtling as it is practised mostly during the night. The record of turtle hunting is shown in Table 6.6.

The record shows that as an economic pursuit in terms of time and labour spent as well as assurance of supply, turtling is not sufficiently rewarding. Nevertheless, as pig hunting was in full swing during that period they did not depend on turtling. A regular pork supply was almost assured. From the number of persons and canoe used vis-à-vis the amount of catch, one can easily guess the adventurous nature of the Onge. It may also be mentioned here that canoe-making is one of their favourite jobs. During our field investigation in 1988, we found a large number of worn out canoes lying around Dugong Creek. This suggests that it was the fag end of the hunting season. On the other hand, in 1986, during the summer months, we had found a large number of canoes just after construction, ready for the coming turtling season.

From the salient features as described below, one can easily appreciate the uniqueness of turtling, Onge style.

TABLE 6.6: RECORD OF TURTLE HUNTING AT DUGONG CREEK
(22 August 1988 to 2 October 1988)

Date	No. of Hunters	No. of Canoes	Amount of Yield
27.8.1988	2	1	Nil
30.8.1988	7	4	30 kg
05.9.1988	6	3	Nil
20.9.1988	4	2	10 kg
25.9.1988	7	3	Nil
26.9.1988	5	2	40 kg

Source: Field study.

1. Turtling is directly related to Onge canoe-making without which it is impossible to practise the same. To be precise during turtling, perhaps, the Onge realize the maximum utility and justification of the laborious canoe-making job. In fact, two small platforms are made on both ends of the canoe for nothing else other than turtling.
2. Turtling is a group activity but the number of participants is generally restricted to three in a canoe for fast and light movement in the sea. In most cases, a medium-size, perfectly built (slim) canoe is suitable for expedition in the open sea with two persons on board, the ideal combination. Generally, a couple of canoes make their journey together.
3. Like reef fishing, the Onge generally select days or nights around the full or new moon but strictly under a clear sky. Weather condition like cloud or strong wind is minutely observed to select the day of turtling. Hence, seasons of strong wind and heavy rains are not considered suitable for such activity. However, the Onge take risks during the late monsoon months when turtles are frequent. Due to better sea conditions, they hunt turtles in *Torale* and *Mekange*. The present-day Onge have gathered adequate experience from the earlier incidents of a canoe capsizing due to wrong assessment of weather that had resulted in a loss of lives.
4. It is observed that the Onge prefer night to day for turtling because in the dark these creatures move towards the shore of the reef for a type of marine grass (*Valosnercia*), their main food, and also for laying eggs. During the night, the Onge carry indigenous torches (*tikwe*) made of twisted palm leaves, tightly bound with fibres and then filled with *dhup* or resin (*bone*), one in each canoe, which burn for several hours and emit good light. The torches are 30"-32" long and 12"-16" in diameter. But they have to be careful in handling the *bone* otherwise they get burns out of drops of burning resins.
5. The harpoon is made up of three basic parts—the 10"-12" long shaft or *kae,* the detachable head (steel made) *nantoranta katebe* (3" without barb) and a 50"-60" long rope, *kao-age* which is tied up with the detachable harpoon head. At one end of the shaft a socket is made accurately to fix the detachable head and the loose end of the rope is tied up firmly to the canoe itself.

Turtle hunting always needs a minimum of two persons. The actual hunter sits on the bow of the canoe, legs hanging in the front, holding the harpoon shaft and the rope with both hands and he helps in rowing with the shaft itself, while the main control of the canoe is left to the man at the rear.

As soon as the raised head of a turtle, slightly bigger than the hood of a large snake, is spotted by any of the members, they start moving in that direction steadily but silently. The stroke of paddle (*ta*) on the sea water becomes almost inaudible. When the hunter, standing on the bow with delicate balance, positioned with the harpoon, reaches within 10-12 feet of the turtle, he jumps on the game to hit the harpoon head as firmly as he can on the hard dome shell. Then the hunter swims back to the canoe. The turtle by that time runs swiftly under water but trapped by the arrowhead on the rope can only move up to a certain distance. The wooden shaft, floating on the sea, is then collected. The Onge let the turtle move around under water for some time and then slowly start pulling the rope and finally catch and lift it on the canoe.

Generally, as the game is bulky, they instantly come ashore. They then put the game in an upside down position on the beach. There they cut it alive into pieces and keep these in the basket. Only the small ones are taken to the settlement. Cipriani says, 'Once caught, the wretched animals are subjected to a form of vivisection utterly incomprehensible to the western mind; they are literally cut up alive and the pieces thrown into the boiling cooking pot. Nor I ever witnessed anything so terrible as they way in which the Onge roast these turtle whole and alive over a slow fire' (Cipriani, 1966: 124). We never came across live turtle roasting except the 'cut up alive' method though a number of turtling ventures took place during our stay.

TURTLE EGGS

Turtles lay eggs during rains, from July to September, on the sandy beaches. These creatures select the spot after several visits and leave footprints on the sand to be easily spotted by the Onge. The Onge search the probable spot, inserting a long stick into the sand. The eggs are generally found buried under 3-5 ft of sand, a depth suitable for incubation. During the entire incubation period (60-70 days), the Onge regard the eggs edible. But the Onge face tough competition and always fall behind in collecting the eggs against more skilled predators like the monitor lizards and jungle cats. The Onge eat these hard boiled eggs as one of their most favourite dishes.

CRAB COLLECTION

Crab species in Little Andaman are numerous. But the Onge eat only one variety of large crab available in the creeks called *tekandu*. This is found on the clay banks of the creeks amidst dense mangrove growth. Both men and women collect crabs from creeks and swamps, though nowadays women rarely go out for crab collection. The most effective method of collection as practised by the Onge is simple. They use a small stick of wood or an iron rod 2-4 ft. long to pierce the crabs right through the centre of its large cavepace. To spot a crab under the muddy water of the creek needs experienced eyes. Sometimes while canoeing down a creek an Onge spots crab and from the canoe itself, collect them from the bank using the paddle (*ta*) as a stick.

Though crabs are available throughout the year, the Onge find it difficult to catch them during the rains when the water in the creek becomes murky. Similarly, it is difficult to get crabs during high tide when the banks are submerged. The most important factor in selecting the days for crab collection is related to the phases of the moon. The Onge know that during the four to five days around the full and new moon crabs become full of water which makes them tasteless and decreases the quantity of flesh in them. If any crab is collected during that period only the large shell is kept and the claws and limbs are thrown away.

Crab collection needs a relatively longer period but produces a negligible quantity of food. Nevertheless, it is a delicacy for the Onge. They, therefore, try to get the largest available ones, weighing around 1 kg or more. Collection of smaller crabs by women has almost become unknown nowadays. This gets corroborated by the absence of the hand-nets (*chikwe*) from the material culture of the present-day Onge.

ONGE KNOWLEDGE OF AQUA-FAUNA

The Onge subsistence activity in their own habitat is guided by knowledge obtained through experience and observations. In the sea and creeks of the Andaman, countless aquatic species reside. A group can survive on these resources provided its members have a sound knowledge regarding the quality of the edibility of the species, its zone of availability, season of occurrence and periodic hazards in its collection, etc.

During our field investigation and from other published reports, it has been observed that only a small fraction of the total of marine species are collected by the Onge. They are, however, very choosy in this regard. For instance, the fish they eat are mostly medium to large in size, with soft and tasty flesh. In the Dugong Creek area itself, some fishes available on a large scale are never touched by them, such as the small *tarini* fish which are only occasionally used as fishing bait. The large *gobra* and *pathar* (butterfly fish) fishes are not liked due to their thick skin and tough flesh. Species like the large and medium sting ray are easier to catch but the Onge avoid it perhaps for its thick skin and bad smell. They can readily identify the poisonous variety of fish, too, such as puffer fish, marine snakes and other creatures. Once a highly poisonous scorpion fish (*murga machchhi*) was hooked by one of our team members. The Onge present there immediately instructed him not to touch it and leave it by cutting the line from a safe distance. Out of around ten available species of crabs in the mangrove creeks, we have seen only one particular variety being consumed by the Onge.

ACTIVITIES OF GATHERING

Plant food is necessary for making the Onge diet a balanced one. In the early stage of technological development of human culture, both men and women were equally responsible for procuring food. Thus we find that the Onge men do the job of hunting and major fishing. Gathering roots, fruits and tubers is done by the women. Once, plant food was the main source of carbohydrates in the daily menu of the Onge. With changing times, the regular activity of gathering by women has decreased considerably.

The Onge women's gathering activity is now primarily limited to firewood collection and picking up of coconuts from the ground for daily consumption. However, during summer, when wild potatoes are available, many of them go to the forest to gather in groups or with their respective husbands. When women go to the forest in a group for collecting tubers, they may return on the same day or stay on for a couple of days. As there are no predatory animals or other people in the forest, the Onge men do not feel scared if the women are away from home for a few days. It may be mentioned here that the collection from such gathering is quite insignificant. Still, the women love to go out on such ventures to overcome boredom of a sedentary and challenge-free life. In the forest, they make their temporary huts and manage their life themselves. If menfolk are around, they kill a pig for the women as it happened during our stay in January 1986. Ten adult women of different age groups left for the forest in the morning and stayed there for two days. They collected wild potatoes, with the exception of one, who was the youngest. They looked very tired and felt hungry when they returned but were in a cheerful mood.

The Onge women at South Bay are still habituated to the gathering activity. Throughout the year they collect some food articles, either from the forest or the sea. For collecting those items they have and other special nets, and other necessary equipment. At times, they go a little distance away from the settlement to fetch sweet water by digging a hole on the seashore during low tide.

Regular food supply may be the sole deterrent factor which keeps the women tied to Dugong Creek and away from traditional gathering activity. The South Bay settlement is free from outsiders and the women feel free to move around while the movement of the women at Dugong Creek is restricted mostly to the settlement due to the presence of too many outsiders.

HONEY COLLECTION

Honey collection from the forest is a special activity traditionally practised by the Onge. The collection of honey, rather than its consumption, is so liked by them that even the oldest person in the community cannot resist it. In the dense equatorial forest of Little

Andaman, different varities of wild bees produce plenty of honey. The Onge collect honey mainly from two particular varities of bees. One is the larger size *badi makkhi* (*Leguki dorsata*) and the other a smaller one, *chhoti makkhi* (*Narele nigrocinta*).

Collection of honey is a more specialized activity than any other collection from the forest. The most important part of the collection is to locate the hives spread over a vast area, and assess the final day for starting collection by which time an optimum level of honey accumulation has taken place. The Onge start searching out the beehives as the temperature approaches its peak in the driest months of January-February. Keeping a keen eye on every hive, they start making wooden buckets for honey collection (*uko*). Generally, they have to wait till the end of February or early March, after a few spells of light to medium showers. After five or six days, almost all Onge men start collection at a very hectic pace. Each individual participating in the collection marks a number of trees having honeycombs in particular places, from which that very person arranges collection. When it is assessed that the comb contains the maximum quantity of honey, the Onge pull it down entirely. The part of the hive occupied by the larvae and young bees is eaten raw as a whole and the other part with honey chambers is taken to the *uko* for extracting honey.

The Onge use a particular leaf (*tongee*) having a peculiar odour which repels bees, specially the *badi makkhi*, having a dangerous sting. Before going for collection, they smear their whole body (and most especially their face) with chewed up portions of this leaf. Another mouthful of this green substance is sprayed on the comb to repel the bees. If proper care is not taken, the men get stung all over the body which causes severe pain for a few days. Nowadays, they come sometimes to the doctor for treatment of such pain. The poor quality of honey from the small bee or *Nigrocinta* which is available during the rainy season is generally not liked or collected by the Onge.

After collection, the Onge men come to the officer-in-charge of the settlement and hand over the honeycombs. The person in charge squeezes out the honey and measures the collection in bottles of specific capacity. The Onge cooperative society pays the Onge Rs. 10 per 750 ml of honey.

The first few collections, however, are mostly kept for their own consumption. As these people have now got interested in cash, they often sell the major portion of their subsequent collection. Besides, they are now habituated to cereals and so do not consume honey as before. Honey is primarily meant for their children and women. It is learnt from them that formerly babies were fed on honey along with mother's milk for a few years. Now this habit is on the wane. However, the Onge women love to consume honey regularly, if available, particularly during pregnancy. We have observed an elderly Onge woman consume about 180 ml. of honey with each of her meals on a day. A pregnant woman was observed to have *paratha* with honey as a regular meal for a couple of days during the honey season in 1986.

Now the Onge preserve honey in glass bottles and also in the *uko* itself. The Onge way of preservation of honey is not at all hygienic. Before extracting honey they do not make any effort to separate the larvae and insects from the comb. They squeeze the entire thing with all organisms within it. Thus the honey gets mixed up with the pulpy juice of the insects and larvae. In such cases if the honey is not treated otherwise it cannot be preserved for long. The Onge, however, consume or sell the honey as soon as they procure it. But the people around Onge settlements are very eager to procure the unadulterated pure honey from them and often buy a major part of this collection at a very cheap price, without the knowledge of the officials of the welfare agency. Since they do not see the actual process of extraction of honey, the craze for honey continues.

The Onge prepare a delicacy by boiling the bees wax with a little honey. During the honey harvesting season, each and every Onge enjoys this concoction by sucking it with a wooden brush especially made for this purpose. It may be mentioned that when no metallic container was available for them, the Onge used to make sun baked clay vessels with rounded bottoms, especially for cooking this delicacy. The brush is a simple one—a piece of soft twig chewed at one end for sucking the sweet wax solution (*tongo*). It has been observed that during the honey-harvesting season of 1986, the Onge supplied 80 litres of honey to the cooperative society at Dugong Creek settlement. The officials, however, were interested in procuring the entire amount of collection for presenting the same at the annual exhibition held in Port Blair. The Onge have also learnt the tactics of retaining the desired amount of honey for their consumption and sale to the neighbouring people without the knowledge of local officials. It is a matter of regret that to keep the product of their own labour and love, they have to take the recourse of surreptitious ways that appear unethical even to themselves.

PLANTATION WORK

Cultivation of plants is considered a major breakthrough in the history of civilization. Though the Onge live in contemporary times, their livelihood is, by and large, pre-modern in character. As part of a development programme, attempts have been made to bring them within the fold of the food producing economy by engaging them in plantation works.

As the soil of the island as such is not sufficiently suitable for cultivation of food grains (as it appears at present), some semi-permanent trees have been selected for horticulture. Coconut plantation was first introduced during the 1950s as a source of steady supply of food to these people. The trees grew well here and the Onge got attracted to it. It is only in the late 1970s that the people have been brought directly under plantation work. At present, there are more than a thousand trees in and around Dugong Creek and officially all adult Onge are employed in coconut farming. Besides, at present, a few more fruit-bearing trees have also been tried which include banana, papaya, areca nut, lemon, some vegetables like okra (ladies finger), pumpkin, etc. There are two plantation-in-charges to look after the plantations and motivate the Onge to work there. The specific jobs in coconut plantation include digging the pit, planting the saplings, clearing the undergrowth, occasional curing of the trees, and harvesting fruit. These works are taught to the adult Onge step by step.

Division of labour is maintained among men and women. Men generally do work like digging the pit and climbing up the trees for harvesting, while women generally take part in clearing the under-growth in the plantation area. It may be mentioned here that we found women more regular in attending to their jobs at Dugong Creek. Going for collection of roots and tubers is not a regular job nowadays, hence the womenfolk are found almost all the time in the settlements.

They go to the plantation when they are called by the in-charge. The men are rather reluctant to work in the plantation. They need lots of goading for such work and do not show any interest in learning them. Though they are paid monthly for this work, actual works like digging a pit or curing the trees are done mostly by hired labourers. However, the Onge get Rs. 200 per month per family (for a husband and a wife) and a single individual gets Rs. 100 per month.

During the drier months from November to April, clearing of undergrowth and harvesting of coconuts are done simultaneously, while during the humid monsoon months (especially May-June), the main job is planting new saplings. Hence, almost all through the year, these people are officially engaged in plantation work from sunrise to 12.30 p.m. for about 6 hours a day. But in fact, it has been observed that only a portion of the total workforce is engaged at a time though no discrepancies are made at the time of payment. Therefore, plantation farming has two objectives—to introduce horticulture as well as build a money economy to the Onge.

It has already been mentioned that women show better performance than their male counterparts. In fact, the Onge do not have much idea of regularity in jobs. They are guided mostly by their personal likes and dislikes. According to the plantation-in-charge, Onge men are interested in collecting coconuts and cleaning the trees, rather than clearing undergrowth and curing saplings. They always give priority to their traditional activities over plantation work. It has been observed that though there is a coconut plantation in South Bay the Onge over there are not interested in any sort of plantation activities. They are more interested in getting money in the name of plantation work like their counterparts at Dugong Creek. The plantation-in-charge at South Bay lives in Hut Bay instead of living within the settlement. Naturally, in his absence, there is no one to goad them to work. As the marketing centre at Hut Bay is close to the South Bay settlement, the men often visit this place. But without any money, they face a lot of difficulties there. So non-payment because of no work in plantation in South Bay causes socio-psychological disturbances among the Onge.

Despite sincere efforts from the development agency, the Onge are apathetic towards adopting any innovation around subsistence activity. They were and still are hunter-gatherers and all their subsistence activities are guided and controlled by the seasonal cycle. Through coconut plantation, the Onge are slowly coming to the fold of an institutionalized market economy, though the people appear least interested in the matter. Without knowing its intricacies, they are becoming victims of consumerism. They have not opted for the wage earning economy yet. It has been thrust upon them. As a consequence, the Onge women suffer doubly. Their traditional subsistence activity in the form of gathering is on the wane. Once they were their own masters. Now they are captives in their own land and work at the dictates of others. Besides, an extra burden of household chores has taken away the fun and charm of a carefree life.

REFERENCES

Bose, S., 'Economy of the Onge of Little Andaman', *Man in India*, 44(4), Calcutta, 1963, pp. 298-310.

Cipriani, Lidio, 'Report of a Survey of the Little Andaman During 1951-3'. *Bulletin of Department of Anthropology* 2 (1), 1953, p. 124.

Tanaka, Jiro, 'Subsistence Ecology of Central Kalahari', in *Kalahari Hunter-gatherers*, Rechard B. Lee and Irvene Devore, Cambridge, Massachusetts: Harvard University Press, 1976.

CHAPTER 7

Evolution of Hunting Technology

It is a fact, that among most of the hunter-gatherers of the world, plant food forms the bulk of food staple, which is collected by the womenfolk. Others hunt for adding delicacy to the food. The Onge practice of hunting, nevertheless, is a daily routine. As hunting is the major subsistence activity for attaining higher efficiency, the Onge always try to improvise hunting strategy in terms of techniques and tools, since any technology is the sum total of implements as well as skill. Hence, the attempt to study the evolution of hunting among the Onge, may throw light on the development of human society, in general, and the Onge society, in particular.

To study the evolution in methods of hunting, one has to go through the methods and implements used in hunting practices, from the earliest available information. While reviewing the different phases of hunting, we have compared the information on pig hunting from the elderly Onges with that of earlier reports of lay visitors as well as anthropologists who visited the island of Little Andaman. Due to various limitations, we have not been able to reconstruct the chronological history of the hunting technology of the Onge. Nevertheless, we have tried to demonstrate the sequence thereof to the extent possible.

On the basis of implements used and methods adopted by them, the Onge way of hunting may be broadly divided into four phases, viz., (1) pre-metal phase, (2) metal phase, (3) dog deployment phase and (4) torsion trap phase.

PRE-METAL PHASE

At one stage the Onge had to depend primarily on their skill for hunting. No metal was available on the island, nor did they attain any knowledge about the use of metal. They used to make their implements from raw materials easily available in their immediate neighbourhood.

The earliest record of hunting implements is available from E.H. Man's collection of the early 1980s of the nineteenth century, partly preserved in Dresden and Leipzig ethnology museums. At present we find the Onge, too, have an almost similar kind of bows and arrows. By and large, the form remains the same, only the material for arrowheads has changed. Previously, the arrowheads were made of hard wood, such as those of areca palm and the hard spines of sea fish and other sea animals like dugong, shark, etc. The hard and sharp nails collected from the base of the long tail of string rays were also used whole as arrowheads or even barbs. During that period, the Onge either did not know the use of iron or it was not available to them. The bow strings were made from different plant fibres. All other hunting implements were made of natural material available in and around the Onge habitat.

Some of the Onges showed us how they used to prepare arrows, choppers, knives, etc., even from the hard and fine textured stems of trees like the wild areca palm. Those wooden implements were sharp enough but mainly used to scare away outsiders from their territory without killing them. This stage of hunting may be called the pre-metal phase of hunting. The implements were relatively crude like long, shafted spears, heavy wooden sticks, knives made of seashell, etc. Without group effort hunting was not possible with all these implements.

Knowledge of animal behaviour is another important matter for the hunters. In accordance with that knowledge, the Onge hunters plan their strategy. In earlier times, as they were poorly equipped to encounter the animals, the Onge used to hunt after dusk. During day time they located the den of pigs. According to them, pigs are not nocturnal in habit and each herd of pigs has one large male pig. Generally, the pigs rest in one place under a thick bush or in the cavity of a large tree trunk formed at the base. At night, Onge hunters reached the night shelters of pigs carrying their indigenous torchs (*bone*) made of resin and palm leaves. Encircling the shelters, the Onge charged after the large male pig with a spear either to kill or drive it away. Being wounded, the pig ran away or died, and it became easier for them to attack the rest. Then all the hunters together killed the remaining pigs, by thrashing and clubbing them with the spear shaft.

In that killing spree, the Onge exercised no choice about the size of the pig killed. It is reported that in general, the large male pig was allowed to escape to avoid a counter-charge from the animal. At that time spears were the main weapon and these were more effective than arrows in that particular mode of hunting.

METAL PHASE

The second phase of development in Onge hunting techniques is marked by the use of metal in the making of implements. Implements became more efficient and durable with the use of metal. The metal era among the Onge started with the availability of pieces of steel as drift materials from the sea and wrecked ships. But the knowledge of the use of steel, as such, was the key to their entry into the metal era rather than its availability. Since steel was used for making ships for several centuries prior to the nineteenth century, and ships were plying on this important international route, the availability of metal was present certainly earlier than its use.

The use of steel might have been learnt from the neighbouring groups like Nicobarese who had more advanced techniques. Whatever it might have been, with the introduction of metal, primarily steel, the Onge hunters got an effective set of weapons for themselves which provided them with an easier and safer way of hunting. Some of the accomplished hunters mentioned that at this stage the Onge started stalking a single or a herd of pigs in the daytime as well. They chased away the large male pig with the help of a deadly weapon operated from a safe distance. The Onge sometimes took position on a low branch of a tree and shot the pigs with either arrows or spears when they were passing underneath. This could kill or injure them sufficiently to make the job easier for the hunters on the ground.

During this period three major changes took place in the hunting method:

(i) The bow and arrow started taking precedence over from spears and wooden club as hunting weapons.

(ii) Timing for hunting shifted from night to day, thus ensuring rest at night to the people.

(iii) With the aid of improved and effective weapons, even an individual could venture to kill a pig by himself.

DOG DEPLOYMENT PHASE

In the next stage of hunting, with the deployment of animal power, the application of human power got reduced. It also improved efficiency. The dog was introduced in Little Andaman in 1858. The use of dog as a hunting aid was a major breakthrough in the Onge hunting history. So far, improvement of weapons helped or increased the efficiency to a certain extent but could not bring about any qualitative change in the hunting technology itself. The aim of higher technology is to minimize the labour, time, and risk involved in the job. The use of the dog as a hunting aid was really an advancement as the dogs could accomplish the task of stalking the game by themselves and thus the Onge were saved from the risk of direct encounter with the wild pigs which could potentially be fatal. Sometimes even the dogs got badly injured from such encounters.

Now the Onge hunt pigs mostly with the help of native dogs. Dogs have the propensity to chase other animals and the Onge make them do the same work for a purpose, by keeping them underfed. When chasing large male pigs, the dogs get injured, sometimes fatally. The Onge give the dogs a reasonable quantity of spoil after every hunting expedition which includes about four-inch long pieces of pig legs with the hooves, attached tail rectum along with entrails. Usually, one man and his dogs make a hunting team. If someone does not have the requisite number of dogs he borrows dogs from others.

INTRODUCTION OF TORSION TRAP

The latest development in the hunting technology of the Onge came about through the introduction of traps. A middle-aged Onge informant said that until recently the trap was unknown to the community. About 35/38 years ago, while going to Port Blair, Chhota, the then community head of Tokoebuea, and another Onge man met a few foreigners, probably Thai or Burmese, who visited this island and Rutland island frequently to collect various, costly shells. The two Onges were astonished to observe that the foreigners could kill quite a few pigs in the forest without any dog or bows and arrows. Upon enquiry, the foreigners demonstrated the use of the trap and its effectiveness to them. The Onge got interested and being good innovators designed a trap of their own with the idea of the trap they could see in operation.

The Onge trap (*koagere*) is technically very simple but effective. Its operation is easy and quick as it does not require a pit to dig. For making the trap, the Onge simply collect a piece of a highly tensile wooden pole or stick (*gulukuche*), about 10 ft. length, and fix it vertically and firmly to the ground. The spot is selected along the probable routes of pigs in the forest on the basis of the hunter's own experience. About 12-15 ft. away from the pole, two small wooden pegs (10"-12") are fixed to the ground in such a way that the pole and the pegs fall on the same line. The pegs between the pole and the farthest peg is grooved lengthwise. The distance between the two pegs is about 2 ft or a little more, falling directly on the path of pigs. A thin nylon string or plant fibre (*kayage*) is tied on top of the farthest peg from the pole and a piece of stick (*thallange*) (8"-10") is attached to the other end of the string which also has a matching knotch like the peg. A strong nylon thread (*erache*), shorter than the pole, is tied on top of the pole and a loop is made at the free end of the string. Above the loop a small wedge shaped wooden piece (*ollotebe*) is tied to the string. Then the *thallange* stick is set against the middle peg by fixing them in the grooves. The grooves in the stick and peg are made in opposite directions so that they get fixed against each other. The grooves are made in such a fashion that when fixed they create an open space/slit through which the wedge-shaped stick (*ollotebe*) is fitted. The entire arrangement rests in delicate balance. Then the loop is spread over the ground. The mechanism of the trap depends on the force of tension. It works on the principle of a torsion trap. With the slightest touch the tension is released and the animal gets trapped. The exact working of the trap is shown in Figure 7.1.

The Onge Pig Trap: *Gulukuche*

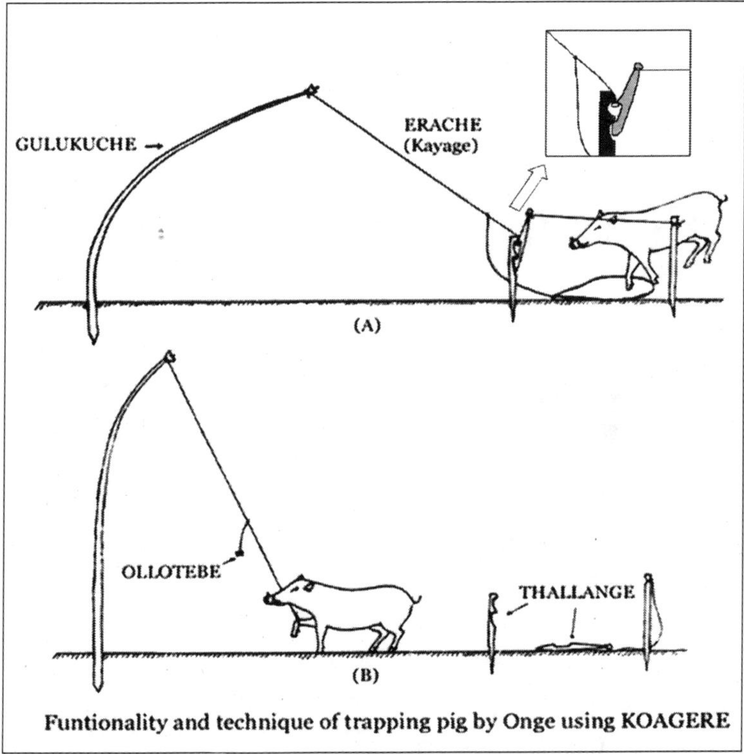

Source: Drawn by the author.

Figure 7.1: Functionality of a trap and the technique of trapping pig.

According to some of the Onge, it is easier to trap pigs during the rainy season. Due to waterlogging during rains, movement in the forest becomes difficult for men as well as animals. The Onge usually lay traps during this season. Since it is easier to locate the path of pigs in the soft damp soil than on dry hard soil, that ensures success. There are some Onge who show a special knack for trapping pigs (they are Timai, Otalate, Billoi, Longoti, Bade Okale, etc.) throughout the year although they are equally successful in hunting by bow and arrow. The record of 16 successful hunts during our stay in the field (42 observed days) shows that 50 per cent of the hunters pursued trapping while the other 50 per cent hunted with the help of dogs. Out of 34 pigs, 17 were hunted with the help of traps and the remaining 17 with the aid of dogs. From this it can be observed that some individuals specialize in a particular hunting technique and none used all the techniques at the same time.

Source: Photo taken by the author.

Figure 7.2: Onge hunter demonstrating the pig trap, 'Gulukuche', laid on the pig trail.

CONCLUSION

Pig hunting among the Onge is not merely a subsistence activity. It is quintessential to their life. Therefore, evolution of hunting has a direct bearing on the process of transformation of Onge culture in general. At the initial stage, the hunting tool was only a simple spear (shaft of spear also used for clubbing) and hunting as such was a strenous job. From spear to trap, group hunting to individual hunting, the darkness of night to broad daylight hunting speaks of a great deal of transformation. This evolution certainly points towards the development in Onge hunting technology imparting ease, accuracy and safety to the hunters. At one stage, dogs started sharing the load of the job and with the introduction of the trap, hunting has become almost a semi-automatic technical operation. More manhours are being saved with the development of techniques in hunting which is

Source: Photo taken by the author.

Figure 7.3: Onge boy aiming his catapult at a bird at Dugong Creek settlement. Bird is never on their food list, but the new equipment is used as an interesting toy.

perhaps utlized as leisure time. It gets reflected in the growing interest of the Onge towards modern entertainment like listening to the radio and tape recorders. Though they spend most of the extra time on these type of entertainment, in reality all these still do not bear any special message to them. For obvious reasons, various programmes on the transistor in different languages do not interest the Onge. They cannot sing a single line of film song though they are exposed to such songs for long hours of the day. Their traditional music has also not been influenced by these songs.

The evolution of hunting techniques has had its reflection on the community life of the Onge. Once hunting was entirely a community activity. It was more laborious and a large number of people were needed for stalking the game and to carry those to the settlement. Lifestyle, therefore, was completely different. Then women used to gather roots and tubers. Often, the major portion of the same was consumed in the forest itself. Besides, the product of such gathering was usually consumed by the immediate kin of the gatherer. Pork at that time was considered a community food. People used to wait eagerly for the hunters to return with game. The arrival of hunters almost amounted to a festivity. Then cooking of pork was a very time-consuming affair. When cooking was done, the people ate to their heart's content. A person was free to eat as much as he could till the stocks lasted. At that stage, life was full of challenges, of course with risks and uncertainty. There was no time to feel bored. The days were action-packed. There was no formal festival in the society. Occasional evening dances added some variety to life.

What does a festival do? It brings variety amid the monotony of life. It brings people together on some occasion and there they contribute their time and labour to share the joy. In the past, the life-style of the Onge was such that every successful hunting day was a festive occasion. They contributed their labour for all and also enjoyed its fruits collectively. Doing things together and sharing made their life more community-oriented.

Contemporary changes in hunting technology have obviously eaten up a lot of the thrill, excitement and festivity that were present in the primordial hunting pursuit. The latest development in hunting has led the Onge people towards a more modern way of living, characterized

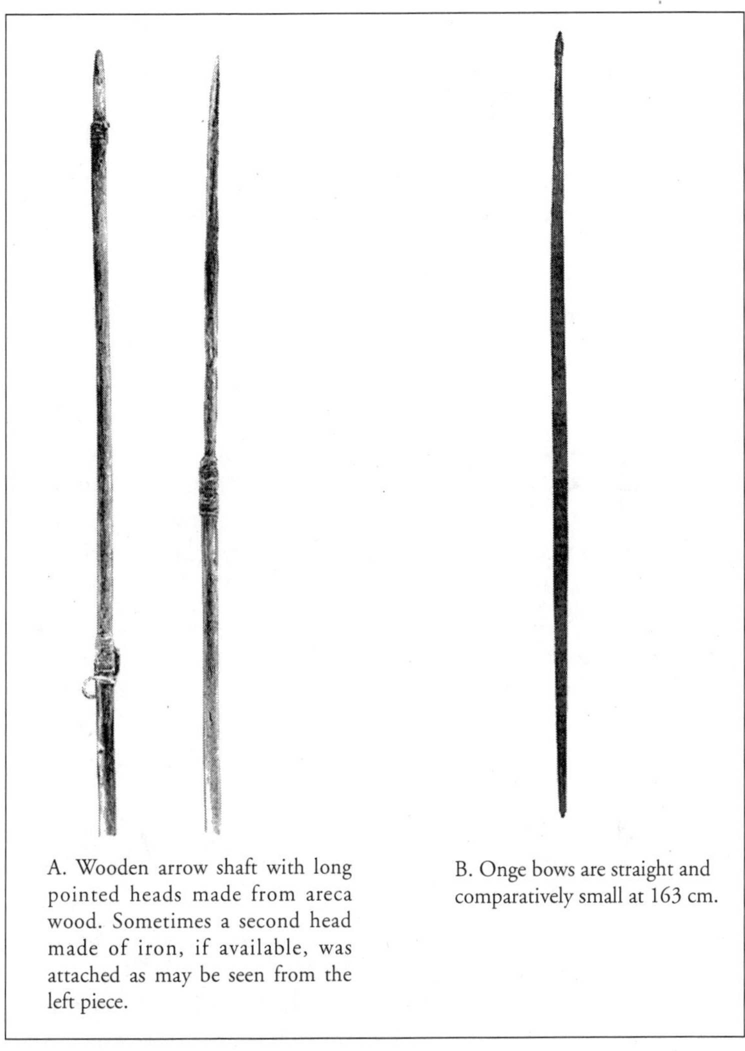

A. Wooden arrow shaft with long pointed heads made from areca wood. Sometimes a second head made of iron, if available, was attached as may be seen from the left piece.

B. Onge bows are straight and comparatively small at 163 cm.

Source: E.H. Man's collection of 1883-7 partly preserved in Dresden and Leipzig Ethnology Museums in Germany. (A). Museum of Ethnography Dresden, cat. no. 45260 c, d. Photo: E. Winkler, (B). Museum of Ethnography Dresden, cat. no. 45248. Photo: S. Weidel [Photos by courtesy of the State Museum of Ethnography Dresden and the Museum of Ethnography Leipzig, cat. no. 45260 c, d (A) and cat. no. 45248 (B)].

Figure 7.4: Onge arrows (A) and bow (B), evolution from the pre-metal and early metal phases.

with relatively more comfort but less manual labour for which they even do not hesitate to take a chance. Now most of them love to adopt time- and labour-saving hunting devices—thus moving towards a more secure life with less hazards. Hunting is basically a full-time job. Previously, during a hunting expedition the Onge could not attend to any other job. Now they can attend the job of canoe-making as well as the setting of traps. However, in this case they do not have any control or command over the game. If hunting is done manually, they have more command over the game. In a labour-saving trap device, the hunters depend more on luck or chance and technology rather than on their own skill or labour. Thus they get more returns with less effort and time to increase comfort in a subsistence economy, contributing to accumulation of leisure time to invest in further development.

It would be rewarding if the Onge could be involved in a number of economic activities and hunting could be a standby subsistence. They could then spend their leisure time in fruitful activities. But what would the Onge do with surplus time? They are not involved in any kind of modern productive activities, nor do they enjoy many recreational activities. Whatever dance and music they once had was associated with community living. All those things have already disappeared as they moved away from that life. Hunting with latest techniques is relatively less challenging and thus less enjoyable though it provides additional physical comfort. If the mark of modern civilization is to have a comfortable life, individualism and nucleated behaviour, the Onge show considerable progress toward this direction with adoption of the new labour saving hunting technique and assured food supply from outside.

From the evolution in hunting, the future trend of Onge society can be foreseen. Even if there is no attempt to induce any change in the Onge life pattern, the people would change on their own volition to have a comfortable and hazard free life. The only problem in the Onge subsistence economy is that they have not yet learnt anything to keep themselves engaged during the surplus time generated by various changes, either induced or spontaneous.

CHAPTER 8

Canoe-making: An Industrial Art

Canoe-making is an indivisible part of the Onge way of life. Once it was a very essential skill when dugong and turtle hunting were important for subsistence purposes. Now, with the improvement in hunting mode on the land, i.e. the forest, as also an assured food supply from an outside agency, hunting in the sea has lost much of its importance. Dugong hunting has almost become a matter of the past and turtle hunting is also not that remunerative. There are many alternatives for conveyance to the traditional canoe, still the Onge men feel an inner urge to make a personal canoe. Canoe-making is quite a time consuming and strenuous job. It appears that a canoe is a piece of art to an Onge for which he spends hours in the forest for days and months. They earnestly love to possess a canoe. In fact, many individuals do not need it urgently, e.g. the men employed in the powerhouse or health centre have not much time at their disposal for this work. Besides, they can use each other's canoe whenever they need one. But these people also cannot restrain themselves from the venture of canoe-making when the season starts for this work. Sometimes, they cannot complete a canoe in a particular season. The entire labour goes to waste because the soft wood cannot last for two seasons. Many a time, it has also been observed that a canoe was never used in that season; even then men start making a new one. In a word, the Onge love to make canoes whether they need them or not.

The physical hardship and monotony of canoe-making is lessened by the Onge through music. The Onge love to sing while at work on a canoe. They rarely sing on other occasions. Canoes are also objects of sentiment and emotion. Ordinarily, the Onge do not express their emotional turmoil at the moment of resentment. But on two occasions we observed that both an Onge man and an Onge woman damaged the canoe to express extreme anger which conveyed that they could hurt the person by destroying his most loved possession.

The extent of importance of the dugout outrigger canoe to the Onge can easily be judged from the labour and time involved in making these non-durable articles. It seems canoe-making has a rather ritual value to them. The Onge believe that once started, a canoe must be completed by the same person, otherwise he will suffer from chest pain. Thus each adult male must undertake canoe-making as long as his health permits it. Even the senior-most members of Dugong Creek do undertake the job at regular intervals. Only one person is an exception to this norm as he mostly prefers to stay with his wife in the deep forest.

Till today, the canoe is the only carriage made by the coastal Onge. From the inventory of material possessions it is evident that the canoe is an item essential to every Onge. During the summer of 1986 at Dugong Creek we found 27 families had 28 canoes in total. Only four adults did not possess canoes and five of them had two a piece. Six out of the 28 canoes were under construction. Though the Onge can identify any canoe by its maker-cum-possessor, in reality all the canoes are basically the property of the entire community.

A canoe has two main parts: (a) the main part to carry man and material and (b) the outrigger or the *bouya* part. The main part or *dange* is a suitably cut out piece of dug out or hollowed tree trunk with two sitting platforms at both ends curved out of the same wood. The outrigger is called *berugu* (*buoya*) and is composed of one light-weight (with maximum buoyancy) log of wood equal in length with the canoe and three or four sticks joining the log and the canoe. Usually, while moving, the buoy lies on the left hand side and the canoe is controlled from the rear. The paddle they use for rowing the canoe is called *naretaknwe* (*tay*). One or more paddles are used for rowing but the direction is maintained by the person rowing at the rear. In most cases the forward and angular movements are both performed by a single person sitting at the bow end.

Canoes are made in widely different sizes. The smallest was found to be only 6.5 ft. in length and could carry two adults at best. The largest one measured about 25 ft. with a maximum carrying capacity of 12 to 15 adults. But on an average, the size of a standard canoe (most common) is 20 ft. long and suitable for 8-10 persons. The size of the paddle also varies with the canoe. Generally, 4-5 ft. length is suitable for most of the canoes. At one end of a paddle, the blade measures 10-12 inch long and is 6-8 inch flat.

Starting from selection of the tree to launching of the canoe in the sea, the whole process involves about 3-4 months, if not more. The different stages of canoe making can be described as follows:

(i) Canoe-making being basically a personal job, an Onge uses his own knowledge and takes precaution in selecting the right kind of tree in terms of species, maturity and shape of the tree. The koallulu (*Thitpok tetrameles nudiflora*), papita and kwera: (*Sterculia companulate*) are some of the common trees needed for making the main body of a canoe. The Onge prefer a mature and straight tree located closer to the sea.

(ii) The next phase is to clear the climbers and undergrowth around the tree and to cut off the branches. These works are done carefully by the person concerned. Then the Onge strip off the bark around the base (1 to 2 ft. above the ground) forming a ring of 1-1.5 ft. wide and leave it to wither slowly so that the main stem will not crack along the cut off branches.

(iii) After a week or two the man again goes to the tree with an axe and felling is done individually.

(iv) The next phase of work involves community effort and the man is accompanied by a group of healthy men to fix the log in the right direction, keeping the convex side of the log on the ground. The log is then fixed up on the ground with the help of several wooden pegs, forming a strong frame. The bark is then chipped off, not scratching the polished outer surface of the log, which serves as water-proof layer.

(v) Then starts the most lengthy phase, demanding high patience and skill of the canoe maker. The top (convex) part is first flattened and two platforms are carved out on both ends. Then with the help of a small *adze*, the man starts scooping and the whole of the trunk slowly becomes hollowed out with delicate strokes of *adze* producing thin wood-flakes. One can only imagine how much accuracy the method needs to leave behind a 1-2 cm.

uniformly thick layer from the whole tree trunk with a length ranging from 12 to 25 ft. or more.

(vi) At the end the tree trunk becomes light enough to carry toward the sea beach for the next phase of work. A day is fixed consulting all the adult male members to bring the canoe out from the forest. It requires days depending on the distance up to the shore to prepare the path by cutting the trees and undergrowth. The cut off branches are placed transversely on the path to serve as a roller for dragging the canoe over it. During the making of such a path, we have observed the Onge generally try to avoid cutting large trees and would rather take a longer route to avoid the unnecessary felling of trees.

To drag the canoe for long distances, the Onge tie up several transverse poles along the top of the canoe and start pushing the poles at both sides of the canoe with their shoulders and hands. It requires the rigorous effort of around 12-20 healthy young Onge. They sometimes use straight tree logs placing those across the path as rollers to drag the hull over, along any uneven ground, especially in the forest. The old and the weak are exempted from this job. But elders also participate by way of giving instructions to the youngsters.

(vii) Once the unfinished canoe is brought on the shore, the canoe-maker needs no more helping hands. He then starts fitting up the outrigger for which suitable wooden poles had already been collected from the forest, while clearing the path. The longitudinal float is taken from a *tayekeye* (*dhup* tree) or the kwallulu tree.

(viii) Now the canoe is standing on its own having a firm outrigger just above the reach of the high tide. Usually, another month or so is required to polish up the inner wall. During this work the man borrows all the available *adzes* in the settlement and regularly sharpens them before work. This is the finest skill required for canoe-making. Any mistake in this regard will lead to leakage and damage the finished product. But the Onge do not feel satisfied until the body of the canoe becomes almost perfectly uniform in thickness and has a smooth touch.

(ix) Ultimately, that happy day arrives not only for the maker himself but the whole community, when the new canoe is launched into sea. Though, at present, the ritual aspect is not so prominent, it was recorded that on the auspicious day women for the first time and perhaps the only time put their hand on the canoe. They decorate it with red clay in celebration of the great achievement. The painting instantly gets washed out as soon as the canoe jumps in the surf but not their enthusiasm.

Once completed, the canoe become the most prestigious property of the whole community even though each canoe is identified by the name of the maker. Anybody can make use of the canoe whenever they need it. Only while going turtle hunting does the maker usually prefers to take his own canoe. Nowadays, the most effective use of the canoe is seen in turtle hunting as the Onge do not sail to any other island with their canoe as before.

The Onge are entitled to travel the entire chain of islands through

Source: Photo taken by the author.

Figure 8.1: A newly completed canoe hull is being prepared for being dragged out of the forest.

the shipping service free of cost. This is why we now observed complete absence of the very big canoes used formerly for long sea voyages to Rutland or even to Port Blair.

Moreover, as the canoes are very much linked with turtle hunting, most of them are perhaps completed before the commencement of the main hunting season of turtle, i.e. September to January. This can be justified by comparing the two canoe enumerations done during March 1986 and September 1988. In 1986, there were 23 canoes in sailing condition while 6 were under construction, but in September 1988, only 6 canoes were in use and 16 were under construction. Moreover, the two figures taken were before and after the main monsoon months (May-July) and hence perhaps pointed to the fact that most of the canoes get damaged during monsoon left as taken are unused and uncovered under the open sky. It is strange to note that the Onge have no traditional method of making waterproof resin for protecting their canoes. They can only repair minor leakages with some natural puddings. Nowadays some of them paint the outer surface with tar.

The canoe is driven on either of its ends and hence there is no fixed bow and stern end. But we found it easier to row with the outrigger on the left. Rowing is done by two persons. The person sitting on the front platform performs the forward movement with a wooden paddle (*ta*), while the man at the rear controls the direction along with the forward movement with a similar paddle. In fact, any canoe can be driven by an expert person sitting at the rear platform when not loaded. But with increase of passengers, additional hands are needed for rowing at a faster pace. In shallow water or while approaching the shore the Onge use long shafts or the paddle itself as point poles to drive by pushing on the seabed.

The Onge at present take precautions to leave their canoe near the beach or nala during movement to ensure that no unknown person can use it. So, they generally keep the canoe in a hiding just above the reach of the tide and keep the paddles separately hidden in a nearby thicket. It is difficult to use the canoe for even another Onge who has no clue of the hideout.

While they make a journey in the open sea, certain precautions are taken to avoid danger, though, according to them, their canoe

Source: Photo taken by the author.

Figure 8.2: A series of newly made hulls of canoe brought out of the forest for fitting the outriggers on a beach near Dugong Creek.

never sinks. First, while facing the high breakers, the Onge cut across transversely and hold the outrigger by leaning on it to make it well-balanced. Second, they usually keep the outrigger on the lee side of the strong wind or current. A person in the boat takes the duty of throwing out the water that enter through several leaks inside the canoe with the help of a small container (formerly nautilus shell) or mug. After each use the accumulated water is carefully drained out from the canoe. The canoe is kept on the shore upside down, especially during rains.

The relevance of canoe-making is decreasing in the present setup of Onge life. How much labour and time is spent on a canoe has already been described. We felt bad when we noticed two big canoes were never used in that season and these were waiting for natural demolition by exposure to different weather conditions. Introduction of motor driven boats had been proposed and might even have been introduced by this time. The Onge feel thrilled with any new object. We are not sure that this thrill would overpower the passion of creativity through which an Onge achieves self-esteem via the art of building the canoe.

CHAPTER 9

Food Culture of the Onge

Once, the life of the Onge was centred around search for food as it happens among any foraging people. Roots, tubers, fruits and vegetables formed the major diet for these people. Food procured through hunting was subsidiary as game is often scarce (Lee, and De Vore 1976). The Onge, being a hunting gathering people, present a rather unique case in this regard. Traditionally, the Onge used to take the meat of wild pig and turtle as staple, and the vegetable collected by women formed subsidiary food.

In the good old days, the first duty of Onge men was to get ready for a hunting expedition in a group. At the day's end when the hunting group returned with the game, it was a great moment of rejoicing for the entire community. As Totanange, Timai and others, the Onge men from Dugong Creek, used to narrate, seldom were days when the hunters returned empty-handed. It is recorded in earlier reports that whenever big game was available, it was an occasion for a great feast. People irrespective of age and sex consumed as much meat as they could. As a result they did not feel hungry for the next few days, and did not go for hunting either. In terms of consumption of food, the Onge were more behaviouristic. There was no regularity in terms of hour and quantity of eating. Their food behaviour was more often guided by the availability of food articles.

The pig population in the forest was much greater than the human population, due to which the Onge never felt any scarcity of game. When food supply was so plentiful, the question of rationing did not arise. People suffer from hunger and frustration when food is scarce as has been observed by Holmberg (1969) among the Siriono. The Onge situation is rather opposite. Here procured food is open to all. Nobody bothers who killed the game or who cooked the food.

Now due to a changed circumstances, community hunting has been replaced by individual hunting. The community mode of cooking has also been replaced by the family kitchen. But the principle of community sharing remains unchanged. No one knows when an Onge man goes for hunting. But his arrival with a headload of meat is known to all. All members within the settlement gather at the hunter's cottage, and get a share. Sometimes, considering the nutritional need by Onge standard, a special portion of the game (e.g. the head of the pig) is given to a family with small children. On such occasions, if any non-Onge people (officially posted there) are present, he/she also gets an equal share. We, during our long stay, were also included in the community, and used to get our share of pork and fish. The Onge are very generous with food. In the matter of other things like bows, arrows, canoes, and some modern dresses, they are quite careful and do not like to share with others. The notion of generosity with food has perhaps been derived from the Onge's subsistence ecology—when nature is so bountiful why will they be miserly?

FOOD ITEMS AND SUPPLY OF FOOD

Since the Onge do not produce any food, they depend entirely on nature for their subsistence. Hence, nature is the eternal donor and they adjust their biocultural needs in accordance with the seasonal cycle of their environment. As they subsist on seasonally available food, they never face any scarcity, rather they are doubly blessed being located in the midst of the sea, and covered by forest. Sometime due to drought or some other reasons they may be deprived of adequate forest products, but the sea never fails them. Their major food item consisted of the meat of wild pig, turtle, dugong, certain varieties of fish, sea shell, vegetarian food like seasonal fruits, roots, tubers and honey. Their food was never deficient in nutrient value, it was rather charged with a protein bias. It may be mentioned here that the Onge do not eat meat of any animal other than that of the wild pig available (*Sus andamanensis*) in Little Andaman. Once during the early phase of the rehabilitation programme white pigs were introduced to them so that they could learn domestication, and also have food supply near at hand. The Onge never liked the meat of those pigs, and in course of time they were consumed by the crew who come to the settlement for transporting monthly rations. The Onge are also very choosy about fish and crab. They relish only a few varieties of these.

Till the introduction of cereal as staple, animal food and plant food interchangeably formed the staple and subsidiary diets of the Onge. In fact, food was a combination of meat, fish, honey, and roots, tubers and fruits. Which of the items would contribute towards the daily meal was determined by its availability in a particular season. The extract from the report based on the work done during the 1950s will give us an idea about the seasonal variation of food of the Onge (Tables 9.1 and 9.3). The present set of data may also be compared in this context.

For comparing the food situation of the Onge at different time intervals, uniformity, and compatibility of data was a big problem. However, we have utilized the data so far available to us which ranges over a long time span from 1953 to 1988. During 1956, the team of researchers from the Anthropological Survey of India headed by Shri Nigam listed the food items only. The quantified data on food was supplied by Dr S. Bose while he worked there in 1963.

This set of data, however, treated pork, fish and other plant food as protein, and carbohydrate as the case may be, without going to the

TABLE 9.1: COMPARATIVE STATEMENT OF AVERAGE DAILY FOOD-GATHERING BY THE ONGE AT DUGONG CREEK (TOKEBUEA)

Period of observation	December-January 1964		August-September 1988	
Food items	kg.	p.c.	kg.	p.c.
Pig	19.23	50.34	13.02	75.96
Fish	7.47	19.44	2.18	12.77
Turtle	1.15	3.01	1.90	11.09
Sea shells	0.46	1.20	–	–
Crab	0.73	1.91	0.03	0.17
Titakala	4.93	12.9	–	–
Titakoru	0.88	2.30	–	–
Gege	2.83	7.40	–	–
Others	0.53	1.39	–	–
Total	38.2	100.00	17.14	100.00

Sources: S. Bose (1964) and authors.

TABLE 9.2: CHANGE IN SEASONAL FOOD PROCUREMENT (1956-88)

Year of study	Food Category	Seasons			
		Dahre (May-August) Humid Rainy	Kolokwange (Sep-Oct) Humid Stormy	Mekange (Nov-Jan) Dry Cold	Torale (Feb-Apr) Dry Warm
1953	Main	Pig, jackfruit, fish, prawn, and turtle eggs	Pig, yam	Yam, pig	Honey, turtle, wild potato
	Subsidiary	Fruits, larvae, and insects, pandenus	Turtle, pandenus, stem-juice	Fish, prawn, stem-juice, turtle	Pig, fish, crab, shell fish, fruits
1988	Main	Pig, fish	Pig, fish	Yam, pig	Honey, wild potato
	Subsidiary	Fruits (lesser quantity)	Turtle, yam	Fish, turtle	Fish, pig, crab, shell fish

Sources: L. Cipriani (1953) and authors.

TABLE 9.3: PROPORTION OF FOOD GATHERED AT DUGONG CREEK (TOKEBUEA) FROM TWO RESOURCE BASES

Period of observation	17 December 1963 to 15 January 1964		3 September 1988 to 2 October 1988	
Resource base	kg.	p.c	kg.	p.c.
Land	851.44	74.32	460.50	79.14
Water	294.15	25.68	121.40	20.86
Total	1145.59	100.00	581.90	100.00

Sources: S. Bose (1964) and authors.

analysis of different nutrient contents of these items consumed by the Onge. This kind of mixed data is apparently not comparable but when treated together throws some light on the food habits of the Onge in terms of varieties, and their change through time.

From the above table, it is observed that up to 1963, practically no marked change has been observed in case of food items. Till then they were entirely dependent on food provided and procured through hunting and gathering. Pig and fish were the major food items constituting 50.31 and 19.55 per cent, respectively. Vegetables also had a significant share in the diet of the Onge. In 1988, when the present authors worked among the Onge, the position of pork and fish remained almost the same, with pigs contributing slightly more, at 75.52 per cent of the food supply. The erratic supply of government food during the study period at Dugong Creek in 1988 might have driven them to fall back on their traditional food sources. Hence, this increase may be due to seasonal variation, though pig hunting may be practised throughout the year. A significant change is marked in case of plant food collected through gathering. The season during which we worked was not suitable for collecting roots and tubers. Besides, in earlier days, roots, and tubers were the main sources of carbohydrate which have been substituted well by cereals. The Onge are not aware of the nutrient value of the different food items that they consume, but unconsciously replaced plant food with the right substitute. It has great implications on the life of the Onge. With this change, the burden of outdoor activities of women is minimized but that has been replaced by domestic chores like cooking and cleaning of utensils, etc. Table 9.3 suggests that there is no marked change in the proportion of food from the source of land and water. It remains almost the same, which suggests that no major change has taken place in their hunting-gathering economy. If the situation demands it, as seems from the above observation, the Onge can still survive on their own. However, in actual practice, their dependence on these sources has been reduced to some extent due to interference of external agencies.

The overall situation, however, changed to a great extent with the introduction of cereal food by the welfare agency, namely, Andaman Adim Janjati Vikas Samiti (AAJVS). Assured food supply has brought about some qualitative change in their lifestyle, which would be discussed in an appropriate place in this section. Now the Onge have adopted rice and wheat as staple, though animal food is still their first preference. Most of the plant foods, like *titekala* and others are no longer consumed, though they are still in the living memory of the people. During summer days they enjoy fruits and yam. Among animal food, dugong has become a rare object nowadays. Consumption of seashells has also gone down. During 1986 we found only few Onge consuming turbo and bi-valve shells.

With the passage of time, food habits of the Onge are changing. They are used to natural food, and these do not have any ill effect on their health. Consumption of more cereal, and a relatively sedentary life tell upon the Onge women's physique. The tendency to grow obese is marked among them. Besides, nowadays, they are exposed to market economy and also have money to spend. It has been observed that whenever they visit the market at Hut Bay or Port Blair, they buy some fried snacks (*samosa, pakora*, etc.). The menfolk eat those things at the marketplace, and often bring some home for their small children. Filial love is so strong that it is very difficult to persuade any Onge not to give such food items to children. Many a time, the children fall sick after consuming such food. The Onge sometimes fail to distinguish between fresh and stale food made by others as they always eat their indigenous food fresh. The concept of stale food is traditionally alien to them.

The wheat flour and rice supplied by the agency are of very inferior quality. We have never seen anybody preparing *roti* or rice without sieving the flour, and cleaning the rice properly. In this connection, some new domestic appliances, like a sieve made of plywood or tin with iron mesh, have been included in the Onge household. In the afternoon, women are found to clean the rice by separating unhusked paddy from stone chips, and other particles like dirt, etc. Likewise, they take extra care about the safety and cleanliness of drinking water. Though there are a number of wells in the settlement, drinking water is fetched from a particular well located a bit far away from the settlement. Incidentally, it may be mentioned here that carrying water is primarily a man's job.

DAILY MENU AND ITS PREPARATION

The adult Onge starts the day with chewing *pan* (betel leaf), followed by black tea. The betel leaf is not purchased from the market. It grows wild in the forest. Tea is taken occasionally but always black without milk or sugar, although they have both things in their stock. However, when they are offered sweetened tea with milk, they do not mind, but never add these things to tea while preparing it in their own house. Tea was introduced to them during the 1950s by the officials of the AnSI. But the Onge were used to drinking some kind of concoction by boiling the leaves of a particular mangrove *more* (*Heritiera littoralis*), and they now identify it as their indigenous tea liquor. It is slightly caustic in taste. At present, however, the Onge never go for this drink as they get a supply of 500 g tea dust per family per month. Surplus tea packets are found in every house.

Preparation of tea is very simple. Early in the morning, as soon as they wake up, a big pan containing about 2 litres of water is put out for boiling. After some time, few tea leaves (not measured by a teaspoon) are added to this water which keeps simmering. This pan full of tea is ready for consumption for the whole day. As it is put by the side of hot oven, the tea remains lukewarm, and ever ready for drinking. Whosoever feels thirsty can take some by dipping a mug or glass in the pan. But the Onge never dips the same glass or mug again without washing it. The Onge are rarely found to drink plain water.

After tea time comes *paratha* time. *Parathas* never make a major meal. They may be treated as breakfast, though among the Onge there is no clear concept of breakfast, lunch or dinner. Though it is called *paratha* (fried chapatti), the preparation of dough and the shape of *paratha* is like chapatti. Dough is made of *atta* (wheat flour) after adding water. As the Onge do not like ordinary baked chapatti, they deep-fry the same in a frying-pan or *tawa*. A gradual change has also been noticed in the preparation of food. During 1986, we never found anybody eating a chapatti. When there was no supply of oil or Vanaspati (saturated vegetable fat) they used coconut oil for frying *paratha*. But in 1988, when they ran short of oil, they made chapatti. However, given the choice, they would always opt for fried *parathas* even today. The Onge are now quite expert in making *parathas*. Among them there is no such idea that cooking is a woman's job. So both men and women are equally adept at preparing food. *Roti* or *paratha* is often taken by itself without a curry. Sometime they eat the same by dipping it in tea.

Rice gruel is strained. The Onge do not consume it. Non-vegetarian food (fish-meat, crab, etc.) and pulse are cooked by boiling. In earlier days, cooking of meat was done by baking/roasting. In that case there was neither any loss of natural juice or any other nutrient content. This traditional mode of cooking is still practised by Onge while inside forests or in transit. In South Bay, this method is still practised regularly. Once, while undertaking a long trek in the forest, we had no food with us. When we felt very hungry, our Onge friends caught some fish with a hook and line, and baked them. So in a natural surrounding they never suffer from starvation.

Nowadays, the Onge are supplied with various spices (turmeric, chilli, and cumin powder) and salt. They season the curry with these spices. In earlier days, they did not use salt in any of their preparations. Sometimes they add onion and garlic to the curry if supplied the same as rations. Vegetable consumption is still limited among the Onge. If any vegetables (lady's finger, pumpkin, etc.) are grown in the kitchen garden under the supervision of the plantation-in-charge, they bring some and cook. However, the cooking method is the same. They never buy any vegetables when they go to the market. Also, they never buy any spices if supply gets exhausted. It suggests that they have not yet been habituated to the taste of spices.

Rice is taken in the evening with a curry. But chunks of pork or a piece of fat is most relished on its own at any time of the day. If there is sufficient stock of pork in the house, they love to eat that.

In Dugong Creek, a new innovation in their cuisine is the soup or curry made from coconut milk. When fish or pork is not available, this curry is prepared for taking with rice. Milk extracted from grated coconut is seasoned with spices. The South Bay Onge do not know this preparation as no outsider lives within their vicinity from whom they could learn how to prepare this. Instead, they prepare delicacies from the mangrove bean and the seed of seaweeds.

To study the food habits in Dugong Creek, 24 households, including adult persons living together, were observed for about two weeks. From the food chart, information on various aspects—like food items, frequency of meals, and eating schedule, etc., could be obtained. These are presented in Tables 9.4 and 9.5.

TABLE 9.4: STAPLE FOOD AND NUMBER OF MEALS CONSUMED

Food Items	Morning Meals		Evening Meals	
	No. of Meals	Total Meals (305)	No. of Meals	% to Total Meals (305)
Rice	31	10.16	193	72.06
Roti	241	79.02	43	16.16
Meal taken without cereal	33	10.82	30	11.28

Source: Field study by the authors.

TABLE 9.5: FOOD ITEMS BY NUMBER OF MEALS CONSUMED

Food Items	Morning Meals		Evening Meals	
	No. of Meals	% of Total Meals (305)	No. of Meals	% of Total Meals (305)
Vegetable	9	2.95	36	13.53
Coconut	14	4.60	42	15.79
Pork	22	7.21	59	22.18
Fish	6	1.97	47	17.67
Crab	–	0	2	0.75
Turtle	–	0	4	1.50

Source: Field study by the authors.

The table shows that the consumption unit of meal with *roti* is higher than that of rice. Various factors may be responsible for this. First, the quantity of wheat supplied through ration is higher (9 kg) than that of rice (5 kg per head per month). From Table 9.4, it is observed that 72.6 per cent of the evening meal was taken with rice and *roti* constituted only 16.16 per cent. On the other hand, *roti* dominates the menu in the morning. It is because fish, pork, etc., are primarily available in the evening and are part of that meal. In the morning, *roti* is taken as breakfast before going to the forest or as and when a person feels hungry. From the same table, it is noticed that the presence of curry with *roti* is negligible but rice is enjoyed with other preparations which gives them a greater satisfaction from the meal after the day's work rather than mere appeasement of hunger. Hence the evening meal may be considered as the major meal. Traditionally, too, they used to take the major meal only in the evening.

From the table, it can be made out that rice or *roti* is one of the major items of the daily meal of the present-day Onge. But till date, pork is their choicest item of food. When there is ample supply of pork in the settlement, they do not bother for rice. Then they revert to their old habit, i.e. subsisting only on pork.

EATING SCHEDULE, MANNERS AND HOSPITALITY

Owing to their hunting-gathering way of life, the Onge have not developed any routine habit of eating at regular intervals. It has been observed from earlier reports that usually the cooking of meat starts with the return of the hunting party in the evening. As the supply of food was not certain and regular, people used to consume as much as they could when food supply was plenty. The climate being hot and humid, meat could not be preserved for long. Hence the Onge have developed a flexible habit of eating plenty or going without food for days together, depending on availability. The surplus pork is kept smoked for a number of days. The way honey is extracted by the Onge, it cannot be preserved for a long time either. Nowadays, however, the Onge get some preservable food items like rice, wheat flour, sugar, milk powder, lozenge, biscuit, etc. But they have not yet developed the idea of storing the food for a lean period. They consume things as soon as they get them.

Wheat and rice are consumed daily, so the stock finishes within a limited period. Milk powder is kept in paper cartons in such a way that it often gets spoilt or consumed by dogs. It may be mentioned here that the people like to eat milk powder directly without mixing it with water or any other fluid.

With free supply of food articles, a kind of regularity is noticed in the food habits of the Onge in terms of timing. It is observed from Table 9.5 that, on an average, the Onge take more than one meal in a day.

It has already been mentioned that in Dugong Creek, 24 households (including adult persons living together) have been observed all through the day for about two weeks to assess their eating schedule, if any. With the change in food items and adaptation of the modern way of cooking, the Onge are now found maintaining a tentative routine for meals, which can be labelled as lunch, dinner and breakfast, etc.

During these two weeks, most of the Onge have taken two meals per day on an average (Table 9.6). Only five families have taken two meals or more. From the table, it seems that the morning meal (taken before 9 a.m.) is the most important in terms of frequency. Out of the total 627 meals observed, 305 were taken in the morning before the hunters go to the forest. Again, 266 meals were taken after the hunters return home in the evening. Midday meals are rare but their occurrence indicates that the days are mostly without any major activity or the presence of the adult male at home. Elderly persons like Tanagiru and Kanjo who mostly stay at home have taken day meals.

The lowest number of average daily meals were taken by households who have joint cooking arrangements. The group in such a case is composed of single individuals, either widowed or unmarried. Often some couples, who were reluctant to cook food regularly, were found to take their food with this group.

In earlier days, there was no gender-specific work schedule for cooking. Now, with the supply of free rations, the responsibility of daily cooking and other domestic chores is gradually being shifted to women. Thus the frequency and regularity of eating depends much on the efficiency and interest of the women in the house.

TABLE 9.6: FREQUENCY OF MEALS TAKEN BY HOUSEHOLD (DUGONG-CREEK)

Name of Head of the Household	No. of Meals Taken at			Total of Meals Taken	No. of Days Observed	Average No. of Meals Taken per Day
	Morning	Noon	Evening			
Tamboli	12	2	10	24	14	1.71
Ramesh	12	2	10	24	14	1.71
Otalate	15	2	8	25	15	1.67
Balla	15	2	8	25	15	1.67
Koira	15	2	8	25	15	1.67
Bada Okale	15	2	8	25	15	1.67
Morai	10	2	11	23	11	2.10
Chota Raju	15	–	15	30	15	2.00
Chota Okale	15	2	14	31	15	2.07
Nabekutte	9	–	6	15	9	1.67
Chogegi	14	–	10	24	14	1.71
Kekele	12	4	12	28	16	1.75
Kanju	13	7	12	32	15	2.13
Kogegili	12	2	13	27	14	1.93
Bara Raju	13	-	11	24	14	1.71
Tejai	11	3	11	25	13	1.92
Tai	15	3	15	33	15	2.20
Bairogegi	12	4	13	29	15	1.93
Kimboi	12	4	13	29	14	2.07
Tenai	13	3	13	29	15	1.93
Totanange	13	2	12	27	14	1.93
Billai	12	2	11	24	13	1.85
Pankaja (munni)	9	1	9	19	11	1.73
Tanagiru	11	6	13	30	14	2.14
Total	305	56	266	627	335	44.93
Mean	12.71	2.33	11.08	26.12	13.96	1.87
Standard Deviation	1.72	2.34	3.97	1.57	0.18	1.86

Source: Field study by the authors.

NOTION OF HOSPITALITY

The code of hospitality among the Onge is altogether different. Apparently from their behaviour, it seems they are at a relatively lower techno-economic level and they have developed their own unique code of education. From the earlier reports, it has been learnt that they had the elaborate custom of greetings the guests. Food was no problem as life was more community-oriented. But at present, people from the two settlements hardly exchange courtesy visits due to the distant locations, except when they visit Hut Bay market occasionally. A lot of changes have taken place in the style of living of the Onge. But their pattern of hospitality has not changed much, when we observed their practice of having food in other Onge houses.

Usually a fixed number of *parathas* are prepared for family consumption in a house. It has been observed that on an average an adult person eats 4 *parathas* for which 200 g flour is needed. It is a very common scene that somebody from another house comes and eats a couple of *parathas,* if, and whenever he/she feels like it, without even asking for permission. In such a situation, the question of hospitality or offering something to a person, as per the value system of the Onge, is irrelevant.

The concept of personal possession is at such a rudimentary level that the demarcation line between 'ours' and 'theirs' is very thin. Though nowadays they have been given individual possession of a hut and prepare their own food at the family level, they did not imbibe the values associated with such modern innovations. The Onge have adopted and assimilated things according to their cultural ethos. Thus the question of asking one's permission to take food prepared by someone or offering food to someone does not occur to the Onge mind. Whosoever needs anything may take it. Putting one's labour to anything does not make it one's personal possession. The people never behave selfishly. It has been observed that a person never takes all the *parathas* or even the quantity which he requires or can eat. Often, he takes one or two, keeping the rest for the person who made it. Many a time, it has been observed that a sick or old person was supplied with cooked food from other's houses. An Onge does not even mind giving his catch of a single fish to someone requesting it. When one's major share of food is consumed by others, the person does not cook a second time. They are so much habituated to uncertainty of food that they do not mind skipping a meal for others. One feels satisfied with whatever is left for him. To test their traditional behaviour we sometimes took few *parathas* from their stock and ate them. The Onge did not react adversely. Neither did they mind or ask why. Many new food items have been incorporated in the Onge diet but the values of their food culture remain unchanged.

DIET AND NUTRITION

It has already been stated that for having an idea about the nutritional value of the food of the Onge at the present setup, we prepared a food chart for 15 days (13 September 1988-27 September 1988) at the Dugong Creek settlement. In South Bay, too, we attempted similar work for seven days. But there the people till today consume a good deal of indigenous food, which could neither be quantified, nor their food value made out. Nevertheless, occasional comparison has been made on the basis of our observations over there.

Though cooking is done on a household or family basis, consumption of food was not always confined only to that household or family. It has already been mentioned that a person is free to take his or her food in any kitchen within the settlement. Keeping this practice in view, we always recorded the number of persons who actually had their food in a particular house and then calculated the consumption unit for a particular date. It may be noticed here that during the season we made the observation, no ready-to eat food like fruits or honey was available in the forest. So the Onge subsisted mainly on cereal food, fish, pork, etc.

According to the Onge, this season is considered to be the leanest in terms of availability of food. For calculating per unit (as per ICMR standard) food consumption we measured all the food items, including, fish and pork, before cooking. Nowadays, as they are used to cereals, in each and every house, we found a fixed measure, glass or cup which can contain 75 to 100 g flour or rice. One such glass full of grains is actually the standard for an adult for one-time consumption. The glass or cup may vary in shape but usually the quantity of the grain remains almost the same in every house. It has often been observed that if some one runs short of rice or *atta,* he/she can take one or two glassfuls from the house of others. As they do not have any concept of borrowing, the question of returning the same does not arise. Sometimes, they take milk powder too, from the person who

TABLE 9.7: PER DAY PER UNIT CONSUMPTION OF FOOD AND NUTRIENTS BY THE ONGE OF DUGONG CREEK

(13-27 September 1988)

Food item	Amount consumed	Protein (g)		Fat (mg)	Energy (cal)	Calcium (mg)	Iron (mg)	Carotene (mg)	Thiamine (mg)	Riboflavin (mg)	Niacin (mg)	Vitamin C (mg)
		Animal	Vegetable									
Rice	70.12	0	0.48	0.28	242.6	6.3	2.8	0	0.15	0.04	2.7	0
Wheat	128.25	0	15.52	2.18	437.3	61.6	14.7	37.2	0.63	0.22	5.5	0
Coconut	63.2	0	2.48	26.29	280.6	6.3	1.1	0	0.03	0.06	0.5	0.6
Arhar dal	17.89	0	3.99	0.3	59.9	13.1	1	23.6	0.08	0.03	0.5	0
Sugar	17.89	0	0	0	71.2	2.1	0	0	0	0	0	0
Vegetable oil	17.89	0	0	17.8	161	0	0	296	0	0	0	0
Pork	273.55	51.55	0	12.04	311.8	82.1	6	0	1.48	0.25	7.7	5.5
Fish (Parse)	59.04	10.33	0	3.48	82.7	501.8	1.6	0	0	0	0.5	3.5
Turtle meat	57.7	9.52	0	0.87	49.6	4	0	0	0	0	0	0
Total	705.53	71.4	26.47	63.24	1,696.7	677.3	27.2	356.8	2.37	0.6	17.4	9.6
Recommended Allowances		55	NA	NA	2,800	400-500	24	3,000	1.4	NA	19	40

Source: Field study by the authors.

TABLE 9.8: FOOD CONSUMPTION OF THE ONGE OF DUGONG CREEK

(13-27 September 1988)

Food Items	Total per day consumption (g)	Per unit per day consumption (g)
Rice	4,050	70.12
Wheat	7,408	128.25
Pulses	1,033	17.89
Sugar	1,033	17.89
Veg. oil	1,033	17.89
Coconut	3,650	63.20
Pork	15,800	293.55
Fish	3,410	59.04
Turtle	3,333	57.70

Source: Field study by the authors.

is able to spare some. Measuring with such a container, the required amount of food is cooked every day. Dogs are also considered members of the family. They are also served food with equal care and love. The children, however, take very little in comparison to the adults. Small babies up to 3 years subsist mostly on mother's milk. There is no definite way of weaning. When they start taking solid food, no restriction is imposed on their dietary habits in terms of food items and quantity. They are given all sorts of food and they consume as much as they want. Often a small piece of meat or fat is given to the young baby who eats the same by licking or chewing depending on its capacity. Similarly, no special food is given to a sick person. It has been observed that whether a child or an adult, during sickness, the Onge reject food.

In terms of protein and fat intake, the Onge food may be compared with that of the Nicobarese, whose per day protein intake from animal source was 103 g. Coconut consumption among the Nicobarese is also very high which is reflected in their fat intake of 116.0 g. But significantly, the calory intake by, Nicobarese is also quite high at 3,050 (Roy, 1967).

The low calory intake (1696.7) of the Onge may apparently suggest that the Onge suffer from undernourishment that might have a reflection in their general physique. With the exception of one or two sick persons, on an average, the Onge do not look famished or undernourished. A relatively higher intake of animal protein makes their food low in terms of calories. In summer, availability of plant food supersedes animal food. In this way, a natural balance is maintained throughout the seasons. If one calculates calory intake of the Onge in terms of monthly ration supply (9 kg wheat flour and 5 kg rice per adult per month) it would be much higher than that of actual intake. Incidentally, the picture presented here is based on our actual observation for a limited period in a particular season.

NUTRITION AND GENERAL PHYSIQUE

To analyse the general physique vis-à-vis nutritional status, we would stress on three aspects of the Onge physique (i) height, (ii) weight, and (iii) skin-fold thickness. The average stature of the Onge males, as measured by us, was found to be 1,515 mm which is considered short. It may be mentioned here that the South Bay Onge are taller than the Dugong Creek people. The average Onge body weight is 47 kg, which, at the first instance, may appear very low. But when weight is considered in terms of height it is not that low, the weight/height index being about 31. The average weight/height ratio is better in South Bay (32.2) than in Dugong Creek (30.5). The value of Pignet coefficient suggests the general physique of a people, which is related to nutritional status as a whole. The mean Pignet index of the Onge is 23.1, indicating an average physique. However, in this aspect, the South Bay Onge show a relatively better performance (20.4) while in case of the Dugong Creek Onge it is 24.2. Skin-fold thickness is another marker of nutritional status. As per recommendations of FAO (1957), the average skin-fold thickness at triceps below 5.0 mm for men indicates definite under-nutrition. The Onge did not show sign of under-nutrition except in case of a single individual. The mean value of skin-fold thickness measured by Harpentine Calliper is as follows:

In this sphere, too, the South Bay people indicate a higher skin-fold at all the sites over the population of Dugong Creek, suggesting a better nutritional status at South Bay. The probable reason of better health of the South Bay Onge may be their relative freedom, and less interference from outsiders. Even now they consume many of their traditional food items which the Dugong Creek Onge have already given up.

Though our observation was made during a relatively lean season, it cannot be said that even in the present situation the Onge suffered from scarcity of food. Nowadays, their food resource is exploited by their neighbouring peoples as well. Often their catch and harvest of honey are shared with others. In this connection, certain observations can be made with respect to the food behaviour of other people living around the Onge. The Onge adopted many cultural traits related to food culture from others, but the neighbouring people, too, have adopted one very important trait from the Onge, i.e. the habit of eating pork. The Bengali refugees settled here nowadays take pork by hunting pigs themselves, which was a forbidden item in their native habitat.

A study of the anthropology of food reflects many characteristic features of the Onge culture, such as the notion towards division of labour, fellow feeling, relationship between man and nature and the transformation process of the Onge as a whole. Food plays a significant role in the process of transformation. Having an assured food supply now, the Onge have adopted a semi-sedentary life and the pattern of division of labour is experiencing a change. Once there was no gender difference in food preparation in their nomadic way of life. There was no such custom that the wife would cook the food and serve the same to other members of the family. Everything was more natural, depending on one's appetite and availability of food. Now, the women do not have to move much for getting plant food and hence they devote more time towards cooking food as the neighbouring women do. The trend is that men would do outdoor activities and women would look after the home.

TABLE 9.9: SKIN-FOLD THICKNESS OF THE ONGE MALE (N = 36)

Site	Mean ± SD (in mm)
Bicep	4.65 + 2.16
Tricep	8.86 + 2.92
Subscapula	9.81 + 4.45

Source: Field study by the authors.

This is the working pattern followed by the people among whom women primarily do not work for subsistence and most often in such cases do not enjoy equal status in the society. Ordinarily, this kind of social change is ushered due to technological advancement in any society. The more there is advancement of technology, the more women go out of employment and become more dependent on others for survival. For the Onge there is no such technological advancement. Only interference from an outside agency has pushed the Onge women to the confinement of their homes. This phenomenon becomes more conspicuous when we compare the situation of Dugong Creek with that of South Bay. There, the women roam about freely and do some gathering activities regularly, whereas in Dugong Creek, there are so many outsiders around, that the Onge perhaps feel insecure to allow their women to go beyond the area of the settlement. The women there are mostly confined in the settlement areas and are gradually getting detached from the world of their own which they had known earlier. A sense of distrust, too, prevails on the minds of their men, so they do not feel comfortable when they are away from the settlement, leaving their spouses behind. Thus the material comfort and security provided by external agency has come at the cost of the internal harmony of Onge society.

REFERENCES

Bose, S., 'Economy of the Onge of Little Andaman', *Man in India*, 44(4), 1964, pp. 298-310.

Cipriani, Lidio, 'Report of a Survey of the Little Andaman during 1951-3', *Bulletin of Department of Anthropology* 2(1), 1953, p. 124.

Holmberg, Allen R., *Nomads of the Long Bow: The Siriono of Eastern Bolivia*, Washington DC: Government Printing Office, 1950.

Lee, Rechard B and Irvin De Vore, 'Kalahari Hunter-Gatherers: Studies of the I Kung San and their Neighbours', in *Kalahari Hunter-Gatherers*, Cambridge: Harvard University Press, 1976.

CHAPTER 10

Load of Material Possessions

How much does a man or a group needs depends on the socio-economic background of the person or the group. The better the economic condition, which is again related to technological achievement, the more the material possession. With this parameter a group like Onge, who are hunter-gatherers and at the lowest level of technological development, would possess the minimum. They had minimum possessions related primarily to food procurement. Thanks to the development agency, today Onge culture is loaded with so many useless material goods which have little relevance to their life situation. Though technology and economy have not been changed, a significant change has taken place in case of Onge food culture. In earlier times they used to subsist only on hunting and gathering. Since the late 1960s cereal-based food has been introduced to them. So eventually most of the newly added household articles are related to the preparation and consumption of food. Even during the 1950s the material possessions of the Onges was dominated by traditional implements related only to subsistence activities, viz., hunting-gathering.

It is a well known fact that with the introduction of a welfare and development programme, traditional subsistence activities and food habits have undergone a major transformation bringing changes all over the Onge culture. As a result, day by day the volume of individual possession of the Onge is increasing. Previously, one big canister served the purpose of cooking meat for the people in a settlement. Now, each household has several pots and pans.

It may be said that the Onge have come a long way on the path of development. How much they have developed may well be debated but there is no doubt about one thing, that these plain-living people are now loaded with a lot of material possessions. The material inventory of an Onge household accounts for the material possessions of the present-day Onge. Their possessions may be classified into four categories:

1. Implements used for procuring food through hunting, gathering and fishing such as bow and arrow, fishing net, baskets, etc.
2. Domestic utensils such as cooking pots and other appliances like plates, bowls, etc.
3. Luxury articles such as garments, *chappals* (slippers), cosmetics, umbrella, watch, transistor, tape recorder, etc.
4. Miscellaneous items like suitcase, briefcase, handbags, sling bags and a few bicycles (supplied by the agency).

The detailed material inventory of an Onge household, as given in the appendix, would prove the significance of the above statement.

From the inventory of material goods one can make a fair estimate about the material culture of the present-day Onge. The items mentioned in the category of household articles are found in almost all Onge households. These may be considered as essential to their daily life. Sometimes, their number varies from house to house.

The Onge buy these articles from the cooperative store in the settlement. Sometimes, they receive items like a stainless steel tumbler and bowl, *lungi*, mosquito net, etc., as gift when any dignitaries visit their settlement. Certain items like jerrycans, buoys, floats, etc., are collected from the seashore which come there as drifted articles. Of all the household articles, except the basket, wooden container, coconut grater and the broom, nothing is made by the Onge. They depend on outsiders for the supply of those articles.

Nowadays, the Onge can cook rice and make *parathas* as well. But their adoption of the cooking vessels, etc., is partial. They use a number of metallic utensils but very few of them realize the importance of the regular cleaning of the same. The same pot is used consecutively for a number of times. As these people did not have any material belongings even in the near past, they do not feel much attachment to these things. They were used to taking food on leaves and Nautilus shells. So it is often found that these utensils are strewn here and there on the veranda or the open courtyard. When the dogs lick the used plates or any cooking vessel left outdoors, they do not consider it unhygienic. It is not that the Onge do not have any sense of hygiene but as these things were not in their traditional culture they do not observe the associated practices of cleanliness. Otherwise, they are always careful about the drinking water and preservation of honey. In spite of lack of hygienic sense they now consider these cooking pots, etc., very essential. That is why when they go to the forest they carry some cooking pots with them. As they do not consider them valued possessions, they do not buy them or take any special care of them.

In the list of material inventory we have included the dress and garments of the Onge as luxury goods, though in general parlance, dress is a very essential item for any human being. It is a known fact that materials and style of dress of any particular people develop according to the availability of raw materials needed and the climate of that region where the people live. The Onge is no exception. The Onge being the inhabitants of a hot and humid tropical region of deep forest and wide ocean have hardly needed any sort of clothing. Perhaps, no dress was the best option in that climatic condition.

So long they had the freedom and choice of living their life in their own way, they did not feel any urgency for dress except for the minimum covering of genitals of both the sexes. Nowadays the Onge have two sets of dress for them—one is their traditional attire which amounts to almost nothing but is very comfortable in their own setting. The other may be called the alien dress, which has been introduced to them not for their own sake but for the sake of outsiders.

TRADITIONAL DRESS AND ORNAMENTS OF THE ONGE

Traditionally, the Onge use minimal attire for both the sexes. *Nakuinege* is made from palm leaves and worn by adult women. Women collect the leaves of a particular type of soft palm and dry them. Then, with the thread of these dried leaves, women make a ball-like tassel. This is tied with the waistband or *enenakwe* made of a string or a piece of cloth. This tassel, they believe, has got some herbal and hygienic quality that protect their vital organs. Adult males also tie a piece of cloth or bark around their genitals with the help of a waistband.

The Onge children grow up completely naked up to the age 5 or 6. Sometimes, girls of this age are found to wear an oversized frock. As there is no winter on Little Andaman Island, there is no need of covering the body with any garment or shawl. However, to protect the tender skin and body of babies and infants from the extreme heat of the sun and numerous insects around them, they paint their whole body, including the face and the head, with different types of clay mixed with water or pig fat. Their traditional decoration is body paint and ornaments include a head dress of palm leaves and a necklace of different seashells.

BODY PAINTING WITH CLAY

Earlier the Onge used to paint their body with white and red coloured clay in beautiful geometrical designs. Today, body painting is not much liked by the adult Onge men. Women sometime daub their faces with clay in no specific design. Bodies of the newborn and young babies are smeared with white clay. There are two types of clay in use among the Onge, which they collect from the island. One type of clay is called *wekala* which is white in colour and used extensively all over the body, including the face but rarely on the head. Children are seen completely smeared with this clay. It serves as their clothing and provides protection against insect bite. Generally, the art of body painting is the arena of women. The mother paints her own child by mixing clay with water. Once painted, the clay remains on the body for about three days on an average. A fresh coat is needed every fourth or fifth day. This, besides being an insect repellent, keeps the body cool under the hot sun by increasing the reflective power of the white colour, as clay is a poor conductor of heat. It has been observed that before eating, if it is pork or turtle flesh, the Onge paint *wekala* around their lips so as to repel flies disturbing them. From its smell it seems that the clay contains a fair amount of sulphur and lime. *Alamu* or *halamu*, the red ochre, is also collected from a particular place on the island. This has a much higher medical value but has a less extensive use than white clay. Usually, this is mixed with pig fat and applied directly on any part of the body affected by muscular pain. It is most commonly used on their head as protection from heat, insect bite and headache. It is not applied on the face.

Other than as a protective measure and medicinal use, body paint has some aesthetic value too. It is considered a beauty aid, specially when done on the face. Self-painting is never practised. Painting is usually done by womenfolk. Custom demands that the wife would paint her husband's body. A mother paints her child and the elderly women paint other women's bodies. Painting on the face is called *enetawa* and that on the body is *enakwanjeme*. The present-day Onge cannot recall any special significance of these designs which are traditionally passed on from one generation to another. However, the Onge do not indulge in body painting now, with the exception of the young babies. Instead, the young people go for modern cosmetics and modern medicine.

For beautification, the Onge used to wear a necklace (*gangitake*) made of *dentallium* shells collected from the sea and creeks. This is not done any more. Now they prefer bead necklaces, which are available to them through gift and local purchase. These are named *enagitoke* and worn by both the sexes. When these bead chains are worn as ornaments around the waist, they are called *torangude. Tamerewe* or *amalukone*, the head band made from a kind of palm leaf, is not used at all now. It may be said that this particular item is now gone from their culture. Instead, sometimes the Onge are found to tie a piece of coloured cloth as a head band or using a cap or a hat in keeping with the fashion of the day.

CONTEMPORARY DRESSES

Before going into the details of modern or contemporary dressing of the Onge we may talk about the attitude of three Onge men of different age groups to dress. Balla is a young man with little exposure to the outside world. He bought two pairs of shirts and trousers which he rarely wears. He mostly wears the traditional dress, which is at best a nylon brief with a pair of *hawai* (rubber) sandals on his feet. He loves to possess the modern clothing items rather than use them. He thinks this dress is necessary for going to Hut Bay. His wife is a middle-aged woman who mostly wears a petticoat over the traditional grass tassel. Sometimes she wears a blouse too. Tanagiru is a middle-aged man working in the powerhouse of Dugong Creek settlement. He is quite an enlightened person among the Onge. He bought four pairs of trousers for Rs. 700. He wears those while attending to his duty, though he feels very hot in them. He thinks this dress is beautiful and suitable for his type of job. He regularly washes his clothes with soap. He also has a pair of shoes and sandals and a wristwatch which he cannot read. Lastly, we will refer to the case of Kanjo, one of the oldest men in the community. He prefers the traditional dress for himself, but wears modern clothes when he visits Port Blair. His second wife is much younger to him. She always wears a petticoat over the tassel and a very tight brassiere on the upper part of the body without any blouse over it. These dresses are rarely washed. Kanjo loves to buy clothes for his children. They wear these for one or two days at a stretch.

From the above, it is evident that the Onge are attracted to modern dress, not necessarily realizing its implications. Precisely speaking, it is more of a craze than a need. The basic need for such clothing is yet to be felt by the people. Modern clothes are worn by the people on festive occasions like celebration of Republic Day, visit of any VIP to the settlement, or going to Hut Bay or Port Blair. A visit to the Consumer Cooperative Store for collecting ration or for other purchases is also an occasion to them. Hence they dress for coming to the shop. In the settlement, men wear briefs or a *lungi*.

MEN'S DRESS

From the material inventory of an Onge house it was found that all adult males and older boys have at least one pair of shirt and trousers in their possession. Often, the men have more than one set of such clothing. Some of them even have warm coats though there is no winter over there. Occasionally, they use briefs, vests, socks, and shoes. They have almost given up wearing the traditional waistband (*enenakwe*) and instead have started wearing underwear and shorts (*nakwakagabe*) regularly. Very few of them are particular about the type of dress and its material. Once Tai, who is perhaps the first Onge who bought two saris for his wife, asked us to teach her to wear it properly. According to him, the sari was a better dress for a woman than salwar kameez. It seems that when they come to Hut Bay, they see the other people and form their own opinion. In this context it may be mentioned here that exposure to other people is more effective for the process of adaptation than introducing some innovation in isolation. It has been observed that the men of South Bay settlement are more spontaneous in wearing the clothing that they have adopted. No outsider or motivator is there to guide them in their day-to-day affairs. In spite of that they wear shirts and trousers more regularly and keep those clean by washing them from time to time. It is due to the closeness of the settlement to the Nicobarese bustee at Harmender Bay and Hut Bay marketplace.

The Onge do not mix much with other people but seeing is learning and exposure has a direct impact on them. The development agency has been in operation in Dugong Creek for quite a long time. Lots of innovations have been introduced there during this period. Still, the Onge there appear to be less open to adaptation and the innovations have been accepted rather superficially. Due to distance and direct supervision of the agency people the Onge do not visit Hut Bay without specific reason. It has been observed that while going to town, they often carry their clothes and shoes in a bag and change in the forest before reaching the metalled road. The same thing is repeated while returning. In the forest they take off their formal dress and feel comfortable in their traditional attire. By now the Onge have realized that whenever they are out of their own world and with other people, they should switch over to a different dress code.

Some of the Onge men wear hats or caps to avoid the strong sun. Tambolai, Totanange and a few others of Dugong Creek settlement have purchased sunglasses from Port Blair or Hut Bay. Tambolai, being a member of the Pradesh Council, visits Port Blair regularly. His friends request him to get a few items for them, which include suitcase, garments, sunglass, belt (leather or cloth), briefs and vests, scarf and even transistor sets. It has been learnt that in spite of continuous efforts of the officials in the settlement, the Onge have hardly accepted footwear, with a few exception like Totanange and Tambolai who wear rubber slippers or shoes regularly while going out to urban centres.

WOMEN'S DRESS

Onge women show better performance in terms of getting used to non-traditional dresses introduced to them. Except for two or three elderly women and very small girls, all others now wear at least a petticoat or a skirt to cover the lower half of their body. Almost 50 per cent of women in Dugong Creek wear blouses. But still one cannot say that they wear these clothes and follow the code of modesty as it has often been observed that they take off their clothes (except the tassel) while taking a bath in the open. Sometimes they wear a man's shirt or a brassiere without blouse. Like their menfolk, they have also developed a craze for possessing some garments. Once, Tejai's wife showed a lot of interest for a blouse in exchange for having a fine cane basket. Women spend a major part of their income from plantation work in purchasing ornaments like plastic bangles, bead necklaces,

Source: Photo taken by the author.

Figure 10.1: Onge women taking bath at the community well as instructed by the health worker. They seldom wash their clothes or themselves other than while being drenched in the rain or fishing in creeks and sea. Now they are instructed and taught personal hygiene as a part of their semi-sedentary lifestyle.

nylon ribbons, safety pins and other trinkets from the cooperative store at the settlement. Nowadays, some Onge women are quite comfortable wearing saris. However, wearing of sari or salwar kameez is more for fun than for any practical use. The petticoat, with a blouse, or a kaftan, is a common dress of the Onge women of today. Very often women have two sets of such attire. Sometime they receive these as gifts and sometimes they buy them. But they are least bothered to wash these clothes regularly. The women at Dugong Creek are found to put on a single garment for days together. It goes on accumulating dirt and sometimes stinks as the small babies are always on the mother's back. Though they do not wash their clothes, the Onge care for personal hygiene. Washing for the women is a matter of community participation. It has been observed that at one point of time all women started washing all their clothes with any kind of soap. During this washing spree, even unused and clean clothes were also washed. In comparison, the menfolk do take a bath more often, as it is a common practice now among the Onge men that after a heavy manual work they take bath. The women at Dugong Creek do not do any hard manual labour, so their frequency of bathing has been further reduced. Women at South Bay are found to pursue some gathering activity. So they take a bath almost regularly. They made an arrangement for washing behind their huts. Though women there have fewer clothes, those are washed regularly. As there is no outsider in the settlement, women usually remain in their traditional attire.

CHILDREN'S DRESS

Children of both sexes go nude up to the age of seven or eight years. There are 22 children in the Dugong Creek settlement. When we took the count of dress (appended), it had been observed that on an average all children had at least a pair of clothes consisting of a shirt and a pant or a frock and knickers according to sex. Two such sets are being supplied by the development agency every year. Some parents love to buy clothes for their children.

It has already been mentioned that the Onge do not realize the significance of dress, that it is related to the code of modesty and is a protective measure against heat and cold. For them, it is more an object of fashion and luxury. Hence, the modern dress is used by the Onge on ceremonial occasions like flag hoisting or visit of dignitaries, as was noticed on the occasion of the Honourable Lt. Governor's visit on 12 September 1988. On that day not only the children but all the Onge gathered at the helipad, fully dressed—men with trousers, shirt and even suit and tie, and women in kaftan or sari. They reverted to their original dress as soon as the VIPs left the settlement. It may be mentioned here after that visit of the Lt. Governor the weather was cyclonic with occasional heavy rains, which continued for a couple of days (17 to 19 September 1988). When we visited the settlement we found that all the babies below one year of age were without any covering and the children, too, were minimally dressed. When we asked Bada Raju to get some clothing for his baby he said that there were no clothes for the children. Clothing being a luxury item, sometimes they bought only costly synthetic garments for the children but never anything for daily use. When we insisted that he should wrap the child with a *lungi* or a sheet he did not do that either.

From their behaviour, it appears that the introduction of dress could not inculcate any sense of practical value to these people. In earlier days, small girls were found to put on *boya* (tassel) even during the activities like fishing (Cipriani 1966). Now they had lost their traditional dress and have also not accepted the new one. We saw girls below ten years of age, whether married or unmarried, roaming without any clothing.

Covering one's body with stitched or unstitched cloth is considered one of the criteria of cultural development. When considered in terms of this criterion, it can be said that the Onge culture does not show much progress. Though they have not adopted clothing for its practical purpose, certain interesting points are noticed in regard to their use of clothes.

1. At present the Onge men and women love to possess a few pairs of trousers, shirts and sari according to their choice.
2. They spend most of their money on these items and sometimes are cheated by unscrupulous traders due to their ignorance about monetary transactions.

3. The use of dress is very much occasional and ceremonial but the sense of possession gives them a kind of satisfaction.
4. They buy more dresses for adults than for children. Children's clothes are supplied mostly by the development agency. When children suffer from any respiratory trouble, they do not put on any extra clothes. Young babies remain bare-bodied most often.
5. They have not discarded their traditional dress. Both sexes wear it under the so-called modern dress.
6. Most often, the Onge are not careful about the cleanliness of their garments.

The Onge have accepted the innovation of clothing in their own way. They maintain a kind of dichotomy so far as their dress is concerned. When they live or move in the forest and are engaged in traditional activities like hunting, fishing, canoe-making, etc., they wear their traditional dress. They prefer modern clothing when they are in the settlement where many outsiders are posted on some official assignment or when they visit any urban centre. Here we may cite the example of Totanange. When he brings water or goes fishing, he does not feel inhibited about his scanty clothing. The same person feels proud of wearing trousers, etc., when he goes to attend his duty at the powerhouse. Another Onge way of adoption is that they have given Onge names to all items of dress. No doubt they love to possess modern dress and wear it on ceremonial occasions despite some physical discomfort. If the people are really to be motivated to dress properly and regularly, they should be supplied with clothes which suit their taste and environment best, i.e. instead of tight fitting, cheap, synthetic or polyester clothes, they should be supplied with airy cotton garments. Above all, it is urgent to make them conscious about the hygienic use of clothes.

Other than clothing, the Onge nowadays love to possess several items. Three persons have watches and two among them have tape recorders. In South Bay there is one transistor radio lying with the chief of that settlement. The Onge have procured tape recorders from a Bengali trader of the neighbouring village on hire-purchase basis. In such a deal, the Onge undoubtedly suffer from losses as they are not well-versed in monetary transactions.

MONEY AND THE ONGE

Money is the most valued possession of the present-day Onge. Until recently, money was an unknown concept to these hunting-gathering people. Most Onge men can recognize currency notes of different denominations by their colour and size. Their economy was self-sufficient and there was no scope for exchange of money in the Onge tradition.

Other than plantation work, at present, the Onge also earn some money in exchange for honey, natural wax, incense, resin and the baskets made by them. It may be mentioned here that though they receive a monthly payment, they do not understand that they are being paid in exchange of their labour. They consider it as a gift as they are used to receiving gifts and objects gratis. Moreover, the fact that human labour is something saleable or exchangeable is beyond their comprehension.

It has already been mentioned that the consumer cooperative store located in Dugong Creek settlement is the main shopping centre for the Onge there. The Onge men of South Bay settlement, however, visit Hut Bay and do their shopping there. The womenfolk of that settlement visit other places very rarely. The consumer cooperatives store also distributes rations. It keeps a stock of almost everything of daily need. The Onge have been found to buy a few items regularly. They are areca nuts, lime (coloured and flavoured), biscuits, shaving blade and pain balm. On an average, an Onge buys 400 g areca nut and one box of lime every week. Sometimes they buy tobacco leaves and *zarda* which are available in the store though there is a directive not to sell these things to the Onge. In the shop, they behave like children. Whatever article attracts them or their children they buy. They never restrain their children from nagging them. Many a time, we found that they were buying a fancy torch for a ten-year-old boy or some balloons for a young baby. They are never guided in shopping by the officials who manage the shop. Even when they do not have money, they are given the things they desire on credit. It is rather distressing to note that a people who are yet to understand the exchange system properly have become the victims of a vicious credit cycle. After getting their so-called salary, the Onge invariably rush to the shop, but the major portion of their earning gets adjusted against the credit purchase of the previous month. However, they are never denied anything that they demand. They are supplied with those materials either against cash or on credit. Thus the Onge have become perpetual debtors, without having actual knowledge about the same. The tentacles of the credit system overpowers them without their understanding it. They do not realize the implication, as they are never paid back the balance of the sum, which they pay for any item. It has been reported by the officials that the Onge cannot count money so there is no point in wasting time to make them understand about the refund of the balance. The balance is adjusted by giving them one or two boxes of lime. During our field stay, some Onge expressed their distrust of those officials. In order to observe their shopping behaviour, when we visited the shop, we requested the official there to pay them their due balance so that they can gradually learn the mode of monetary transaction. At this, the Onge, for the first time, could realize that they could get some of their balance back. Then onwards, the Onge men at Dugong Creek always requested us to be in the store when they went there. It is interesting to note that when the Onge were given the credit voucher, without our asking, they came to us and handed over those vouchers (appended at the end of this chapter). From those vouchers, it appears that interest has been generated among these people to procure certain things.

Upon enquiry it was learnt that the Onge never bought several of the items mentioned in the credit voucher. The records show that many people bought a spanner set costing about Rs. 26 for repairing cycles. It is interesting to note that cycles have been given to the Onge as gift and cycle riding is more of a fun activity for them than a means of conveyance. It is unfortunate; that they cannot read or count money and so are ignorant about the money required to spend for the fun. But in reality, most people have not bought the items and kit for cycle repair; it has already been supplied in the settlement free of cost. Sometimes the Onge of Dugong Creek settlement make some transactions with the merchants of the neighbouring Bengali village. In such transactions the official posted at the settlement works as the middleman. Three persons bought two-in-one transistors through these transactions.

The South Bay Onge do not enjoy a market within the settlement. But the men over there are more exposed to other people. They have developed friendly relations with the Nicobarese of a neighbouring village. A mutual give-and-take relationship has already been started between them without exchanging money. Young boys of South Bay often visit Hut Bay and spend money in video shows. Such practices may lead to prodigal habits among the Onge youth as they do not have to spend on basic needs of life.

Because of such exposures, Onge nowadays appreciate the value of money in their life. They are aware of the fact that the government is spending a lot of money for their development but the lion's share of it is being usurped by others. If they had handled the money matters themselves, that might have resulted in a good deal of benefit.

Due to their exposures to urban population, primarily through government officials and the market centre, a sort of consumerism in a rudimentary form engulfs the Onge mind. What would they do with the money which is given to them at regular intervals? They spend their money according to their perceptions, mostly whims.

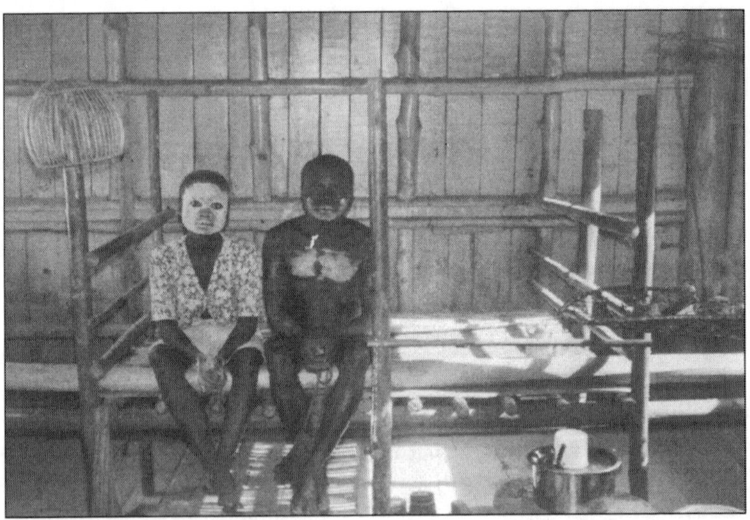

Source: Photo taken by the author.

Figure 10.2: An Onge couple inside their allotted hut along with some cooking utensils bought by them from the Dugong Creek store.

To use currency notes and coins, one must have the minimum knowledge of counting and recognizing the value of currency. The Onge perhaps present a unique case of having a pocket full of money but never knowing how much. In Dugong Creek, only four men can identify currency notes and can count money up to Rs. 20 and two persons can count up to Rs. 100. But none of them can add or subtract while doing any monetary transaction. They depend completely on others in this respect. They are completely ignorant about the value of coins.

Until recently, the Onge did not use any bag or purse to carry money. Now they are conscious that they should have a place for storing their valuables. It may be mentioned here that once the Prime Minister (Shri Rajiv Gandhi) visited the settlement at Dugong Creek and asked them about their needs. Most of them said, 'We want a *peti* (box) to keep our clothes. Otherwise, mice will destroy them.'

As already stated, after receiving it, the Onge generally spend the entire amount of money as early as possible. The habit of spending of money instantly might have been derived from the hunting-gathering economy of the Onge. They are used to consuming things just after procurement. Storing anything for future use or the propensity for hoarding is alien to them. Besides, considering cash as potential capital which might be multiplied through reinvestment is too much for an Onge mind. Nevertheless, they understand that it is a valuable thing to be kept in a safe place. Normally, they are not apprehensive of theft within their own community. But once we found, Tambolai, who has the maximum exposure to the outer world, had locked his cottage while going out to the forest for gathering. It was because there were a few outsiders in the settlement for repairing the helipad, he explained.

From the behaviour and attitude of the Onge it seems that they have developed a strong passion for more money. They are becoming money lovers without being conscious or aware of the modern monetory system. Initially, it may cause some problems in society but with proper guidance in future, they may be involved in a productive economy through horticulture or handicrafts. So far, the Onge have not showed much interest towards any type of agriculture. But on account of their desire for money, they are unknowingly heading towards commercialization. The Onge sell almost 80 per cent of their annual collection of honey instead of consuming it freely. In this way, they also sell 50 per cent of the baskets they make every year. It may be maintained that in the case of the Onge, the process of involving the people in a productive economy has been started from the reverse, i.e., not from work to money but from money to work.

APPENDIX I

Material Inventory

I. HOUSEHOLD ARTICLES

Onge Term	*English Term*
Bachu	Aluminium cooking pot
Thali	Aluminium plate for having food
Tirabokhale	Jerry can
Tochaya	Cannister for storing flour/rice
Tebile	Rolling pin
Tamborakhejibe	Wooden plate for making *paratha*
Longothi	Enamel mug
Ketile	Kettle
	Tinned milk
	Aluminium tumbler
Bati	Stainless steel bowl
Tatakoable	Coconut grater
Tobulebe	Aluminium ladle
Tawabe	*Tawa* (frying pan for preparing *paratha*)
Tukogebukoge	Sieve
Totale	Broom
Tole	Basket (coarse)
Boya	Buoy
Uku	Wooden container
Jhola	Cloth slingbag
Tebo	Strainer

II. IMPLEMENTS RELATED TO FOOD PROCUREMENT

Tochyanduba	Axe for cane work
Kwene	Iron digging stick
Ley	Chopper

III. DRESS ITEMS

Kuindewey	Tassel (traditional women's wear)
Enitatekute	Traditional man's wear
Inechequine	Blouse/skirt
Enekugagare	Pants
N.A.*	*Lungi*
N.A.*	Napkin

N.A.*	Brassiere
N.A.*	Brief
N.A.*	Banian
Koilaboi	(not known)
Onotaykute	Sandal
N.A.*	Wristwatch
N.A.*	Sun hat or cap

IV. OTHER ITEMS

Tebagi/beti/peti	Box
Bajage	Transistor/tape recorder
Bone	Torchlight
Onotabotabo	Mosquito net
Anaikute	Bed sheet
Totiebe	Pillow
Botua	Small bag for carrying areca nut, lime, etc.

* There is no specific Onge term but they pronounce name in broken English.

APPENDIX II

Credit Sale Account of Onge Individuals Entered in the Ledger of the Cooperative Store, Dugong Creek, for June 1988

Name	Credit Sale Account (Rs.)	Article Purchased	MRP (Rs.)	Remarks
Botalai (F)	77.00	*Chuna* (lime) 6 boxes	15.00	*Chuna* boxes are often supplied to adjust money against balance amount but never given out six at a time.
Nabekutti (M)	58.70	Belt 1	30.00	
Chota Raju (M)	93.47	*Chuna* 6 boxes	15.00	Onge are seen to buy balloons at best of Rs. 2.
		Balloon ½ groce	11.00	
		Spanner set	26.82	
		Sukha (tobacco) 1	9.25	
Koria (M)	101.14	Pencil 1pkt	32.50	Two cells were purchased by him. Coloured vests. He was actually given 3 boxes of *chuna*
		Banian 1	36.85	
		Chuna 6 boxes	15.00	
Bada Okale (M)	67.15	Shorts 1	33.00	
		Sukha 1	8.25	Sukha charged at Rs. 9.25 from Chota Raju
Balla (M)	97.43	Pencil 1 pkt	32.00	
		Spanner set	26.82	
Otalate (M)	45.16	Balloon ½ gross	11.00	
		Zarda 1	15.25	
Ramesh (M)	124.27	*Banian* 1	36.85	All for cycle repair. The cycle has been given to them as a gift.
		Chuna 6 boxes	15.00	
		Spanner set 1	26.82	
		Gum tube 1	6.05	
		Emery paper	2.75	
		Old tube 1 pc	5.50	
Tolatobegi (F)	54.10	*Chuna* 6 boxes	15.00	

Name	Credit Sale Account (Rs.)	Article Purchased	MRP (Rs.)	Remarks
Tambolai (M)	300.00	Perfume 1	46.20	The credit amount could not be adjusted from his wage. It is to be adjusted from the next month's wage.
		3-celled torch 1	74.00	
		Brief 2	66.00	
		Leather belt 1	30.00	He never purchased the brief. (The same item was sold to Otalate for Rs. 15.25)
		Zarda 1 box	14.30	
		Old tube	5.50	
		Spanner set	26.82	
		Gum tube	6.05	
Timai (M)	232.72	*Sukha* 1 box	9.25	
		Brief 2	66.00	
		Vest 1	36.85	Coloured *banian*
		Spanner set	26.82	Cycle repairing items
		Gum tube	6.05	
		Emery paper	2.74	
Mayai (F)	119.00	Perfume 1 bottle	47.50	Rs. 46.20 was charged from Tambolai for the same item.
		Chuna 6 boxes	15.00	
Kogegeli (M)	108.81	Vest 1	36.85	
		Zarda 1	15.25	
		Ballon 1	22.00	
Tejai (M)	83.45	*Chuna* 6 boxes	15.00	
		Balloon ½ groce	11.00	
Bairogegi (M)	163.72	Old cycle tube	5.50	
		Hawai sliper	33.00	
		Cell 1 dozen	64.20	
		Chuna 6 boxes	15.00	
		Gum tube	26.82	
		Emery paper	2.75	
		Old tube	3.30	

Source: Field study by the authors.

CHAPTER 11

Development and Transformation

'Development' speaks of a course—a gradual process of growth for the betterment of all concerned. In order to ensure development, certain goals are often set out to be achieved. It is expected that through the process of development at a certain point of time, a person or a community will experience transformation, ensuring betterment. However, more often than not, in case of developmental initiatives, experiences are rather painful, if not frustrating as well as downright discouraging. This is especially true for the small Negrito populations of Andaman Islands.

Andaman Islands are traditionally the abode of Negrito populations represented by four groups: the Great Andamanese, Onge, Jarawa, and the Sentinelese. They were confined to their respective niches and survived with their age-old mode of hunting and gathering. Nevertheless, the hunger of civilization is so overpowering that no area could remain out of bounds. The remote areas of Andaman Islands have not been the exception.

An area has to be developed on the plea of extending the benefits of advancement and progress of civilization to the people living therein, even if it is not according to their felt needs. The island communities of Andaman lived in relative isolation for long. With the advent of British colonial rule in India, these small communities could not protect their exclusiveness any more. Prior to contact, owing to physical distance and isolation, there was a visible hiatus between the indigenous island communities and the mainland people. They could roam about freely within their territory practising their age-old culture of foraging and associated practices. However, their land was needed in the interest of the larger society and thus South Andaman Island was selected as the site for penal settlement of the then Government of British India. This initiative disturbed the rhythm and tranquility of the indigenous people's lives who then registered protests in their own way. As the agents of development gave no importance to such protests, several incidents of encounters between the native people and outsiders followed. The results of these unequal battles, between guns and arrows, were obvious. We all know that the ten tribes that constituted the Great Andamanese have been reduced to a handful within a span of only about a hundred years. Most of those who survived are not independently identifiable any more. A large number of Jarawa also got killed. The remaining few took shelter deep inside the forest. Through this process, one could hardly escape the oppression of 'civilization'. The Sentinelese are perhaps the only exception known so far in this respect.

The Onge of Little Andaman, too, could not escape the onslaught. Contact with the outside world was perhaps never as impossible, as it is often imagined. The issues could only be a matter of time and degree. It is, nevertheless, a fact that the Onge were not directly responsible for such a contact. It is primarily the outside communities, who usurped these simple folk in order to fulfil their own desires. As is the case with the Onge, the shell poachers used to visit Little Andaman Island and engaged the Onge men as divers for collecting valuable shells. It is claimed that the poachers tried to introduce opium and alcohol among the Onge. The people were habituated to tobacco and tea but they refrained from cultivating taste for opium and alcohol. Nevertheless, the tradition of getting harmed on the way to progress through contact still seems in operation. To be very candid, the overall situation has aggravated the condition of the people seriously during modern times. In the name of development, it has actually set in motion a slow process of degeneration, which is being sanctioned and legitimized in the name of development initiatives and transformation of the welfare state of India.

Though historically, the first contact with the Onge took place as early as 1886, their land was laid open to outsiders only in the late 1960s. During the span of over a hundred years of contact with civilization, the Onge had to pay a heavy price. A vibrant nearly six hundred strong population got reduced to less than a hundred.

The Onge have been deprived of their absolute control over their resource base. In the natural state, a balance is ordinarily maintained between the living population and the resource base of an area. During the pre-contact days, the Onge were well-adjusted to that eco-system. When the measures for developing the area of Little Andaman were initiated by settling other people, constructing a jetty, setting up some small industrial establishments, developing red palm plantation, the traditional right of the indigenous population over their resource base was altogether ignored. The carrying capacity of the land for a people having hunting-gathering as their livelihood received no consideration, though it was generally appreciated that these simple people cannot survive by pursuing their primordial way of lifestyle, living side by side with other people having knowledge of advanced technology. As a result, the weak had to make sacrifices beyond their capacity, just for the maintenance of the larger society. In the tussle for survival of the Onge and the development of the area, the latter got priority. Admittedly, the development planners are not totally insensitive to this background, and in order to compensate their loss, several measures have also been initiated. The first and foremost among them is to rehabilitate the people into the comfort of two reserves equipped with modern facilities: one at Dugong Creek and the other at South Bay at the southern extremity of Little Andaman Island.

Development programmes are supposed to be all-pervading, taking care of basic needs like food, shelter, clothing, health, and education. It had been presumed that the Onge would adopt the modern way of life, without much loss of time. While introducing different development programmes, the people's capacity for absorption of innovations have not been considered. In fact, though the Onge are existing in contemporary time, their cultural clock is turned to an early era. Until recently, they were in the state of nature with minimal dress, having no knowledge of how to make a fire or to grow their food. Even then they were a self-sufficient community residing in the lap of nature. They were happy in their own niche living a life of their own choice, holding their own cultural values and self-esteem in high premium.

Usually problems arise when a group of people with low techno-cultural efficiency come in close contact with people equipped with modern technology. It usually results in disaster for the former group. The Onge of Little Andaman suffered exactly the same.

It has already been stated that the Onge were the only inhabitants of Little Andaman, an island with an area of 731 sq. km. They were living in perfect harmony in three separate niches. Each region was inhabited by a number of local groups (*beyra*). *Beyra* is actually the term for a beehive type communal hut where a number of consanguineally-related families live. Their residential affiliation acts as a social institution in the life of the Onge, since they do not have any clan-like organization. As an institution, the communal hut performs the function of a clan, especially regulating the bio-cultural life of the people. It determines the marriage rules and the degree of incest.

During summer months, the Onge used to move deep into the forest, partially to avoid heat and also to save the trouble of travelling a long distance for hunting at a time when the pig population too, by and large, moved deeper into the forest. The Onge used to rest in the communal huts during the peak rainy season.

The shrinking habitat

- Till 1940: The whole of Little Andaman (731.5+ sq. km) and nearby islands covered under dense forest.
- 1957: The Onge reserve in Little Andaman (520 sq. km) Hut Bay Harbour constructed.
- 1972: Resettlement of refugee and oil palm plantation—denotification of 200 sq. km from Onge Reserve.
- By 1990: Onge forest resource has been reduced to 15 per cent of the original.

In earlier days the communal huts were spread out almost all over the island. On the basis of field studies made during 1955-6, it was learnt that the Onge population, not exceeding 200 then, were distributed over about 30 *beyras*. Now the population has reduced in strength to less than a half, even with utmost healthcare provided by the public health care programme of the government.

After Independence of India, various welfare measures have been introduced for the welfare and development of the tribes of Andaman Islands. Before launching any such programme, there was hardly any serious endeavour to appreciate the culture of the people and their necessities.

As already stated, Little Andaman was once the exclusive preserve of the Onge. Now fewer than 100 Onge people share the land with 7,214 non-Onge persons. Naturally, the area available for foraging has shrunk drastically. The Onge habitat has now being restricted to 'reserves', as prescribed by the government. Other technologically developed people, like the Bengali refugees and Sri Lankan expatriates, have been rehabilitated near the Onge reserves. In this new environment, such aliens are required to adapt themselves for survival. Accordingly, many of them have cultivated the taste for pork. In search of pigs, they often poach into the Onge territory. Honey, which was once largely consumed by the Onge women and children, is now purchased by these other people from the Onge at cheap rates. All these are the outcome of various welfare/development programmes for the Onge. This is more so because the Onge have developed a craze for paper money. So they do not hesitate to sell the honey depriving their own children and women.

Source: Photo taken by the author in 1988.

Figure 11.1: A Bengali fisherman throwing his net in the shallow sea just opposite the Dugong Creek settlement, well inside the Onge reserve.

As our development planners are primarily concerned with the economic development of the people, attempts have been made to compensate the Onge for the loss of foraging land. Hence, a programme for distribution of free rations in the form of rice, wheat, milk powder and other articles has been drawn up. A consumer cooperative store has been set up in the settlement of Dugong Creek. By supplying them free food, the Onge have been virtually deprived of the dignity of earning their own living. Through such programmes, a slow process of degeneration has been set in motion to destabilize the internal balance of the people, which ultimately results in a process of decay, cultural as well as biological. Gradually, a vibrant, lively human population has turned to an indolent, dependent, parasite group. The strength of a tribal society is in its self-sufficiency and sense of pride. Unfortunately, the development planners have wilfully chosen a formula evolved by our colonial masters which erodes these values. The quality of life of any group of people may be improved if their basic needs can be addressed duly. We can scan the process of development and its outcome by analysing the basic needs of the people.

The most important basic need is food. The life of the Onge was once centred around the quest for food, as usual to any foraging community. Roots, fruits and vegetables formed the major food items for such people. Food procured through hunting is subsidiary food as game is often scarce (Lee & Devore 1969). The Onge, in this respect, presents an almost exceptional case. Traditionally, they used to have the flesh of wild pigs and turtle as their major food and vegetables collected by women formed the subsidiary food.

One from the mainstream may consider that surviving on hunting-gathering is a very arduous job, full of risks and hazards and practically without any comfort. But these perceptions are relative, varying from culture to culture. For the Onge, life and livelihood are not two separate realities, rather their entire culture is one and well-integrated. The whole nexus of life and living is tuned to that particular mode of livelihood. For that reason, going out on hunting expeditions for Onge men or crab collection for Onge women remain something more than earning one's livelihood. These are refreshing ventures full of excitement. So the question of individual hardship and drudgery does not arise. There is no master like the plantation-in-charge to dominate or overrule their decisions. Whenever they need anything it is always available in the neighbouring forest or sea. They never return from forest empty-handed. So in the midst of the nature's bounty, they never feel insecure. Insecurity, in fact, leads to tendencies to hoard, which the Onge avoid. Even today they do not preserve any provision for the future.

In earlier days, pig hunting by men and collection of plant food by women were routine subsistence activities of the Onge. Usually men devoted more time to pig hunting than fishing though, in those days women's collection of seashells and molluscs was also quite important. The responsibility of women as food provides has been reduced to a great extent with the introduction of free rations. On the other hand, womenfolk, at present, act more like lower middle class housewives who spend time cooking. Cleaning paddy grains or frying *parathas* by Onge women have become a common sight in the Onge settlement.

Pig hunting was so important in Onge society that it may be called the pivot of their culture. Pig hunting is intimately associated with initiation ceremony, which is very important in transforming an adolescent Onge boy into an adult in the society. Among the Onge life is community-based. Nobody would hunt for himself. The individual hunter does not have any special claim over the game as is found among the Sirionos who enjoy certain privileges while distributing meat to others. The concept of community sharing is unknown among the Sirionos. The hunter may offer some meat to anybody who asks for it. Most often, he enjoys sex with a woman in exchange for meat (Holmberg, 1969). Community sharing comes from community hunting. With distribution of free ration to individual families, community hunting and sharing has lost much of their charm. Still, culture never dies completely. Community hunting is no longer there but the spirit of community sharing persists. At present, there is hardly any excitement or purpose in Onge life. Carbohydrates were never their first choice, but now the food group play a major role in Onge food culture.

The Onge did not know the art of producing food. Nor do they know it even now. Previously, they depended on the supply of nature for their subsistence. For them, nature was the eternal donor and always bountiful. They never suffered from any anxiety regarding shortage of food. But now the donor-cum-benefactor is the welfare agency and the people have become their dependents. The Onge also have started believing that the officers posted there are their food providers and money distributors. Hence they have learnt to place themselves in a subordinate position. They wait eagerly for the ship that carries rations to the settlements to arrive and thus suffer from a sense of insecurity if it does not reach on time. In pre-development days, the Onge never suffered from food insecurity. Any kind of insecurity creates stress which is associated with the modern way of life. What a transformation of the people from an independent self-reliant race to meek dependents!

During our stay among the Onge, once we had experienced such a situation, and realized the helplessness of the people. Out of desperation, they turned finally to the forest for pig hunting, though they knew that it was not the right season for such an activity.

They still practise hunting but not with as much vigour as in the olden days. The style of hunting has also changed. Community hunting is not there any more. Nowadays, they cannot go too far for hunting as they have to return to the settlement before sunset. It is also difficult to carry a large pig by oneself. So they remain happy with small pigs with less fat, but which they do not relish sufficiently. The excitement and joy associated with hunting is almost gone. Now it is only a matter of hunger satiation and a way of escape from boredom. Can we really call it an improvement in the quality of life of the Onge? Most of the plant food is not consumed any more though they are still there in the living memory of the people.

The overall situation changed to a great extent with the introduction of cereals by the welfare agency, namely Andaman Adim Janjati Vikas Samiti (AAJVS, 1976). The assured food supply brought about a qualitative change in their lifestyle. Now the Onge have adopted rice and wheat as staple, though meat is still their first preference. In earlier days, roots and tubers were the main source of carbohydrates, which have been substituted by cereals. Previously, the Onge were not used to this kind of food. This type of food is consumed primarily by those who know the art of producing them or can buy it from open market. The Onge neither produce them nor can they afford to buy it from

Source: Photo taken by the author.

Figure 11.2: A young lady, Mrs Sheela, adopted the sari from Bengali settlers and developed the habit of using a fancy umbrella while carrying home her share of pork from a hunter in Dugong Creek.

the market on their own. We do not know for how long they will be provided with free food. If the same practice continues for an indefinite period, the Onge will be far removed from their traditional mode of livelihood and it will not help them to integrate with the national mainstream. It is doubtful whether their subsistence economy will be replaced by any type of food producing economy. They now work as wage labourers in the plantation, but it is also not desired that in distant future, they will be transformed to wage labourers as a community working in the farms of settlers in the neighbouring villages or at Hut Bay.

The replacement of plant food has had a far-reaching effect on

Onge life, especially on women. With the introduction of cereals, the usual load of outdoor activities of women have been reduced considerably. Nevertheless, that has been replaced by domestic chores, like cooking and cleaning of pots and pans. In fact, in the earlier days, women were almost free from cooking since meat was the major item of food and it was roasted/baked by the menfolk. Then the Onge women had more leisure and enjoyed more freedom. They had the dignity of sharing equal responsibility in terms of subsistence activities and enjoyed an equal status in society. The introduction of cereals has also affected the gender relationship in society, assigning the women a subordinate position to the men.

Having an assured food supply and a permanent shelter, the Onge have now adapted themselves to an almost sedentary lifestyle. Consequently, division of labour has undergone a sea change. Now, a trend has been set that men will do outdoor activities and women will look after the domestic chores. This is the working pattern followed by the people among whom women primarily do not work for subsistence and often do not enjoy equal status in society either. Ordinarily, this kind of social change comes about due to technological advancement in a society. In the Indian situation, the more the advancement in technology, the more the women (especially of the unorganized sector) get displaced from their traditional way of life and become more dependent on others just for survival. For the Onge, there is practically no technological advancement whatsoever. Instead, increasing interference from outsiders have confined the Onge women within the four walls of their huts. In the name of development, a new food culture of an alien nature has been thrust upon them. As a result, the Onge women are required to sacrifice their freedom, leisure and enjoyment. Now, they evidently suffer from purposelessness in life.

After food comes the question of shelter—the other area of adoption of innovations in the form of housing and settlement pattern. It is reported that during the 1950s, two types of shelters were found in Little Andaman—(i) the large beehive-type communal huts and (ii) temporary camping huts comprising a number of lean-to sheds. These are known as the *beyra* and the *corale*, respectively. A number of families used to live in a *beyra.* The inmates were, as indicated, identified by their *beyra* affiliation. Nowadays, no Onge lives in the *beyra* or communal hut. Instead, they live in huts provided to them by the welfare agency or they make their semi-permanent huts at suitable locations.

Wooden cottages have been introduced to the Onge during the early seventies of the previous century at both of the Onge settlements under the tribal rehabilitation scheme. Initially, when the cottages were handed over to the Onge, the people had shown no interest in them.

After a due probe, facts revealed that they were not used to the elevated floor of the cottages. They were not comfortable with this type of dwelling and the stairs were not considered safe for the children. Another aspect of poor planning about the settlement also came to our notice. The site of the settlement was totally cleared of greenery. Coastal sandy lands, once deforested, can hardly be brought under any vegetation. Under the scorching equatorial sun, especially during the dry period, the sand absorbs enough heat to compel the forest dwellers to leave the settlement and stay inside deep forest most of the time. Besides, the settlement being devoid of any green cover, its surroundings need regular cleaning. The Onge do not have any habit of regularly sweeping the floor because they are not accustomed to living in any particular place for long. Moreover, regular consumption of coconut adds to increasing garbage in the neighbourhood. They were given permanent shelters but no effort was made to make them aware of public hygiene.

Till the early 1980s, the Onge stayed away from these cottages. Finally, these were rebuilt at Dugong Creek, lowering the floor level. Gradually, people started living in these cottages allotted to them as individual families. These cottages were provided with electric power supply, which is available only for four to five hours in the evening powered by a diesel generator installed at Dugong Creek. In 1986, on the plea of avoiding the scorching heat, the Onge of Dugong Creek settlement was tutored to demand electric fans and they were supplied the same accordingly. But they could not foresee the immediate effect of the new incorporation. They had to shift the cooking arrangement from the room to the open space outside. They were not habituated to the modern way of cooking, so cooking in open space could not be the preferred option from the hygienic standpoint either. Traditionally,

Source: Photo taken by the author.

Figure 11.3: A bicycle gifted by the welfare authority and the cottage on raised floor at Dugong Creek settlement.

they did not have any concept of a kitchen or a permanent hearth.

The individual cottages have been provided to them to change their nomadic habit and make the Onge settle down at one place. As other people have already been rehabilitated in the once exclusive Onge habitat, the movement of these people got automatically restricted. Though the people have not been settled in the true sense of the term, nevertheless, the administration, could, in this way, introduce the notion of private property to them.

The sense of private property among the Onge is hardly developed. Allotment of a cottage was the first step towards the development of the notion of personal property. When a man goes out for a long period, he keeps the cottage locked, though there are no valuables inside it. Adoption of any idea is much more important than any material goods, such as clothings or utensils. For this new type of accommodation, they had to change some of their important ritualistic practices. This again suggests a serious infringement upon their culture. The Onge funeral custom demands that the dead body be buried under the sleeping platform used by the deceased and that the house is abandoned. In the present set-up, it is not possible to desert the hut. To overcome such problems, the Onge made some adjustments. They selected an open space within the settlement area and prepared a bed under a makeshift thatch in the dead man's name and buried the dead body beneath the bed. Two such thatched structures were shown to us at Dugong Creek. They also modified the custom of burying the placenta after a childbirth. These suggest that the practical wisdom of the people can help them cope with any innovation, if they act on their own.

The next important item is clothing. The Onge shows an interest towards modern dress without understanding its optimal use. It has already been stated that the people have developed a craze for money and they love splurging. They love to buy anything and everything without knowing the proper use of what they are buying. It has been observed that they bought wristwatches, though they cannot tell the time. Suddenly they were exposed to many consumer goods and the market sells these goods to them irrespective of their felt needs. They have not learnt the art of earning money to procure consumer goods. Their only source of money is the dole distributed to them on the plea of plantation work done.

CHANGE IN VALUE SYSTEM

Long exposure to development and welfare programmes as well as the programme executors has affected the value system of the Onge directly and indirectly. The change in this respect is very slow, gradual, and almost imperceptible. At the first instance, it seems that the people are not conscious of such a change. But outsiders like us who have experience of these simple folk over a period of time can feel the slow change in their traditional value system or mindset.

It is well-known that the Onge society has an egalitarian base with no occupational specialization or social hierarchy. For operational advantage and more so with the prevalent notion of hierarchy, the officials responsible for development work choose two Onge men: one each from the two settlements as representatives or spokesperson of the community and treat them differently by addressing them as *Raja*. Traditionally, the Onge do not have any formal council or headman, as such. The officials ascribe a superior position to these so-called *rajas*, though the Onge are not much aware about the relative superiority inherent in the term. Once while returning to Hut Bay from the settlement, one of the *rajas* and another Onge man accompanied us. The officials suggested to us not to give our luggage to the *raja* to carry, even if we feel any difficulty carrying them ourselves. We were carrying the luggage ourselves. It was a long journey and the two Onge persons could feel our plight. Their original self came out automatically, throwing aside the artificial coating of superiority imposed on them by the outside agency. Forgetfully, they volunteered to help us in carrying the luggage. We paid some token money to the other man for his assistance before departing. He didn't expect we would pay him, because they do not have the idea that human labour is a saleable commodity. However, so-called superiority imposed by the others on individual Onge may hit the egalitarian base of their society in times to come.

The Onge love to share everything they procure from nature like pork, fish or honey. Community sharing is still very much in practice, though community hunting is not as much in vogue. The Onge never refuse anything when asked. But the people who are there to do good to them often take away the major share of meat or fish. Fishing is mostly an individual effort and done for pleasure, and hence the catch is usually not large. The officials do not hesitate to take out the large or tasty fish from the basket of an Onge when he passes through their quarters. The Onge do not refuse him, though they might not appreciate the behaviour as they spent long hours fishing. Nowadays, the Onge have also learnt the behaviour of the so-called civilized people. Those who are intelligent try to avoid the regular path to the settlement to escape the notice of these usurpers. For a long time they have been robbed of their catch, otherwise they voluntarily give fish to others. Their inborn innocence and sense of sharing are getting replaced by a certain slyness, selfishness, and distrust for the surrounding people. The same has also been observed when the hunter returns from a pig hunt. For the first time, they were offered money by us for pork and we made others (non-Onge) pay and fixed a price for that. Even without any measuring tool, the Onge used to give almost equally to all those who were interested to have some pork about 500 g and we gave Rs. 5 in a currency note for that as it was easier for them to identify the particular denomination. As long as we were there, other people also followed the practice but there is every doubt whether it has been continued after we left the place.

From our experience it may be said that close contact with the change agent within the settlement has had far more damaging effects on their values, particularly when it comes to the adoption of vices of modern society. Though special treatment is offered to one or two persons as stated earlier, most often the officials treat them as subordinates or lesser human beings. By now the Onge men also treat the officials as superior and try to emulate their lifestyle and language. The change agents posted within the Onge settlements introduced alcohol among these people. During our initial sojourn among them, we observed that the so-called development agents of various designations were addicted to alcohol but no Onge was found to have the habit of drinking. They were rather skeptical about it. Ramu, a young boy who worked in Port-Blair, once came to the settlement with a bottle of liquor. The elderly Onge men were visibly angry and he was compelled to leave the settlement. It has been reported by scholars who worked among the Onge in recent past that the Onge men cultivated the habit of alcohol which had a serious reflection on the gender relationship in the society (Venkateswar 2004).

We may examine how much the Onge could absorb or adopt the new innovations in their day to day life. From the perspective of development, the attempt to settle the people in two areas is partially successful. The Onge have accepted those two locations as their permanent dwelling places. This has been possible mainly due to free supply of ration and other essential articles. However, this innovation of modern housing is yet to fully penetrate into the core of the Onge culture.

The Onge, in general, were not used to sedentary life and they had very little material possessions. Use and throw was their life-style. When so many material objects, including utensils, were introduced to them, they were not tutored properly about their hygienic use or purpose. So most of the adoptions were partial. Besides, the people around them responsible for making them aware of all such things inculcated a sort of divide between the programme executors and the target group. Thus, gradually, a sense of inferiority overpowered the Onge mind, a phenomenon that was a deterrent in upholding their pristine cultural pride and self-esteem in a changed situation.

From the subsistence point of view, hunting is still their basic economy. In the changed situation, they only modified their hunting habits and techniques. Nevertheless, their habit of animal protein consumption remains almost unchanged when compared with the data on food intake during the pre-development period.

With so many development initiatives, to what extent could we solve the problems of the Onge? Scholars have tried to identify the problems of the small populations like Onge. Sarkar (1993) classified their problems under two categories: (1) the socio-economic problems due to increase of non-tribal populations around and establishment of settlements close to where they live, (2) the problem of depopulation. Sarkar discussed these two issues fairly extensively. Along with these two, we propose to identify two more areas of problem that the Onge face today and that need special attention: (1) loss of identity, (2) loss of self-esteem and dignity.

It is not very clear to us yet what we propose to achieve through the introduction of the so-called welfare measures and developmental initiatives. Often, development aims at economic betterment and the result is measured in terms of amount of money spent on the target group. By now some crores of rupees have been spent in the name of development of the Onge. But the net result is that the Onge have made practically little progress in the economic field. They have not cultivated any interest as yet to adopt any food producing economy directly. No change has ever been observed in the attitude or activities of the people, responsible for executing the development work. Since the beginning the people were supplied with free rations, a practice which is still continuing. Through the passage of time, their lifestyle has changed in terms of material possessions. Their houses have become crowded with unnecessary material items which they do not need. The administration has thrust an alien life pattern on these simple folks to bring them at par with other citizens of the country. With this set model, an urge could be cultivated for apparently useless material possessions which has no meaning in their given eco-cultural setting. Most often, the Onge procure the things with the dole money they receive on the pretext of doing something while practically doing nothing. Once the source of this system is blocked or gets dried up, we cannot even imagine what will happen to them. Would they go to the neighbouring people merely as wage-earners? What goal have we set for these nature-nurtured people! The prospect is frightening!

Certain measures had been initiated to change the socio-economic life of the Onge by making them interested in horticulture and the domestication of animals. However, no significant progress is visible. So what development did we do for them for decades together? We do not have any ready answer for this. In the name of working on the plantation, the Onge are paid monthly wages, though they are not interested in this kind of employment at all. By now they have got used receiving a salary even without contributing any labour. Through this endeavour, we could not inculcate the value of dignity of labour in them. Instead we could only create a craze for money among them.

It would not be out of place to add a few words about the role of money in the day-to-day life of Onge. Until very recently, money was an unknown concept to this hunting-gathering people. But it is now apparently the most valued possession of the present day Onge even as he does not know the real use of money. The implication of this has been discussed in detail in the earlier chapter.

Due to their exposure to urban populations, primarily through government officials and the market centre, a sort of consumerism pervades the Onge mind.

The South Bay Onge do not enjoy the market facility within the settlement. But the men over there are more exposed to other people around them. They have friendly relationships with the Nicobarese of a neighbouring village in little Andaman island. A mutual give-and-take relationship has already been started between them without exchanging money. The young boys of South Bay often visit Hut Bay and spend money on video shows. Such practices may lead to prodigal habits among the Onge youth as they do not have to spend for basic needs of life. However, their womenfolk very rarely visit other places.

Because of such exposures, the Onge nowadays appreciate the presence of money in their life. They are aware of the fact that the government is spending a huge amount of money for their development but the lion's share is usurped by others. If they could have handled money matters themselves, that might have resulted in a good deal of benefit.

To use currency notes and coins one must have the minimum knowledge of counting and recognizing their value. The Onge perhaps present a unique case of having a pocketful of money but never knowing how much. In Dugong Creek, only four men can identify currency notes and count money up to Rs. 20 and two persons can count up to Rs. 100. But none of them can add or subtract while doing a monetary transaction. They depend on others completely in this respect.

From the behaviour and attitude of the Onge it seems that they have developed a strong passion for money. They are becoming money lovers, not being conscious or aware of the modern monetary system. Initially it may cause a malady in society but with proper guidance in future they may be involved in a productive economy through horticulture or handicrafts. So far, they have not showed much interest towards any type of agriculture. But on account of their craze for money, they are unknowingly heading towards commercialization. The Onge sell almost 80 per cent of their annual collection of honey instead of consuming it freely. In this way, they also sell 50 per cent of the baskets they make every year. It may be mentioned that in case of the Onge, the process of involving the people in a productive economy has been started from the reverse end, i.e. not from work to money, rather from money to work.

We have the records to demonstrate that the Onge are being robbed of their money in the settlement itself. Now with better transport facilities, the menfolk come to the bigger market at Hut Bay easily and pick up many vices with the easily available cash. Adoption of vices is multiplying day by day and sometimes proves life-threatening (as it happened in recent past—a good number of young boys of Dugong Creek died due to consumption of spurious liquor). It may be summed up that the benefit Onge derive from the development/welfare work is relatively less compared to its hazards—a comfortable, sedentary life, associated with a degenerated health condition, loss of population and loss of cultural landmarks leading to loss of identity and cultural pride.

The degree of direct involvement or supervision of the welfare agency also matters for transforming the target group towards the desired end. This issue may be examined through the mode of development work executed in the two locations of the Onge.

The Onge of Dugong Creek settlement are always under the direct supervision and guidance of the agency people, who are stationed there for the overall management. The Onge there have restricted choice and movement. The Onge of the South Bay settlement are relatively free from such direct supervision. Often, they visit Hut Bay and the nearest settlement of the Nicobarese. Thus the Onge of the South Bay have developed a friendly relationship with them almost on equal terms. The Dugong Creek settlement is surrounded by a non-tribal rehabilitated Bengali population. These people look down upon the Onge as *junglees* or savages. Naturally, no friendly relationship is possible in such a situation. Rather, sometimes, they try to take advantage of the ignorance and simplicity of the Onge, while making a transaction through barter or cash.

The Onge of South Bay can pursue their traditional mode of life by subsisting mostly on gathered food. As no plantation-in-charge is stationed there, the women can move freely. They go to the forest regularly for collection of various kinds of plant food. The people in general are physically more fit and joyful. In Dugong Creek the Onge women are captives in their own settlement. Their physical movements are minimal and they are becoming obese day by day. Their overall nutritional and health status also show significant difference between the two groups of the Onge. Thus, it appears that the less the interference of outside people, the better it is for the Onge. The South Bay situation suggests that developmental supervision is needed but that should allow for some breathing space between the welfare agency and the target group. Too much interference from a close quarter takes away the freedom of the people and curbs their inner strength and vigour. Development work is to be planned and executed in such a way that the people feel happy, well-cared for, but not overwhelmed or subjugated.

We have depicted the result of a development that are, by and large, questionable. Is there not anything positive in the development measures initiated for the Onge? Surely, there are some. The most important one is the introduction of healthcare system within the

Source: Photo taken by the author.

Figure 11.4: Ramesh and Baby, one of the most eligible couple in reproductive age are visibly down with obesity and other psychosocial conditions.

settlement. Though public health and hygiene are not given due importance, medical care at least is available for the Onge. The Onge can understand the efficacy of modern medicines. Through medical care, infant mortality could be checked to some extent and the lifespan of the Onge definitely recorded a rise. In case of men, less physical activity led to obesity, which may ultimately create many more diseases. However, mortality rate has come down but unfortunately the rate of morbidity has gone up in society.

In sum, we could not achieve many of the desired results because the model of development used for the people appears to lack sensitivity and perspective. No serious exercise has so far been done for improving the quality of life of such marginal people. Instead, we rushed for as easy solution by borrowing models from our colonial masters.

The cases of the Onge or the Great Andamanese pose many serious questions involving the functioning of our development planners and executives. A detailed account may not only embarrass them but put their developmental initiatives into extraordinary scrutiny for judiciousness. Are such initiatives really directed towards conservation of the people and preservation of their beautiful culture, at least for some more time to come? Or they are ever eager to usurp their land and other natural resources as quickly as possible, even if such actions lead to their early degeneration? If the present trend continues or goes altogether unchecked, in the near future the Onge men would make mere imitations of other poverty-stricken people as often found in the mainland of India. If this is what is meant by bringing the people to the national mainstream of India, it would perhaps be better if the process gets delayed rather than being rushed through. It is highly important that we review the matter afresh in the historical perspective taking the ground realities into account and try to evolve a model for development out of our own experiences.

REFERENCES

Agrawal, S.N., 'Reproductive Life of the Onge Women', *Vanyajati*, vol. 15, 1967.

Awaradi, S.A., *Master Plan (1992-2021) for Welfare of Primitive Tribes of Andaman and Nicobar Islands*, Port Blair: Andaman and Nicobar Administration, 1990.

Cipriani, Lidio, *Andaman Islanders*, London: Wedenfeld and Nicolson, 1966.

Ganguly, P., 'The Negritos of Little Andaman Islands', *Indian Museum Bulletin*. vol. X, no. 1, 1975.

Govt. of India, Planning Commission, *Primitive Tribal Communities of Andaman and Nicobar Islands*, New Delhi: Planning Commission, 1988.

Pandit, T.N., 'The Tribal and the Non-tribal in Andaman Islands: A Historical Perspective', *Journal of the Indian Anthropological Society*, vol. 2, no. 2, 1985.

Sarkar, Jayanta, 'Endangered Tribes and their Development in Andaman and Nicobar Islands', in *Andaman and Nicobar Islands*, Calcutta: Indian Anthropological Society, 1993.

Venkateswar, Sita, *Development and Ethnocide: Colonial Practices in the Andaman Islands*, Copenhagen: International Work Group for Indigenous Affairs (IWGIA), 2004.

CHAPTER 12

Excerpts from Field Diaries

In the field-based research format that we followed, there is a vast scope of acquiring data beyond structured instruments, interviews and observations. Pages of the field diary or special notes on personal interactions and events related to the people of the community, local residents or visiting personalities, can add a valuable dimension to such empirical studies. During our long stay with the Onge in their habitat, both of us regularly jotted down several narratives and expressions of our emotional reactions and experiences in their raw format. In this chapter we have included extracts and select clippings from the pages of our diaries which, we believe, will fill the aspects left untouched even after the preceding chapters.

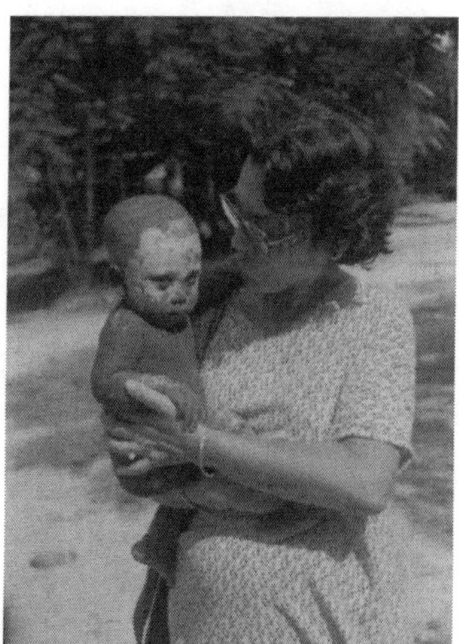

Source: Photo taken by the author.

Figure 12.1: Dipali Danda soothing an ailing Onge baby at Dugong Creek Settlement.

EXTRACTS FROM DIPALI DANDA'S DIARY

I have had a fairly long acquaintance with the Onge of Little Andaman. At first, I had seen them at Port Blair participating in the Republic Day Parade. Their complexion appeared so dark that it was as if they were painted black. When they used to come out of the sea after a bath, their skin looked shiny.

Over the years, their skin lost their natural shine. During the subsequent years, every time I visited them, I noticed deterioration of their health condition in some form or the other. Young kids had potbellies and sometimes rickets, too. During our initial visits, we did not find any trace of alcoholism among the Onge. I have narrated an incident related to the reaction towards intake of alcohol by an Onge boy. But we were shocked to hear the news that most of the Onges had got addicted to alcohol when we reached Hut Bay in 1988. I was rather surprised that when there was so much development all around the Onge were getting lustreless, listless, and adopting so many bad habits.

When I revisit my personal diary certain things pop up, which may throw some light on this aspect. Dr S. Bose conducted his field study among the Onge in 1963. During that period, they used to have their traditional food only, and never liked any non-traditional item, like fried *paratha.* If they were supplied with these, they used to throw them away. Now they are very fond of such food items. May be, this is being considered as a marker of success in development initiatives. Our tireless effort has been to lure them to our life pattern leaving their own. To some extent that goal has been achieved. Now they like our food but even our vices are being adopted, too. Previously, they never had any stale food because they had no idea of storing or hoarding for future. Now they are often found to take the leftover fish curry of the previous night. In humid warm climate, how far those are fit for eating is anybody's guess. No effort had ever been made to teach them any hygienic practice whatsoever in terms of food. The unhygienic practice of defecating through a hole made in the wooden floor of their cottage makes their environment detrimental to public health. In 1987, the AAJVS constructed community latrines which the Onge never used.

During our long stay among them many small incidents recorded in my diary made a deep impression on me, which I would like to share with our readers. Strictly speaking, these small things may not be treated as data but these are reflections of the values of the Onge and views vis-à-vis those of others.

ATTITUDE OF THE CARETAKERS

One morning, Moroi and his wife were leaving for the forest. On their way to the forest they did not forget to take their dogs and puppies along with their meagre personal belongings. The puppies were too small to cover the distance, so Moroi put them in a basket. Three dogs, including the mother of the puppies, followed them. On the way one of the dogs caught a chick belonging to Saiburam, a non-Onge staff of the development agency living in the settlement. Saiburam chased the dog and hit it mercilessly. At this, Moroi's wife got angry and rushed to the dog (or the chick!) with a chopper in hand. Saiburam's wife became furious at this and said very caustically, 'We are giving you free rations and you people do not care for us.' I felt rather awkward listening to such comments. Saiburam's wife was in no way involved in the work of welfare agency and, more so, her husband was holding a very insignificant position among the development workers. This was the attitude of most of the people who were entrusted with development work. Even the observation of the teacher reflects an almost similar prejudice. According to her, 'They are *junglees*, there is no point teaching them'. There was, of course, a school over there for the Onge with a single teacher but no student to attend it.

Nevertheless, Moroi could not protest as he was a meek person. Besides, he also believed that the agency people were their food providers. After getting a good thrashing the dog fell almost unconscious. Moroi very carefully took the dog on his lap as if he was carrying a sick baby and came to the shore. There, Bairogegi gave his canoe to them to cross the creek. In the boat, they tied the dogs by the neck with fibre so that the dogs do not fall in the water as there was a crocodile around. Then they left for the forest. I still remember the gesture of Bairogegi and the love of a human for a non-human being.

THE CARING AND SHARING COMMUNITY

When we exhausted our stock of rice we had to prepare chapatti. But we had no proper utensils for making them. The Onge women voluntarily supplied us their utensils. Sometimes it happened that there was no ration with us and the market was far away. We survived on biscuits and green coconuts. During those difficult times, the Onge men came to our help. They gave us fish, crabs, pork, etc., without expecting anything in return. It is inherent in their culture. Whosoever needs food, he/she may have it from anybody's house, of course leaving something for the owner. There is no exaggerated sense of reciprocity. Nevertheless, the principle of sharing ensured food security to them, which they had imbibed from their foraging heritage.

AMAZING DISPOSITION

Let me narrate another incident which provoked me to think that the disposition of the Onge is very different from what we see among ourselves. When we interact with these simple folk for a good length of time, we also learn many things from their way of life. When I tend to reflect back I still cannot decide which one, ours or theirs, is the better way to encounter a critical situation like death.

Bara Raju lost two children within a month. They had been sent to Port Blair on 4 August 1988 by helicopter for treatment, but they could not be cured. The local doctor at the settlement was sceptical about the proper treatment of the kids at Port Blair hospital. However, their dead bodies were brought back at Dugong Creek on 28 August 1988. With the arrival of the bodies, close relatives started weeping. Others gathered at the burial place observed silence or participated in ceremonial weeping. Only the parents of the dead children looked grave and sad. For others, it was almost a casual affair. It surprised me to see that most of the women were busy looking at the articles brought from Port Blair and some were also eating bananas which are not ordinarily available at the settlement. It seemed that in their lives, events like death, bereavement, etc., are taken very much for granted. The couple lost two children within a month, but they looked composed, not complaining as if life was like that. No loss or grief is everlasting. These are very transient in nature—the flow of life that never stops is the only permanent thing.

STAY AT SOUTH BAY

I will end with the sweet memories of our stay at South Bay settlement, though it was for only a very brief period. We did not have any cooking arrangement with us, so we stayed with the Onge and also ate with them. We found them to be very gentle and warm-hearted. When I joined the Onge women in collection of seaweed, they felt very happy. They were like little children; how easily some of them could relax with their heads on my shoulder as if they had known me for years. Similarly, Sumit ventured to join fishing expeditions with the Onge men. They, too, enjoyed his company very much. In other words, they were very spontaneous in expressing their joy and emotions. They looked very healthy, too, in comparison to the Onge of Dugong Creek, though their dependence on supplied ration was relatively less.

I had an interesting experience of night stay at South Bay settlement in a godown where the rationed articles were being stored along with many random things like garments, saw, tortoise shells, etc. Sumit was lucky to share a room with the unmarried men of the settlement. At night the storeroom became the playground of rats and mice. Sometimes it appeared that snakes caught rats. After mustering some courage I switched on the torch and discovered that rats of different sizes were busy ripping open the sacks containing rations. They never found any human beings in that room, so they did not bother about my presence over there. I could feel the peaceful co-existence of human and non-human beings, in this case the latter being a bunch of rats. The Onge never complained about loss of grain or the rat menace. I discovered one lantern in that room. I could not sleep any more. With the help of the light from the lantern I concentrated on my field notebook and enjoyed seeing the rats play in the room. By then, it was 4.30 a.m. My transistor radio started the broadcast of the Mahalaya programme of All India Radio. I came out with the lantern and transistor to wake Sumit up for the programme. But he was in deep sleep with the Onge men. Perhaps they were sufficiently tired after the lengthy fishing operation. I left the lantern in their room and came

Source: Photo taken by the author.

Figure 12.2: Sumit Mukherjee with a group of Onge men of Dugong Creek going to bring the large canoe hull from deep inside the forest.

out. It was a lifetime experience listening to the melodious Mahalaya programme on the transistor in South Bay with the backdrop of the vast sea behind me.

EXTRACTS FROM SUMIT MUKHERJEE'S DIARY

I had the rare opportunity of accompanying the Onge in several of their foraging and other activities, both inside the forest and in the open sea. Other than the details of hunting and canoe-making techniques I have already included in the preceding chapters, I cherish the personal interactions during the course of my participation in those ventures. I have felt in my heart the fellow feeling and concern among the Onge about my safety and well-being. The most memorable and valuable part of my experience with them is my peak into the mode of survival as a forager when in real wilderness.

As the Onge families accepted me as one of their fellow men, particularly when I took my wife Amiya to Dugong Creek, though for a very brief period, sharing of food items as well as their knowledge became more regular. We used to accept the offered share of raw and cooked pork, *paratha*, etc., from them and in return they also accepted the share of my fish catch but only the fresh ones and not even the half-a-day-old catches. The womenfolk became crazy about the inner garments of Amiya, just like children who react trying on seeing a new exotic item. Some younger women had even shown interest in learning how to wear the *sari* from her.

In a rare incident, Bairogegi's wife finally allowed me to take her two-year-old baby in my lap as the baby had high fever and medicines were being administered to it in regular intervals. The doctor in charge and, myself, took care of the baby for almost a whole day as the mother sat at a distance weeping.

THE INCIDENT OF *MURGA MACHCHI* (COCK/SCORPION FISH)

One afternoon I was alone fishing with my set of hook and line standing at the far edge of the jetty (wharf) on the Dugong Creek. I started exploring just beneath the jetty where certain fishes gather during afternoons. In fact, I got quite amused watching some hungry, foolish fish approaching my hook. After a couple of minutes to my surprise, a long, red and yellow fish with two large, red and pink side fins and equally large, top and tail fins came up gracefully and gulped the hook. Being excited on sighting the amazingly beautiful fish never seen before, I brought the line closer to watch.

Before I attempted to unhook the fish with my right hand, Kanjo, an elderly Onge man who was fishing at a nearby location, came rushing to me waving his right hand and head and shouting in broken Hindi not to touch the catch. The first question that came to my mind was what had gone wrong catching a fish which otherwise was appreciated and enjoyed by the Onges so far. As Kanjo came closer he started pointing to the fish shouting, 'Murga Machchi, Murga Machchi…'. He snatched the fish away holding the line and tried to throw it back into the creek, snapping the line. I stopped him for a while and took a picture with my camera which I used to carry almost always. There was a big smile of satisfaction on his face. In his broken Hindi he narrated that this fish bore highly poisonous spikes all over its colourful fins and anybody who touched them would experience severe pain for the next three to four days. Later that evening a local Bengali fisherman from a nearby refugee settlement narrated his painful experience of being scratched by this species of fish on his leg while fishing in the creek several months earlier.

THE NEW CANOE OF BOTALE

For more than a month before, I was actually informed about his new canoe from Botale himself, who had been visiting the forest almost daily to finish the most laborious part of the work, i.e. to dig out the core of the tree trunk and complete the hull of the canoe. Around a week ago, Ramesh, the son-in-law of Botale, informed us with his usual big grin that the hull was ready to be brought to the shore for fixing the outriggers on it. We had to coax him and Botale a lot to take me and the doctor with them on that occasion.

Around 7.15 a.m., we reached the Onge dwelling area to find nine of the ablest and most experienced Onge men waiting for us. They greeted us warmly as we joined the team but with a smattering of doubt about our ability and adaptability for such a venture deep inside the forest. All of them were carrying *dao* (chopper and adze) while Kanjo, the oldest, was carrying his *pan* (betel leaves) and *chuna* (lime) in a sling bag hanging from his right shoulder. Three younger men were wearing T-shirts with shorts while three others wore vests with Kanjo only in traditional dress the *chaddi*. Interestingly, only the youngest Otalate was wearing rubber slippers in contrast to his barefooted brethren.

Botale and Kanjo took the lead and all of us, a group of eleven, started following them northward along the eastern shoreline. The yellow beach stretched quite wide that day due to low tide. For about half an hour briskwalking we turned left to enter the dense forest. Here lay three-newly made canoes of varying sizes. All were at various stages of being outrigged. There was a makeshift shade close to the forest with a bamboo bench to sit and relax. Only about 12-15 ft. ahead an open path approximately 10/12 ft. wide had already been created through which all those canoe hulls made inside the forest were brought out to the sea beach. Throughout this path straight tree branches of medium thickness had been placed across at a regular interval of about 5-6 ft. During the journey only Kanjo took a short break to have a betel leaf. Others preferred not to have anything to eat or drink.

Our pace of forest-walking became almost half that of beach-walking as we had to hop over and dodge those cross-laid branches and numerous debris from cleared smaller tree and bushy plant base. But the Onge men were walking on, unfazed by those obstacles.

We reached our destination after about a 25 minute walk inside the forest. It was located deep in the core of the forest with towering trees standing tall spreading the huge buttresses of their roots. The undergrowth had already been cleared where the newly curved hull of the boat was lying. That particular tree, about 30 ft. tall, was cut for making one canoe.

Botale, the maker and owner of his new boat, was in a happy mood, bearing a prominent smile on his face. His teammates, who had joined hands on the day of felling the tree, again accompanied him voluntarily and cheerfully at this final stage to drag the huge hull out to the beach. There the outriggers would be fixed to it before launching forth to the sea. As we all reached the spot first they appreciated that we had taken the trouble to see the boat and that the two of us were safe and sound. Then, for a while, they sat on the ground having examined the hull. Some of them took a betel leaf or two and exchanged some happy words or thoughts. It was around 8.30 in the morning but there was hardly any direct sunlight. Rather, the scattered inclined sunbeams cast a graffiti on the forest canvas. After a round of *biri* and betel leaf, the Onge discussed the day's job at hand. Then, led by Botale, they picked up their adzes one by one and started giving final touches, especially to smoothen the outer surface of the hull. Some made wooden poles and sticks and started tying those across through the holes made for fixing the outrigger to the hull. Each pole measured about 6.5 ft. and was very straight. Two such poles, of the length of the hull itself, were then laid over the crosspieces and tied at every intersection using a particular fibre strip made from the outer bark of a tree. It took them almost two-and-a-half hours to make the hull ready to be dragged to the beach.

The next job was to transport the hull. Then we decided to take a break. It was necessary to soothe our thirsty throats and fill our hungry stomachs. In fact, we had exhausted our stock of 200 g biscuits and 2 litres of water we had carried from the settlement. Understanding the poor condition of their urban guests, the ever-smiling Ramesh pointed at a huge tall tree close to where we were standing. Kanjo and Botale also came forward, and examined a high branch to show us a very large honeycomb hanging with thousands of bees in it. Those were the larger variety of honeybees found in the Andaman forests in abundance. The three of them took a little time to find a particular bushy plant and then broke from it a small branch full of leaves. It was handed over to Ramesh who carried those and the *dao* up the tall tree.

Ramesh, climbed the tree as smoothly, as if walking, sans climbing gear. On close observation, I found, it was the soft but elastic soles of their feet that helped them get a good hold on the moderately rough outer bark of the tree. Climbers get this kind of support using high grade rock-climbing shoes with thick rubber soles during rock climbing events. My observation was in concordance with Lidio Cipriani's remark about the high elasticity and softness of the skin of the Onge.

At about 25 ft. above the ground, Ramesh was nearly 3 ft. away from the honeycomb. He stopped and started chewing the green leaves carried by him. Then he smeared some of the green paste on his face, neck, and hand. Then he started spraying the remaining paste from his mouth directly on the honey bees using long breaths. Within a minute he started cutting the hive with the *dao* in his right hand while keeping his hold and balance with the other three limbs, almost sticking to the tree trunk like a giant lizard.

Climbing down to the ground, he started cutting the hive into two halves with the help of Bairogegi. The one with larvae inside was chosen by the Onge. Each one of them was enjoying his share of the piece of the hive with honey and larvae. At the same time Bairogegi offered me and the doctor a 6×3 inch cube of the hive full of only honey. I was astonished to find a few bees were still on the hive but they looked very docile, as if they had been tranquilized. As we chewed and sucked on the piece, the honey entered into our throats like very sweet, thick nectar with a high sugar content. Though the two of us chewed the piece and discarded the wax, the Onges mostly took their pieces whole along with the larvae.

Having consumed this pure instant energy booster, I witnessed my body temperature rise a bit and felt terribly thirsty. Perhaps a similar feeling happened to the Onges as they were looking for some water. But both of our bottles were already empty. The Onge men instantly found a nearby hollow on the ground with some water, removed the decomposed leaves there by hand and started drinking the brown water using an enamel mug. They did not even bother to check whether the water was clear. As we refused to drink that water, they smiled but did not insist. The ever-smiling Ramesh arrived as a saviour and we started following him far into the forest. After 15 minutes of walking amongst tangled bushes, a relatively open forest area suddenly appeared the soil was softer and damp under our feet. It can best be described as a thicket of full-grown cane. I was looking keenly for a cleaner source of water in the form of a stream or pool. But to my utter disbelief, Ramesh pointed out the cane, saying: *enge!* (water). Upon querying, he narrated that this type of cane and bamboo mixed forest areas are called *Tambojoko*. He then chose a large cane of nearly 4 inches in diameter hanging 3/4 ft. above the ground resembling a sagging rope. He instructed us to stand on either side of the cane approximately 10 ft. apart. Then he cut one end of the cane and asked me to hold it. It was pretty heavy and both of us were at our wit's end by that time. Then the same act was repeated by Ramesh and this time the end was held by the doctor. As he supported the piece of cane in the middle, he instructed the doctor to raise the end by his side slowly and that I should place my open mouth below the opposite end. I can never forget the first few drops of sweet and cold water dripping into my mouth. It was an almost divine feeling. Then I raised the end of the cane on my side, and the doctor drank from the cane. We repeated the process four or five times and every time some of the 'nectar' entered our throat.

Then, with the sudden outburst of the shrill sound of a species of forest cricket, I came back to my senses to find it was already 1.45 in the afternoon. These crickets, present in hundreds, practically invisible in the forest have the habit of making a loud chorus suddenly breaking the silence.

At the call from Botale and Kanjo, all of the men were back at work. They started adding some more thin logs and branches tangentially across the cleared path made for the canoe hull to be dragged to the beach. The transverse logs were placed almost at every 5 ft distance. As they started pushing the hull along the cleared path, the logs laid on the ground acted as castor wheels. Once the hull was moved 10 to 12 ft. forward, the logs left behind were brought to the front and again laid out similarly. Thus, the huge hull was transported relatively easily at an average pace of almost 50 ft. per six to eight minutes by those nine men. There was no performance of any kind of ritual offering or prayer that came to our notice at any stage of the work so far.

We reached the sandy beach around 3.00 p.m. They placed the new hull stably parked on the upper end of the sandy beach and tied a nylon rope they had carried for fixing and anchoring it to the mangrove tree. After another break for rest and cleaning our hands and feet (as did most of the Onges) in the sea water, we started our return journey after a truly memorable venture.

THE ONGE YOUTH WITH HIS BEER BOTTLES

Another incident I remember is from the time when Ramu came into Dugong Creek settlement with beer bottles. I was amazed to see the community's reaction and revulsion to alcohol and their expressions of disapproval. Totanange, who was fishing in the reef at the head of Dugong Creek since morning, came rushing to his senior, Kanjo, at the settlement to inform him that Ramu, an Onge youth, had arrived at a point on the other side of the creek and has been consuming beer. In fact, Ramu had been staying in Port Blair for the last four years or so and had somewhat spoilt himself by developing several bad habits like begging and drinking alcohol. He preferred to stay away from his community, though he received various doles from the welfare organization.

The news of his appearance near the Dugong Creek settlement instantly made all the adult men and women present there very agitated and fearful. They decided unanimously to stop him from entering the settlement and pushed him back to Hut Bay. Around late afternoon, Totanange and two other Onge men took a canoe and moved fast across the creek to reach the spot where Ramu was enjoying his booze behind a large rock on the sea beach. We, standing on the jetty, could not really make out what happened there.

The next morning around 9.30, while on my morning stroll along the beach near the jetty, I spied Totanange was rowing towards this end. He disembarked from his small canoe with a strange grin all over his face. By that time Bairogegi and some others had gathered there and Totanange narrated what had happened. The previous afternoon they had asked Ramu to leave the place and go back immediately to Hut Bay. But he reacted angrily in his inebriated state. Being denied entry to this side of the creek, he took the canoe, which was kept near Bara Nala (the large river) for community use, and started rowing away. This morning Totanange could spot something unusual lying scattered near the place where they left Ramu. Upon reaching the spot he found that the canoe near Bara Nala was lying in pieces all over the sandy beach. This was an expression of anger from poor Ramu, which was a common behavioural pattern found among Onges. Earlier, an Onge man chopped off all the plants in the garden of the social worker posted at Dugong Creek after he denied him some petty articles from the ration shop.

The most significant takeaway that emerged from the incident is the degree of dislike and non-acceptance of alcoholic drinks by the Onge society in general. In fact, such intoxicating stuff, other than betel leaf and nuts, were treated as taboo items by Onges.

A SMALL GIFT FROM A CHILDLESS COUPLE

The most touching and humane gesture from an Onge couple is perhaps the most precious memory I still nourish. During the last few minutes of the second and final phase of our three-month field study, most of the Onge men gathered at the Dugong Creek jetty, along with some officials posted there. As we were loading our baggage into two large canoes to travel up to the head of Bara Nala to the nearest road head, Otalate, the Onge, appeared with his wife. It was rather pleasant to have them there as they were the only couple who, for some reason beyond our perception, kept themselves isolated from the rest of the Onge in Dugong Creek and stayed inside the forest. The only probable reason we could find was the loss of their little son the previous year before proper medical treatment could be provided. Otalate came straight to me and took a small cane basket *tole* from his wife and offered it to me with a soft voice '... *ni ale*'. With my limited understanding of Onge dialect, I could translate that this was the gift of a toy for my newborn son at my home in Kolkata. I was completely astonished that he remembered me mentioning my baby son when his wife inquired about my wife a week back, whom she had met during our previous field study. There can be nothing more touching and precious than this gift from such an innocent group of beautiful people I had met.

CHAPTER 13

Postscript

In this volume we have tried to view the Onge life trajectory through time, beginning from the mid-1950s. That was actually the period when scholars, particularly anthropologists, had taken an interest in studying the life and culture of this isolated island community. It was not our intention to prove or disprove any theoretical model of culture change or to demonstrate how a dominant group overpowers a smaller one in the name of development that results in the ultimate degeneration of a pristine apparently archaic culture.

We came to learn from the writings of earlier authors that the Onge were a vibrant people holding their values and self-esteem in high premium. They were happy in their own niche living a life of their choice, depending primarily on the foraging technology. Detailed accounts of such lifestyle become evident from the descriptions of Ganguly and Bose that have been incorporated in this book.

Contact with the outside world was perhaps never that impossible as it is often imagined. The issues could be only a matter of time and degree. It is, nevertheless, a fact that the Onge were not directly responsible for such a contact. It is primarily the outside communities, who, in order to fulfil their own interests, usurped these simple folks. The shell poachers used to visit Little Andaman and engaged the Onge men as divers for collecting valuable shells. It is claimed that the poachers tried to introduce opium and alcohol to the people. Though the Onge were habituated to tobacco and tea, they refrained from cultivating tastes for these two items. Nevertheless, the tradition of getting harmed because of contact seems to be still continuing. To be very candid, the overall situation has seriously aggravated the condition of the people. The pursuit of development has actually set in a slow process of degeneration which is being sanctioned and legitimized in the name of welfare by the welfare state of India. Change agents employed and posted within the Onge settlements introduced alcohol among these people. During our initial sojourn among them, we observed that the so-called development agents of various designations were addicted to alcohol but no Onge was found to be in the habit of drinking. They were rather found to be skeptical about drinking. Ramu, a young boy, who worked in Port Blair, once came to the settlement with a bottle of liquor. The elderly Onge men were visibly angry at him and he was compelled to leave the settlement.

A major research study done by Sita Venkateswar (1989-1992) and published in 2004 throws considerable light on the change in Onge culture, mainly due to introduction of welfare measures. Some of her observations are totally similar to what we have seen happening to the Onge. As she emphasizes, the process of the decay of Onge culture was accelerated, especially with the introduction of alcohol among the Onge men. She described meticulously the effect of alcohol on Onge men, each by name. We could identify one and all who once abhorred drinking, as already mentioned.

Today, the Onge men enjoy drinking alcohol, a habit which they have cultivated through their association with the welfare staff. In traditional Onge society, no clearcut distinctions could be made between family and society. This had helped in maintaining an extraordinarily harmonious way of life, devoid of any gender discrimination. The male members of the Onge now appear to be more under the influence of the welfare personnel. Their women maintain a distance from those people. Thus, women are being segregated from public life and, by and large, remain within the domestic sphere.

While individually, within the domestic space, Onge men concurred with their wives' grievances, as a group, they tended to keep this area of interaction with the welfare personnel separate. This was the arena of collusion that provided access to alcohol, and with alcohol they could all 'be men' together. A dramatic transformation is effected in the behaviour of Onge men, once they have consumed alcohol.

The remarkable feature of this change was how closely they mimicked the behaviour of the welfare staff or the drunken exhibitions they had witnessed in the nearby towns. When drinking, Onge men spoke only Hindi, the most halting speaker discovering an amazing fluency with the language. In that language, their conversation acquired a certain lewdness and the kind of discussion they engaged in was one they shied away from when sober (Venkateswar, 2004: 167).

The drinking habit of the Onge men has a serious reflection on gender relationships in their society. The Onge women enjoyed equal status with their men folk in the traditional Onge society. Sometimes they were found more dominating in certain spheres of life and activities. Men always cared for their wish as well as demand. An incident as narrated by Ganguly, during mid-1950s, will substantiate the point appropriately.

Premarital and extramarital sexual relations are not common perhaps because it is difficult to secure a paramour in Onge society. But sexual misdemeanour sometimes occurs. In Tokoebue communal hut, an attractive young woman was sleeping with her husband. Another married man living in the same hut stealthily approached and had sexual intercourse with her. The woman at first thought in her sleepiness that the man was her husband and accepted him but she was later able to recognize the man. The following morning when she narrated the incident to her husband he got extremely angry and chased away the culprit who fled into the jungle. He climbed on a lofty tree and hid himself among the leaves. But the aggrieved husband searched him out and shot an arrow which inflicted a deep wound in his buttock. The angry husband was soon pacified by the elderly of the camp. When the wounded man returned to the camp, instead of taking care of him, his wife scorned him and kicked him repeatedly. It may be pointed out here that among the Onge there is no tribal council or any other organization to administer justice.

This incident demonstrates what sort of authority and power the Onge woman had in the olden days. Now the Onge men demonstrate a sense of ambivalence in their behaviour. In the domestic sphere, like pregnancy, childbirth, etc., they behave traditionally. In other spheres of activities, they appear to be indifferent. This has become a fact of life. 'For the Onge women, who, in other respects, tended to keep a firm check on their men, drinking and alcohol became the means through which the men evaded and eluded them. The deference shown to them by their husbands in their daily lives was erased at a single stroke with alcohol' (ibid.).

Scholars who worked among the Onge during the beginning of the present century observed that there was a gradual increase of obesity among the Onge, especially among the males. It is because they have been far removed from their own culture-bound lifestyle as well as habits. Their food had high protein content once. Now it is more loaded with carbohydrate and fat. A study of the year 2001 shows that '... fat and carbohydrates content of their diet is high due to use of refined oil, coconut, as well as processed food grains, sugar and jaggery as major food items, but their traditional diet were devoid of these items.... Their Physical Activity Level (PAL) is decreasing gradually but fairly significantly. On the other side, food availability is secure with enhanced food intake. Thus, Physical Activity Level and food intake play major roles for the existing overweight and obesity' (Sahani: 2011) among the Onge. Sahani further comments that the Onge males are more influenced than females in this regard and the difference has widened due to rehabilitation.

ANNEXURE I

The Onge of Little Andaman: A Vanishing Tribe

PRANAB GANGULY AND ANADI PAL

Our earliest information about the Onge dates back to 1825 when T.E. Alexander landed on Little Andaman and gave the first news of its inhabitants (Cipriani, 1953). In 1867, the captain and seven members of the crew of the ship *Assam Valley* landed on Little Andaman, but were never seen again. A punitive expedition was sent to the island after this incident and the remains of the Europeans who had obviously been murdered were found. Some seventy Onge were killed in skirmishes with the members of the expedition (Bonnington, 1932).

Homfrey, Stewart, Cadel, Man, and a number of other persons visited Little Andaman during the period 1867-84, but their attempts to befriend the aborigines yielded no results. In 1885, a few Onge, including women and children, were captured in South Cinque Island and their enmity was overcome by kind treatment and offering many gifts. They were subsequently released. Since then the aborigines began to become friendly towards foreigners. In the years 1886 and 1887, Portman made many trips to Little Andaman and the natives behaved very congenially with his party. Lapicque visited the island in 1893 and Eickstadt in 1927. In 1948, a short visit was paid by Dr B.S. Guha, the then director of the Anthropological Survey of India. Following him a number of officers of the Survey started anthropological investigations on the island.

One of the present writers (Ganguly) made many trips to Little Andaman during 1953-7 and stayed there for more than eight months. A summary of the survey of our knowledge is presented here with the hope that it will be a useful record for future reference. Apart from the Jarawa and Sentinelese, the Onge are the most highly inbred population and may be considered to be the purest representatives of the Asiatic Pygmies.

The Anthropological Survey party working in Little Andaman during 1955-6 under the leadership of R.C. Nigam, of which one of us (Ganguly) was a member, actually saw, counted and photographed 161 individuals, comprising 46 adult males, 61 adult females, 30 male children and 24 female children (Nigam, 1960). The sex ratio among the adults was 75.4 males for every 100 females, whereas the sex ratio among the children was 125 males for every 100 females. There were 45 families, all belongings to the nuclear type, which consists of the father, the mother and their unmarried children, yielding a total of 138 individuals. The remaining 23 individuals did not belong to any regular family. They were old unattached widows, grown-up unmarried persons and widows' children. About one-third of the married couples were found to the childless. Careful enquiries revealed that in addition to the 161 individuals, already seen and photographed, there were very few Onge, possibly not more than a dozen, with whom we had not come in contact. From this it can safely be concluded that in 1956 the total Onge population was not more than 180.

Male predominance among the children, small size of the average family (3.07) and high percentage of sterility indicate that the population is in decline. Onge men and women are very fond of children, but the birth of a child occurs infrequently and many of the children born die young.

The Andamanese languages, including that of the Onge, show no demonstrable affinities with any known linguistic family of the world. The Onge language has closer affinities with the Jarawa language, both in respect of lexicon and morphology, than with the other languages of Great Andaman.

In this connection it may be pointed out that the change in Onge vocabulary that has been going on over a period of time, is ascribable to a certain extent to a peculiar custom found on the island. When an Onge dies, his or her name is tabooed for an indefinitely long period, for it is believed the utterance of the name will displease the spirit of the deceased and have harmful effects on the living. As most of the personal names of the Onge are ordinary words in daily use, new expressions have to be constantly coined to take the place of the tabooed words and, thus, the vocabulary changes considerably over the course of a few generations.

SOCIAL ORGANIZATION

(a) *Territorial arrangement*: In the olden days there were two divisions among the Onge, *embelakwe* or coast dwellers, and *engeakwe* or forest-dwellers. The coast dwellers were more expert than the forest dwellers in seafaring, canoe-making and in hunting turtle and dugong. They visited the nearby island frequently in outrigger canoes for fishing and collecting turtles' eggs. The forest dwellers, on the other hand, were more skilful hunters and better acquainted with the interiors of the island. They never travelled by sea and used canoes only occasionally for crossing the creeks. Recently, owing to great decrease in their members, the two divisions have merged together.

The whole of Little Andaman island can be divided into a number of territories. Each territory is owned by a local group consisting of 10 to 15 families. It serves as the hunting and collecting ground of the local group and has one or two communal huts and several recognized camping places within its boundaries. The boundaries, however, are not clearly demarcated.

The different local groups usually live in peace. The people of one group are not only allowed, but actually welcome to enter their neighbours' areas for some days and hunt, fish and collect food. But when two local groups are not in good terms, the intrusion of one group into another's land is much resented and may lead to skirmishes and even murder.

When two Onge meet each other after a long interval, the person who is older sits on the ground and the younger person sits on his or her lap. They then embrace each other and remain silent for a few minutes. At the time of such greeting, they are often found weeping, with tears rolling down their cheeks. When a number of persons arrive together, they embrace their hosts, one after another.

The membership of a local group is acquired by birth, adoption or marriage. The women usually come to reside with their husbands' local groups after marriage. We did not find any case of expulsion from a local group for bad conduct. A local group is independent and autonomous. Its members have exclusive rights over a certain area for hunting, fishing and collecting fruits and tubers. A great deal of cooperation exists among the individuals of a local group and they participate jointly in various activities, such as construction and repair of communal huts, canoe-making, dancing, feasting, etc.

Chieftainship is unknown among the Onge. The natives do not recognize anybody as headman or chief having the authority to give them orders. In each local group, however, there are several senior persons who are respected and obeyed, not because of any authority wielded by them, but because of their age, experience, wisdom and personal qualities.

A local group as such has no name. Its members are recognized by the name of the communal hut situated within its territory. The hut is the headquarters of the group and each family has a sleeping place in it. Owing to the great reduction in numbers, the survivors of two local groups have sometimes merged to form a single group with a larger hunting and collecting area. In such cases, there may be more than one communal hut in the possession of single group.

Communal huts are inhabited mostly by the people during the rainy season. At other times the aborigines wander in their own territories in search of food and seldom stay at one place for more than a fortnight. Each local group has a number of recognized camping grounds in the vicinity of which fresh water is readily available. Temporary shelters are constructed at these places for living for a few days only.

There is no political framework which unites all the local groups. But they speak a common language and, from a cultural point of view, constitute a tribe.

(b) *Family*: A local group consists of some ten or fifteen families and some unmarried and widowed individuals. The families are elementary, consisting of a father, a mother and their children. When a widowed person remarries, the children of the previous marriage, if any, are included in the new family. The children of others, particularly orphans, are occasionally adopted. The children, however, do not stay with their parents or depend upon them for food supply for many years. Young boys of only ten or twelve have separate sleeping places in the communal hut. When hunting in the jungle, the boys construct for themselves separate lean-to sheds in the hunting camps. They start hunting, fishing and collecting food for subsistence even before reaching puberty. Little girls accompany their mothers to the jungle for collecting tubers and fruits. They also go to the streams and creeks for catching prawns and fishing by small hand-nets. The girls enter into matrimony after the appearance of the menses and developing of breasts.

The Onge are strictly monogamous and a great deal of harmony exists between the husband and wife. Marriage is dissoluble at the beginning but it becomes stable after the birth of a child. We did not find any case of divorce taking place after the birth of a child. Each family has a sleeping platform in the communal hut where the husband, wife, children and even their dogs sleep. There is very little privacy or shyness in sexual matters. At night the sexual play and coitus of a couple can easily be observed by other inmates of the hut in the light of the fire which is always burning.

Disagreements or quarreling between the husband and wife are rare phenomena. Both are jointly responsible for household management and collection of food. The wife collects the bulk of the vegetable food. The husband hunts pig, turtle and dugong with bow and arrow and collects honey and fruits by climbing trees. The parents are very affectionate towards the children and treat them with extreme tolerance.

THE FOOD QUEST

The Onge do not know agriculture. Their subsistence activities are limited to food gathering, hunting, and fishing.

The main division of labour is based on sex. Hunting, fishing by bow and arrow, honey collecting and plucking fruits from tall trees are done by men. The women, in addition to their domestic duties, collect edible roots and stems, fruits, crabs, prawns, larvae of insects, shells, etc., and also fish with the help of small hand-nets.

Usually the people get up early in the morning and go to the jungle for easing themselves. They use leaves for cleaning themselves. Then, after having breakfast, which usually consists of boiled tubers and pork, they get ready with their weapons and implements to go out in search of food.

(a) *Food-gathering*: Vegetable foods are collected mostly by women. Several women go out together for the digging of yams and tubers. Children are sometimes left behind in the custody of the elderly staying in the camp. Young babies are carried on their mother's back when they go only a short distance. Women usually carry some food with them for eating in the jungle, baskets for keeping the collected materials, and long iron rods to be used as digging sticks. They also carry with them smouldering pieces of wood for making a fire, if necessary. As the Onge do not know how to make a fire they always take burning wood or resin with them, particularly when moving from one camp to another. *Chendalu*, *gigi*, and *toredalu* are the three most important varieties of tubers. These are available in large quantities during the northeast monsoon period. Women recognize the plants from their leaves and start to dig up the soil with an iron rod or digging stick. The soil is loosened and removed, exposing a part of the tuber. The distal and bigger part of the tuber is cut and put into the basket. The remainder with the attached stem and leaves is left in the ground so that it may grow again (Cipriani, 1953).

Among the other vegetable foods, mention may be made of *titekala* and *tamboala* stems which become soft and edible when boiled or roasted over fire. There are also more than a dozen varieties of edible fruits growing in the jungle. The most important of them is the monkey jackfruit, called *bulundange* in Onge language. These are available in large quantities during the months of May and June. Collection of *bulundange* fruits from tall trees is usually done by the men. Women sometimes pluck *bulundange* and other fruits from lofty branches with the aid of a very long hooked pole (*chale*). The seeds of *bulundange* are highly relished by the Onge. It may be mentioned that within the territory occupied by a local group, the rights of particular families over specific *bulundange* trees are recognized. Indiscriminate collection of fruits from other trees may lead to serious trouble. The wild variety of pandanus that grows in Little Andaman is of inferior quality and is seldom eaten by the Onge.

Several hundreds of coconut seedlings were planted near Dugong Creek on the east coast of the island by the Anthropological Survey parties during 1952-4. The trees have now grown and started bearing fruits. Some of the trees have unfortunately been damaged by rats and insects. The milk and kernel of coconut are relished a lot by the Onge. Near the communal huts on the east coast some plantain and papaya trees were also planted by the Survey parties, the fruits of which are enjoyed by the Onge. A few plants yielding small, red, very pungent chillies were found growing around some huts. The Onge, however, do not like the taste of chillis, nor do they take salt.

Besides collection of vegetable food women also collect edible shells from the reefs. Many kinds of shells are available in the creeks and in the sea around Little Andaman. Among these the Cyrena and Arca varieties are most popular. The women also catch several types of crabs which are edible. When a crabhole is found, a long stick is inserted into it. Water crabs are collected using handnets. Among the crabs the large *tekandeue* variety is considered the most delicious.

(b) *Honey collection*: Collection of honey is exclusively a man's job. There are two varieties of bees in the island. *Nareleve* is a stingless, black and small variety of bee, producing honey which is dark in colour. The hive of this bee is built in the hollow of a tree trunk having a small opening for entrance. The cavity of the tree is required to be opened for taking out honeycomb. As the bees are stingless, no protection is needed for such honey. *Leguki* is the other variety of bees (*Apis mellifica*) which is large and yellowish in colour and possesses a venomous sting. The honey produced by this type of bee is golden-yellow in colour and superior in quality. They build large combs on high trees. Honey of this variety is available in abundant quantities in Little Andaman in the months of February and March. For protecting themselves from stinging bees, the Onge use the leaves of *tonyoge* plant which have very effective bee-repellent properties. Before going up the tree a man puts some *tonyoge* leaves in his mouth and chews them into pulp. Then he takes out the chewed leaves from his mouth, squeezes out the juice and apply the paste all over his body including the head and face. He chews some more leaves and keeps the pulp in the mouth. When climbing the tree he carries a bucket on his back and a knife attached to his waist-band. After reaching the beehive he drives away the bees from the comb by spitting out the chewed *tonyoge* leaves, cuts the comb with the knife, places it in the bucket and climbs down. Many a time, we observed that while collecting honey the Onge got bitten by bees. The people do not seem to be much bothered by it. The right of an individual to collect honeycomb from a particular tree is clearly recognized.

(c) *Pig hunting*: Pig hunting is the most important of all subsistence activities in which Onge men are engaged. Pork is the major item of the meat eaten by the Onge. Little Andaman pigs (*Sus andamanensis*) grow fat and become available in adequate numbers during the rainy season. In the dry season they become lean and their meat is not so tasty. Men usually set out for hunting pigs early in the morning. Several men go together with a number of hunting dogs. They take with them bows and arrows or spears to be used as hunting weapons and also some food, several empty baskets for carrying the pork when returning, and smouldering pieces of wood. Some men, who are expert pig hunters, often go alone.

The hunting dogs are carefully chosen; sickly and wounded dogs are eliminated. Cane strips are tied round the necks of the dogs. The unwilling dogs are dragged behind by their masters. It should be stated here that the dog is a recent introduction in Little Andaman. Previously, the Onge had no dogs and as such pig hunting was much more difficult. The Onge are now extremely fond of dogs and never beat them even if they prove to be a nuisance.

As soon as the hunters reach the area, which is frequented by wild pigs, the dogs are set free. The dogs spread over a wide area and smell the presence of pigs, if any, in the vicinity. Following the scent they soon find out the pig and encircle it. The hunters follow the dogs. If the game is a small one, the dogs themselves are able to dispatch it, but if it is a large boar with sharp projecting tusks, the dogs are afraid to charge at him directly. In that case the hunter shoots an arrow as soon as the game comes within his range and climbs a tree very quickly to avoid the attack of the wounded boar. If the hunter fails to get out of the way in time he may be injured seriously by the boar. Such mishaps happen occasionally during pig hunting. The dogs are frequently wounded by the pigs.

Spears can be used for hunting only from close quarters. When a pig, being chased by dogs, takes shelter between the buttresses of a large tree, the hunter goes close to the tree from behind and leaning forward across the buttress, pierces the pig with the spear.

The Onge do not usually eat monitor lizard (*Varanus*), frog, rat and birds. They, however, accepted cooked pigeons from us on certain occasions. There is no deer in Little Andaman, but large herds of deer are found in the North and South Cinque Islands. These islands are frequently visited by the coastal Onge, but they never hunt deer, nor take its meat even if offered by others.

(d) *Turtle and dugong hunting*: The coastal Onge have great skill in using the harpoon for capturing turtles and dugongs. Turtle hunting is done mostly on moonlit nights. Two or three persons set out in an outrigger canoe when the sea is calm and the moon shines brightly. The canoe is at first poled by the harpoon as long as the ground can be touched with it. On reaching deeper water the men start paddling. Now the man sitting at the stern end steers the canoe towards the direction of the shore again. The canoe moves silently along with the waves. Paddles are used minimally to avoid noise. When a turtle is sighted by the man standing at the bow end with the harpoon, the canoe is taken near it very cautiously and the hunter jumps down piercing the turtle with the harpoon with all his body weight behind it. The iron head of the harpoon gets stuck in the hard carapace of the turtle. The turtle dives down but is again pulled up by drawing the three-ply cord attached to the harpoon head. When hauled up in the canoe, the turtle does not offer much resistance. The man in the water returns to the canoe after collecting the detached pole of the harpoon. The method of catching dugong and large fish by harpoon is essentially the same.

Turtles are available in large numbers in the sea around South Brother Island which is situated several miles towards northeast from Little Andaman. The island is frequently visited by the coastal Onge during the dry season for harpooning turtles and collecting turtle eggs. Female turtles dig up holes on the shore of the island and lay eggs there, numbering more than a hundred at a time. The eggs are covered by sand for protecting them from predators. The Onge can trace the hidden eggs moving along by following the trail on the sand left by the turtle in its wake. The place is dug up with long wooden stick (*ketele*) and the eggs are collected.

(e) *Fishing*: There are many varieties of fish in the sea around Little Andaman. Next to pork and yam, sea fish is the most important item of food for the coastal people. Some varieties of fish are, however, excluded by the Onge from their menu. They are also not accustomed to eating shark, sting-ray (*Urolophus*) and eel. Men usually catch fish with bow and specially made fishing arrows. Women use hand-nets. Men also use hand-nets for catching sardines and other varieties of small fish.

An Onge generally goes out alone for fishing with a bow and a number of arrows. He also carries on his back a basket for keeping the fish. During low tide he moves up and down in search of fish along the shore and in the shallow water among the reefs. It is extremely difficult to find the fish swimming under the rolling waves and more difficult to transfix them. But the Onge's vision is so sharp and they are so skillful with the bow and arrow that a fish, once detected, can seldom escape. The fish is shot at as soon as it comes within the range. If vitally injured and unable to move, it floats to the surface. The man plunges into the sea, returns to the shore with the fish and takes out the arrow from its body. If the fish is still alive, he breaks its head with a stone and puts it into the basket. If the fish is not very badly injured, it may dive down into the sea. The Onge follows the fish till it is completely exhausted and then catches it. If the fish, hit with an arrow, escapes, the Onge regrets the loss of the arrow more than the loss of the fish because the making of a barbed arrow-head is difficult and time-consuming. The Onge also catch river fish by shooting arrows from the bank.

Women catch small fish and prawn in the streams and creeks with the aid of hand-nets. Sometimes a woman holds two nets by the cane-frame, one in each hand, and draws them together to entrap the fish between them. A fish may also be hit by a *dah* (chopper), a long and heavy Indian knife, and captured. The Onge have recently learnt from visitors to their island the use of line and barbed iron hook for fishing. They can make strong lines for themselves from vegetable fibres. Fishing hooks are in great demand in Little Andaman. Whenever a party arrives at Little Andaman from Port Blair or elsewhere, the Onge try to obtain hooks from them.

The vegetable food and the fish and prawn obtained by a woman are her private property and are consumed by the members of her family. Similarly the fish and fruits collected by a man belong to his family. But when a man hunts a large pig, turtle, dugong or big fish, or cuts down a large honeycomb, the food is shared by all inmates of the camp. After keeping aside sufficient food for his family, he distributes the rest among others. As a result of this custom, the hunters who return empty handed in the evening without being able to secure any game do not have to starve. In difficult days when food is scarce, if only one hunter succeeds in hunting a large boar, everybody else in the camp, including the dogs, are assured of some food. On occasions, however, the Onge have to go without any food for a day or two in spite of all their cooperative efforts.

CONTACT WITH OUTSIDERS AND ITS EFFECTS

It has already been mentioned that the Onge were hostile to all strangers prior to 1885-6. The Onge did not, however, confine themselves to Little Andaman, and moved northward upto Rutland Island in search of food and. A section of the Onge lived in Rutland. There is a series of Onge hunting camps, spread in a chain along the shore between Little Andaman and South Andaman. After entering into friendly relationships with the settlers, mainly through the efforts of Portman, the Onge began to pay visits from time to time to South Andaman and, particularly, to Port Blair. At present they come to Port Blair every year in the month of October during the lull period following southwest monsoon when the sea remains calm. They have to cross a distance of about 70 miles over the sea in their frail canoes. The main purpose of their visit is to obtain pieces of iron with which to make weapons and implements, strips of cloth, tobacco, tea, etc. They usually arrive first at Maymyo-Ghat on the west coast of South Andaman and keep their canoes and weapons hidden in the jungle near the coast. The Burmese settlers living at Maymyo and Wandur are very friendly with the Onge visitors and give them shelter. Prior to the visits of Anthropological Survey of India parties, Onge women very seldom visited South Andaman. But nowadays they occasionally come up to Port Blair. A party usually consists of 8 or 10 adult males and several grown up boys. From Maymyo they come to Port Blair covering a distance of about 20 miles on foot. The Onge bring various kinds of seashells, bottles of honey and shells of turtle with them for barter.

Of all things, dried leaves of tobacco are most eagerly appreciated by the Onge. The tobacco that an Onge obtains from the settlers, either as gift or in exchange of honey and shells, are carefully packed in small tins and taken back to Little Andaman. For keeping the tin hidden, his wife digs up a small hole in the floor of the communal hut and buries it there. Only a small quantity of the stored tobacco is taken out at a time for consumption and kept in a netted bag. The *chela* (dactyl part of Chila of Chiliped) of a large crab is used as the smoking pipe. The tobacco collected by a person is his individual property but the pipe, when filled and lighted, is passed on from one person to another, including the boys and girls, and enjoyed by all of them.

Tea is prepared and consumed collectively. In a large metal vessel a certain quantity of tea leaves are boiled in several gallons of water for about half an hour. Then one bucketful of cold water is fetched from a well or stream and poured into the vessel to make the decoction cool. This is stored in large bamboo vessels by each family. It is poured into nautilus shells from time to time and drunk till satisfaction. Milk and sugar are not added.

Some shell poachers, who visit Little Andaman at times and want to employ the coastal Onge as divers for collecting valuable shells, have tried to introduce opium and alcohol among the aborigines which are more injurious to health than tobacco and tea.

As a result of their prolonged contact with outsiders, the Onge have come to appreciate a number of foreign articles, such as rice, sugar, safety matches, aluminum utensils, mirrors, implements of iron, etc. Owing to the introduction of metal vessels, the art of pottery making has got lost. Though unable to count beyond three, they have come to recognize the use of money. Some Onge have been found asking for small coins from the passers-by in the streets of Port Blair for purchasing tobacco leaves and other articles from the shops of the town. Our observations fully confirm Datta Majumder's (1957) comments on the Onge culture in transition which are as follow:

> ... the Onge are in a process of transition from a pre-lithic age to the iron age, and from a pre-barter economy to a barter-cum-money economy. In other words,

the hunting- and food-gathering Onge culture, which had been an autonomous cultural system in the past, is now breaking down, and becoming a part of a wider and more complex civilization represented by the culture of the mainland of India.

Note: This has been summarized from the original unpublished report written by the authors based on field studies during 1953-7.

ANNEXURE II

Economy of the Onge of Little Andaman

SARADINDU BOSE

(*Received on 21 July 1964*)

Introduction

LITTLE Andaman is the southernmost island among the Andaman Islands in the Bay of Bengal. Situated between 10°25′N and 10°55′N and between 92°20′E and 92°40′E, the island is roughly 24 miles long and 16 miles wide.

Climate is controlled by its position in the sea and nearness to the equator. Equatorial as well as maritime types of climate prevail in this region. Temperature is almost uniform throughout the year and varies only from 72°F to 96°F. The difference is also less near the coast than in the interior. There is no remarkable change of season. Yet a little difference of rainfall and temperature can be noted during the months of January, February and March, which may be considered as the dry season with lower temperature. The climate of the island is not healthy and rainfall, of both monsoonal and equatorial type (convectional), prevails over the region during the nine months from April to December. April-May is the season for cyclonic weather and near Duncan Passage, which is a few miles north of the island, the weather becomes furious during these months over the sea and islands. The total annual rainfall in the neighbouring islands is said to be 150 in.

The island is almost flat and only towards the southwestern corner a contour line rises to 400 ft. It appears that from this 400 ft. hilly region the altitude of the land decreases gradually towards the north until it reaches the sea. Comparatively, the slope towards the opposite side of the hill, that is the southern side, is steep. The coast line is very irregular. Due to the tides, the net area of the island varies, and during high tide, water from the sea penetrates the interior of the island through creeks, creating thereby marshes and swamps. Mangroves are the typical natural vegetation in this swampy region.

The interior of the island has a luxuriant growth of tall hardwood forest often covered by tremendous climbers. The density of vegetation is sometimes so high that it is very difficult to penetrate the forest without cutting trees and climbers.

Occupation

The Onge depend on a primitive type of production, namely, hunting, fishing and collecting. There is absolutely no production of food by cultivation. Little Andaman has enough wild animals and birds, and the sea-coast also has a good stock of edible fish, crabs, bivalve shells, turtles, etc. The Onge prefer to hunt pigs on the ground by means of spears or shoot fishes in the shallow waters by means of bow and arrows. They do not generally shoot birds for fear of losing their arrows in the thicket.

There is a division of labour among men and women in hunting and collecting. For example, items which require hard labour are in charge of men only, like the hunting of pigs, turtles, collection of honey, etc. On the contrary, women collect wild roots and tubers and small fishes only from the creeks and streams. But fishing in the sea is the work of men only. Little Andaman has a rich stock of wild pigs. Onges always keep with them a number of dogs for hunting. The dogs are not allowed to eat much as it is believed that overeating makes them too lazy for hunting. As these dogs are always hungry, they are very keen to find out any pig in the deep forest, and when one is available all the dogs surround the animal from different directions. It happens sometimes that a big wild boar with long tusks charges so violently that the hunter loses his dog. That is why immediately after the dogs spot game, the hunter tries to kill the animal either with bow and arrow or with a spear.

Generally small pigs are not killed as their meat is not considered tasty. They have too little fat on them.

It seems from this that Litte Andaman has plenty of pigs to feed the Onge, otherwise they would not have released small pigs. An interesting habit is that a day after a good collection, the community takes rest, and even if anybody goes for hunting he always avoids bad collection.

Fishing is practised both by women and men, previously by a bow and arrow and now, besides bow and arrow, with net and fishing line and hook. But women do not use bow and arrow and do not go out to fish in the open sea. They always prefer to catch in the creeks and streams with the help of nets. Men are now accustomed to using even nylon lines presented by the Government for fishing in the open sea.

Turtle hunting is also an adventure, and in time of emergency they proceed up to South Brother Island for turtles. It is said that due to the absence of pigs in that island, turtles lay their eggs safely and the Onge are occasionally able to collect huge quantities of turtle eggs. For turtle hunting, they use harpoon and rope from their boats. A turtle sometimes weighs 80 pounds. Crabs and bivalve shells are also collected. The crab of Little Andaman has some reputation for size and taste. It is sometimes more than 4 pounds. These crabs are found under rocks or shelters in shallow water and it is only possible for the Onge to find out crabs from these hidden places.

Though proportionately less important, yet besides hunting and fishing, the Onge also collect wild roots, tubers, fruits, honey, etc. But these are seasonal in supply. Moreover if meat is available they are not interested in collection.

Among their collections the Onge are very fond of honey. Collection of honey starts from the middle of January and continues up to the end of March or middle of April. Before collecting honey the Onge manufacture wooden buckets from logs for collecting and storing. It requires craftsmanship to manufacture these fine thin buckets purely carved out of wooden logs. Before climbing a tree for collection, they smear their body with the juice of a leaf called *tongee* for protection against the sting of bees. Collection of other items like jack fruit, wild roots and tubers, nuts and fruits is specially the work of women. It starts from the month of January and the peak season is the rainy season when hunting is difficult. It is customary for women to go collecting in a group. Otherwise a woman is generally accompanied by her husband during travel.

Hunting is collective. A hunter is responsible only up to bringing the kill to the settlement, and after that the meat is cut into lumps and boiled by other persons. There is no particular system of distribution of meat. Everybody is free to take according to his choice and there is no quarrel over shares. This also indicates that there is enough for everybody.

As wild roots and tubers are collected by groups of women, these are sometimes treated as personal collection. Yet there is a custom that if anybody takes any food from a hut, the owner may never object.

Food from any item, either meat or root-crop, is prepared either by boiling, which is now popular, or by roasting. Only some fruits and honey are consumed raw. So far they have learnt only boiling for cooking of food, otherwise no spices, not even salt is added to the Onge diet.

There is no specific time for eating; nor is there any average rate of consumption of food. It depends on the supply. When a hunter supplies the village with a number of pigs or food the Onge observe no limit to eating. They have a good, probably exceptional capacity of digesting meat; and it has been observed that even a young man can digest 6 pounds of meat or other food withi a day. So also just after this type of overeating Onges do not go out next day for hunting and it is generally presumed that unless and until they are hungery they would not move. The Onge do not generally store any food for the future. It is done only when they migrate from place to place for a short term. On such occasions smoked pork or honey is preferred.

On the contrary, they have also the capacity of going without food for even a couple of days. It happens sometimes, though on rare occasions, that they come back without any collection and then the general practice is to go hungry without complaint.

Though on an average they consume a good amount and quality of food yet the consumption and supply is very irregular. This can be clearly seen in the graph.

Consumption

So far it was known that the Onge are dependent on hunting, fishing and collecting. We also knew about the items of their collection, method of preparation of food, system of distribution, etc. But we had no knowledge about the rate of collection, rate of consumption, systematic and serial importance of each item of food in their daily diet and so on. In order to gain a quantitative estimate, we tried to keep a day-to-day record of all collections of food by weighing the items in a machine. The weights of each edible food collected were measured separately for a continuous period of 30 days, from 17 December 1963 to 15 January 1964, at Tokebuea and a chart is attached herewith for explaining the rate of daily collection of food. We have also given in the same graph, the fluctuating size of the population. A relationship can be established between the quantity and nature of food and the population size.

It appears that according to demand they try their best to collect meat food, as we see that within the first 15 days pigs were in good number. Similarly collection of root-crops during this time was not necessary as the population in the settlement was not so high. But as the demand for food increased with the increasing size of the population, they went in for more hunting. If there were not enough game, as in the first half, they tried to collect more roots and tubers. The curve for both protein and carbohydrate has less variation in the second part than in the first part of the month. This is due to the continuous demand of food for the increased population. But in the first part the population was less and supply of food was irregular.

As already stated, collection of food by the Onge is very irregular. From the table it appears that collection of food per day per capita varies from 8.73 pounds to nil. So also there is no uniformity in the consumption of food. It depends on the supply. An Onge can fast for 2-3 days continuously, and on the contrary can consume 6-7 pounds of meat within a day. There is no fixed time for their diet in the day. But generally a hunter comes to camp with game in the afternoon or evening. Pigs' meat is boiled throughout the night. Some portion of it is consumed in the night, and from early morning they start eating irregularly until the stock is exhausted. They do not like to keep food in storage. Only fat is kept sometimes separately and is considered to be a delicacy.

The amount of collection of food is not merely controlled by the stock of the surrounding region but also to some extent by the population. Though they migrate from place to place in search of food, yet Little Andaman has enough stock of food for this limited population of the Onge.

It was observed on several occasions that the Onge generally roam in the jungle or near the beach or near the creeks in searoh of food within a limited regon. But there is no territorial division as such between the Onges of each region. Every Onge is free to hunt animals in the any part of Little Andaman. But they generally roam within a radius of 4-5 miles of their settlement. And when they feel that the region is unable to supply food, they migrate to other regions. The people who lived near Dugong Creek in 1955-56 are still there, as proved by the names and photographs collected by previous workers of the A.S.I. Similarly those who stay near Nachuge or Tulah in the south, never settle in the northern part. But they occasionally come to Dugong Creek with the coming of a motor boat in expectation of presents.

On an average an adult consumes 2.34 pounds of raw food as evidenced by the measurements taken during December and January. But within this total food of 2.34 pounds, protein diet, which is a combination of pigs' meat, fish, turtle, eggs, crabs and bivalves, constitute 1.78 pounds. Carbohydrate food, which is a combination of all root-crops and tubers, forms 0.53 pounds and other food-stuff, a combination of

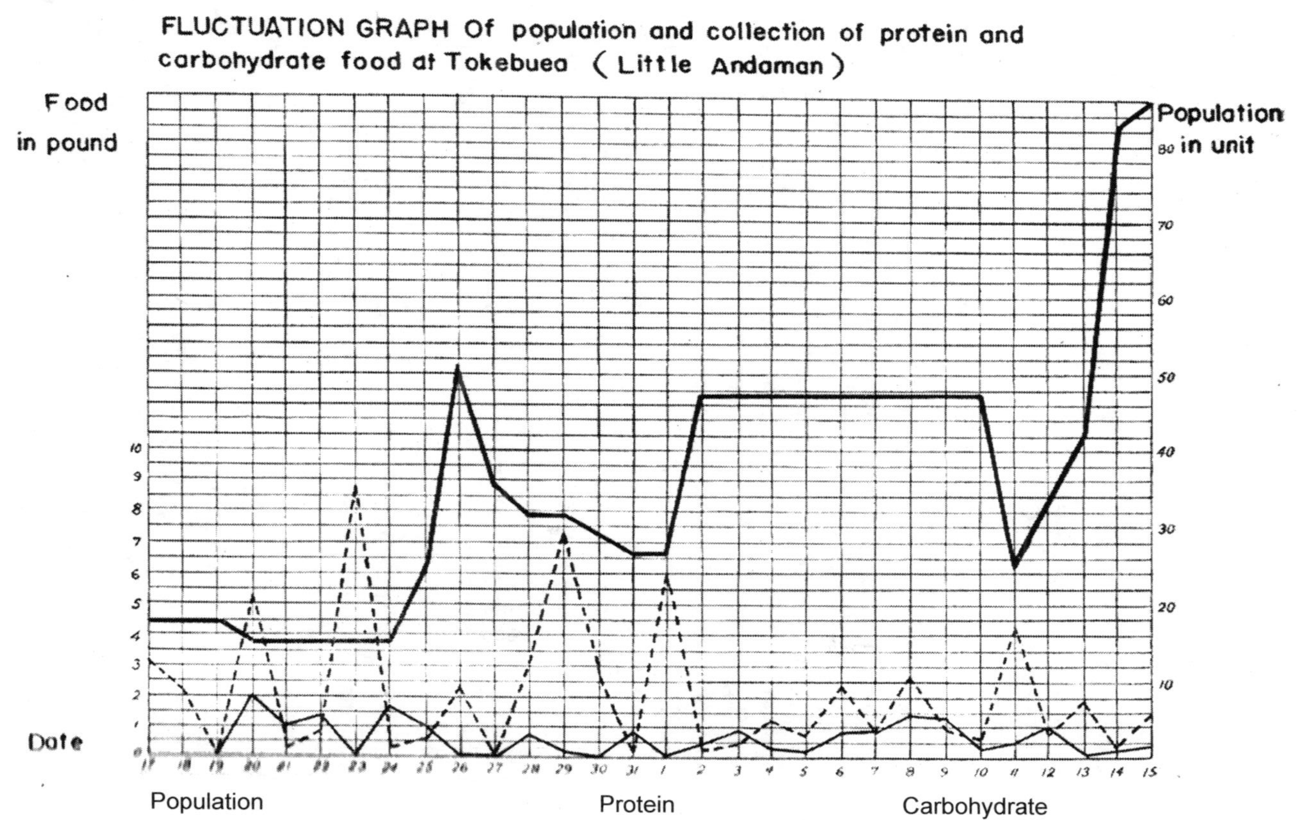
FLUCTUATION GRAPH Of population and collection of protein and carbohydrate food at Tokebuea (Little Andaman)
Food in pound
Population in unit
Date
0 1 2 3 4 5 6 7 8 9 10
10 20 30 40 50 60 70 80
17 18 19 20 21 22 23 24 25 26 27 28 29 30 31 1 2 3 4 5 6 7 8 9 10 11 12 13 14 15
Population
Protein
Carbohydrate

fruits and honey, forms only 0.03 pound per adult per day. Though this 0.03 pound is negligible in comparison with protein and carbohydrate yet it has some special food value which cannot be neglected.

If we take the average of one month's collection of food in percentage for each unit then the figure is as follows :

Protein	76
Carbohydrate	22.6
Others	1.4
Total :	100

The total area of Little Andaman is roughly 270 sq. miles. Within this region there are at present 24 communal huts or settlements (9 jungle huts and 15 coastal huts). The population of this island is not correctly known. Dr. Cipriani in 1953-54 estimated the population of the island, counting family beds in communal huts, as 569. According to the 1951 census the population was only 150, and again in the 1961 census the figure decreased to 129. During our observation in 1963-64 we have counted up to 132 persons and photographed them individually. We have the impression that there are also a few persons whom we were not able to count. However, even if the population is roughly about 150. the density of population is only 0.56 persons per sq. mile, or roughly one person has got within his command an area of 1.8 sq. miles.

If we convert the population into units of adults then more area may be allotted for each person or density may be less. But if we want to know how far the Onge are dependent on this land or what is the relation between land and man so far as their economy is concerned, then certain other factors must be taken into consideration.

The Onge in the forest region are completely dependent on their surrounding land. Density in this remote region is less than the density in the coastal region. In other words, the Onge of the jungle area use more land for hunting and collecting than coast dwellers.

On the contrary the majority of the people live near the coast where the density of population is naturally high. They have no facility of exploring land in all directions as the sea forms a barrier. Side by side, it is also to be noted that the water region, that is either sea or creek, supplies about 25% of their food.

So it may be said that the land, which can support a man within the forest region for 9 months, is sufficient for him for a complete year in the coastal region for the sea is also there.

Conclusion

Till now we have not been able to form a correct idea about the carrying capacity of this region under this type of primitive occupation. We do not know the optimum capacity of food gathered either from forest or from the sea. We have observed that besides the collection of food by the Onge, other seasonal settlers, like labours of the Coconut Development Department of Andaman Islands, also collect food from this region by hunting pigs and collection of honey, etc., and the figure is not negligible. It shows that the region surrounding Tokebuea can supply more food than the requirement of the local people.

In order to find out the optimum capacity of feeding people in this region by the existing means of production we should collect data on the same lines from all the regions of Little Andaman for more days than already noted. As there is no traditional boundary among each group of Onges, at least so far as hunting is concerned, a survey of the whole island will be effective in finding out the carrying capacity of land under the present type of occupation.

Daily food of the Onge at Tokebuea

(weight in pounds)

Date	Protein					Carbohydrate			Others		Total population	Unit of population	Collection of protein per unit per day	Collection of carbohydrate per unit per day	Collection of other food per unit per day
	Pig	Turtle	Fish	Bivalve shells	Crab	Titakala	Gege	Titakoru	Honey	Fruits					
17. 12. 63	57	×	×	×	×	×	×	×	×	×	19	18	3.17	×	×
18. 12. 63	40	×	×	×	×	×	×	×	×	×	19	18	2.22	×	×
19. 12. 63	×	×	×	×	×	×	×	×	×	×	19	18	×	×	×
20. 12. 63	75	×	5	×	×	30	×	×	×	×	16	15	5.33	2.00	×
21. 12. 63	×	×	6	×	×	15	×	×	×	×	16	15	.4	1.00	×
22. 12. 63	×	×	8	×	4	20	×	×	×	×	16	15	.8	1.33	×
23. 12. 63	115	×	16	×	×	×	×	×	×	×	16	15	8.73	×	×
24. 12. 63	×	×	×	×	5	15	10	×	×	×	16	15	.33	1.66	×
25. 12. 63	×	×	10	×	5	30	×	×	×	×	28	25	.6	1.2	×
26. 12. 63	×	×	120	×	×	×	×	×	×	×	60	51	2.35	×	×
27. 12. 63	×	×	×	×	×	×	×	×	×	×	41	35½	×	×	×
28. 12. 63	85	×	10	×	3	25	×	×	×	×	37	31½	3.1	.78	×
29. 12. 63	160	×	66	×	2	×	1	6	×	×	37	31½	7.23	.22	×
30. 12. 63	80	×	5	×	×	×	×	×	×	×	35	29½	2.8	×	×
31. 12. 63	×	×	5	×	×	15	5	×	×	×	32	26½	.18	.75	×

Daily food of the Onge at Tokebuea

(weight in pounds)

Date	Protein					Carbohydrate			Others		Total population	Unit of population	Collectoin of protein per unit per day	Collection of carbohydrate per unit per day	Collection of other food per unit per day
	Pig	Turtle	Fish	Bivalve shells	Crab	Titakala	Gege	Titakoru	Honey	Fruits					
1. 1. 64	120	×	40	×	×	×	×	×	×	×	32	26½	6.0	×	×
2. 1. 64	×	×	10	×	4	×	15	5	×	×	56	47½	.29	·42	×
3. 1. 64	10	×	4	×	5	30	5	5	×	×	56	47½	.40	·84	×
4. 1. 64	×	×	46	3	7	10	×	5	×	×	56	47½	1.17	·31	×
5. 1. 64	30	×	4	×	×	×	×	10	1	×	56	47½	.71	·21	.02
6. 1. 64	64	×	30	15	5	4	26	6	1	¼	56	47½	2.4	·75	.02
7. 1. 64	16	×	26	4	1	×	34	4	1	×	56	47½	.98	·8	.02
8. 1. 64	85	×	55	3	×	56	7	×	½	1/10	56	47½	2.58	1·32	.01
9. 1. 64	30	×	10	×	×	36	24	×	×	×	56	47½	.84	1·26	×
10. 1. 64	30	×	3	×	×	14	6	×	1¼	1	56	47½	.69	·42	.04
11. 1. 64	104	×	4	×	×	×	12	×	2	×	26	25	4.32	·48	.08
12. 1. 64	20	×	1	4	×	16	12	1	10	×	41	32½	.76	·89	.3
13. 1. 64	70	×	4	1	6	4	×	×	12	×	46	42	1.92	·09	.28
14. 1. 64	20	10	6	½	×	1	10	6	×	×	98	82½	.44	·2	×
15. 1. 64	60	66	×	×	1	5	20	10	5	×	102	86	1.4	·4	.05

Total consuming units for 30 days=1081.5

Collection of food for 30 days (in pounds)

Pig	—	1271	Protein — 1919.5 or 76%
Fish	—	494	
Turtle	—	76	
Crab	—	48	
Bivalve shell	—	30.5	
Titakala	—	326	Carbohydrate — 571 or 22.6%
Gege	—	187	
Titakoru	—	58	
Others	—	35.1 or 1.4%	

Total : 1919.5 + 571 + 35.1 = 2525.6

Average consumption rate for protein per unit per day	— 1.78
,, ,, ,, carbohydrate ,, ,,	— .03
,, ,, ,, others ,, ,,	— 0.03
Average consumption rate of food per unit per day	— 2.34

Relation of land and sea in supplying food

Production from land :

Pig	—	1271	1877.1
Titakala	—	326	
Gege	—	187	
Tetakoru	—	58	
Others	—	35.1	

Production from water :

Fish	—	494	648.5
Turtle	—	76	
Crab	—	48	
Bivalve shell	—	30.5	
			2525.6

Percentage of consumption of food from land and sea is 74.6 and 25.4 respectively.

List of different types of food collected by the Onge during our observation

1. Pig — *Kuea*
2. Turtle — *Narelange*
3. Turtle egg — *Toikala*
4. Bivalve shell — *Totule* (edible) or *Tojala* or *Todadalu* (ci pi)
5. Crab — *Kotole* (of sea) and *Tekande* (of creek)

6. Fish — (a) *Toichu* (from creek)
    (b) *Tekocho* („)
    (c) *Ukechenge* (carnayx or popularly Kukari)
    (d) *Okala* (Bhetki type)
    (e) *Tiuga* (spotted Bhetki)
    (f) *Timondalu* (Tarini)
    (g) *Owgage*
    (h) *Koral* (Bhetki) and others
7. Pigs fat — *Giri*
8. Edible plant — *Titakala* (grass family)
9. Yam or potato — *Gege*
10. Root (thin and long) — *Titakoru*
11. Jack fruit — *Buludange*
12. Root — *Tebogeta*
13. Root — *Ynayna*
14. Root — (small and round) — *Gine*
15. Root — *Tejokoage*
16. Honey — *Lei* (big type of bees)
    Tanja (small bees)
17. Wild nut — *Dambora*
18. Fruit (red 1″ long) — *Chadalu*
19. Fruit — *Naragero*

Bibliography

Adhikari, A.K., *Society and Worldview of the Birhor: A Nomadic Hunting Gathering Tribe of Orissa,* Kolkata: Anthropological Surveyor of India, 2008.

Barnard, Alan (ed.), *Hunter-Gatherers in History, Archaeology and Anthropology*, New York: BERG Oxford, 1993.

Bhattacharya, S.K. et al., *All India Anthropometric Survey: Basic Anthropometric Data: Andaman,* Kolkata: Anthropological Survey of India, 1993.

Binford, Louis, 'Human ancestors: Changing views of their behavior', *Journal of Anthropological Archaeology*, 1986, pp. 235-57, https://en.wikipedia.org/wiki/Onge - cite_ref-14.

Budjeryn, Mariana, 'And Then Came the Tsunami: Disaster Brings Attention and New Challenges to Asia's Indigenous Peoples', *Cultural Survival Quarterly Magazine*. Retrieved on 3 August 2018.

Chawla, S. and T.N. Pandit, *Bibliography of Andaman and Nicabar Islands,* Kolkata: Anthropological Survey of India, 1981.

Dasgupta, D. and S.R. Sharma, *A Handbook of Onge Language,* Kolkata: Anthropological Survey of India, 1982. https://en.wikipedia.org/wiki/Onge-cite_ref-7.

Devi, L. Dilly, 'Sociological Aspects of Food and Nutrition among the Onges of the Little Andaman Island', Ph.D. dissertation, Delhi: University of Delhi, 1987.

Dutta, P.C., *The Great Andamanese: Past and Present,* Kolkata: Anthropological Survey of India, 2004. http://www.censusindia.gov.in/2011census/PCA/SC_ST/PCA-A11_Appendix/ST-35-PCA-A11-APPENDIX.xlsx.

Endicott, M. Phillip et al., 'The Genetic Origins of the Andaman Islanders' (PDF). American Journal of Human Genetics. 72 (1): 178-84. doi: 10.1086/345487. PMC 378623?[* | In-line.WMF Retrieved 21 June 2018. https://en.wikipedia.org/wiki/Onge-cite_ref-Moorjani_23-0.

Justin, A., *Tourism in the Andaman Islands: An Anthropological Perspective*, Kolkata: Anthropological Survey of India, 2012.

Lal, P.N., *Great Nicobar Island,* Kolkata: Anthropological Survey of India, 1977.

——, *Andaman Islands,* Kolkata: Anthropological Survey of India, 1979. https://en.wikipedia.org/wiki/Onge-cite_ref-Ethnologue_19-0.

Lewis, M. Paul, Gary F. Simons and Charles D. Fennig, eds., 2013 *Öñge, Ethnologue: Languages of the World* (17th edn.), Dallas, Texas: SIL International, Archived from the original on 9 March 2016, https://en.wikipedia.org/wiki/Onge-cite_ref-LipsonReich2017_21-0.

Lipson, Mark and David Reich, 'Working Model of the Deep Relationships of Diverse Modern Human Genetic Lineages Outside of Africa', *Molecular Biology and Evolution*: msw293. doi:10.1093/molbev/msw293, 2017, https://en.wikipedia.org/wiki/Onge-cite_ref-endicott2003_22-0.

Portman, M.V., *A History of Our Relations with the Andamanese*, vol. II, Calcutta: Office of the Government Printing, 1899.

Malhotra, R., *The Indian Islanders- An Anthropological Perspective*, New Delhi: Mittal Publications, 1989.

Mandal, H.K., S. Mukherjee and A. Dutta, *India: An Illustrated Atlas of Tribal World*, Anthropological Survey of India, Kolkata, 2002. https://en.wikipedia.org/wiki/Onge-cite_ref-8.

Mann, Rann Singh, *Andaman and Nicobar Tribes Restudied: Encounters and Concerns*, New Delhi: Mittal Publications, 2005.

Misra, P.K. and K.C. Malhotra, *Nomads in India: Proceedings of the National Seminar*, Kolkata: Anthropological Survey of India, 1982.

Mukhopadhyay, K. et al., *Jarawas Contact: Ours with Them, Theirs with Us*, Kolkata: Anthropological Survey of India, 2008.

Niyogi, T.K., *Kerala Evam Andaman Nicobar ke Adibasi* (Hindi), Kolkata: Anthropological Survey of India, 1977.

Pal, Anadi (in press), *Physical Anthropology of the Negritos of Little Andaman*, Anthropological Survey of India, Kolkata, https://en.wikipedia.org/wiki/Onge-cite_ref-Pandya1993_5-0.

Pandya, Vishvajit, *Above the Forest: A Study of Andamanese Ethno-anemology, Cosmology, and the Power of Ritual*, New Delhi: Oxford University Press.

Rao, V.G. et al., 'Malnutrition and High Childhood Mortality among the Onge Tribe of the Andaman and Nicobar Islands', *Public Health Nutrition*: 9(1), 2005, pp. 19-25.

Reich, David et al., 'Reconstructing Indian Population History', *Nature* 461 (7263): 489-94. doi:10.1038/nature08365. PMC 2842210. PMID 19779445, 2009.

Seksharia, P., 'A People in Peril', *Frontline*, Chennai, 16 (9), 1999, https://en.wikipedia.org/wiki/Onge-cite_ref-9https://en.wikipedia.org/wiki/Onge - cite_ref-gob_10-0.

Sharma, A.N., *Tribal Development in the Andaman Islands*, New Delhi: Sarup & Sons, 2003.

Singh, B. and A.K. Danda, *The Kodaku of Surguja,* Kolkata: Anthropological Survey of India, 1986.

Singh, K.S. (ed.), *People of India: Andaman and Nicobar Islands,* Kolkata: Anthropological Survey of India, 1994.

Sinha, Dikshit, *The Hill Kharia of Purulia: Impact of Poverty on a Hunting Gathering Tribe*, Kolkata: Anthropological Survey of India, 1984.

Sirajuddin, S.M., *Human Biology of the Chenchus of Andhra Pradesh: A demomorphogenetic Study,* Kolkata: Anthropological Survey of India, 1993.

Venkateswar, S., *Development and Ethnocide: Colonial Practices in the Andaman Islands,* Copenhagen: International Work Group for Indigenous Affairs (IWGIA), 2004, https://en.wikipedia.org/wiki/Onge- cite_ref-2https://en.wikipedia.org/wiki/Onge-cite_ref-weber_3-0.

Weber, George, 'Maurice Vidal Portman (1861-1935)', *The Andamanese* (Appendix A: Pioneer Biographies of the British Period to 1947).

Index